D0362636

A QUESTION OF CONSCIENCE

A QUESTION OF CONSCIENCE

By CHARLES DAVIS

HARPER & ROW, PUBLISHERS

NEW YORK
AND EVANSTON

The Scripture quotations in this publication are from the Revised Standard Version of the Bible, Catholic Edition, copyright 1966 by the Division of Christian Education, National Council of Churches, and used by permission.

For Florence

Contents

PART ONE

A PERSONAL DECISION

1. PUBLIC BREAK WITH
THE CHURCH

The purpose of this book is to take stock of my present position as a Christian.

On 4 December 1966 I decided to leave the Roman Catholic Church. For myself personally no decision could have been greater. I was born of Catholic parents and brought up, though without an oppressive piety, in an atmosphere where the claim of the Roman Church to be the one true Church was taken for granted as an assured fact. The Catholic Church remained for me right into adult life an unquestioned and unchangeable part of reality; it dominated my world. From the age of fifteen I had pursued an ecclesiastical vocation and was ordained priest on 15 June 1946. I had no reluctance for the priesthood or the celibacy it carried with it. No one had done anything to urge me in that direction; my choice was truly personal, my enthusiasm deep and without pretence. And for over twenty years I worked in the Church as a priest, wedded to the ministry, immersed in theology and ecclesiastical matters, absorbed in Church concerns. To renounce the priesthood and to reject the Church I served—it was an almost unthinkable step. However carefully thought out my decision might have been (and I did take pains over it), I need to write a book to get my bearings.

But I also owe others a full account of my present convictions.

My departure from the Roman Catholic Church was a public event. After I had finally made up my mind to leave, I still let ten days pass before doing anything about it. I wanted to make sure that my decision was in truth firm and final. Then on 15 December I wrote to Cardinal Heenan. He was my bishop, since I was a priest of Westminster diocese, even though at the time I was working outside that diocese at Heythrop College, Oxfordshire. I had a personal interview with him a few days later, after which I felt free to announce my break with the Roman Church. I did so on Wednesday, 21 December. I had already told my relatives and a few friends privately. The news was released by a brief statement of fact sent through the Press Association. It was accompanied by a notice that I would be available to answer questions at a meeting-place in the afternoon. I wanted reporters to have the opportunity of getting the full story accurately and in correct perspective. I achieved my purpose. The Press handled the difficult story admirably. The story *was* difficult: a prominent theologian, giving reasons of faith and criticising official attitudes and policies, leaves his Church, but at the same time, hitherto a priest bound to celibacy, he declares his intention of getting married. To assess the matter carefully and then treat it with fairness required judgement and honesty. Both were there. While understandably with a varying presentation due to different readerships, the newspapers all reported the event in a serious and balanced manner. This confirmed my view, formed through daily contact with journalists during the Third Session of the Second Vatican Council, that the most frequent reason for distortion in the newspapers is lack of information. Make the facts available and answer reasonable questions in a straightforward fashion and the reporting will be skilful and honest. Wanting my own action to be reported correctly and with understanding, I took steps to help the Press to do this.

At this point I must express my thanks to Mr Desmond Fisher. During the first noisy, disturbed days after the news had broken, he and his wife, Peggy, offered me the hospitality of their house. I am grateful to them both for that—it was not easy to live in a state of constant interruption. But Desmond also helped me further. As an experienced journalist he gave me the professional advice I needed to release the news in an appropriate manner and to cope with the pressure of the resulting wave of publicity. People with no *parti pris*, including journalists and others working in the communications media, have commented on the dignity and skill with which the affair was handled. That this was so is due in large measure to Desmond's help. We worked, I think successfully, to ensure that the public, whether in agreement or disagreement, had before them a reasonably complete and balanced account of my case.

Desmond Fisher was and remains a Roman Catholic by conviction, but he saw no reason to deprive me of a hearing or to let my case suffer from uninformed reporting. Quite a number of Roman Catholics, however, did resent the publicity. They thought I should have left the Church quietly, at most merely issuing a statement. According to them I should have thus shown some consideration for the Church that had nurtured me, for the simple faithful liable to be hurt by the scandal and for my former colleagues, fellow priests, students and readers. Instead, I have forfeited respect, they said, by seeking publicity and exploiting the occasion in an unseemly fashion. I must confess I find the objection disingenuous.

The publicity was inevitable. Whether with reason or no, I was regarded as the leading Roman Catholic theologian in Great Britain. I was Editor of *The Clergy Review*, which under my editorship was gaining a much wider reputation than before. I was well known as a lecturer and writer and prominent in a fair range of ecumenical activities. I was probably as familiar a name in the United States and Canada as in Britain, because I had crossed the Atlantic several times to lecture and my writings had a wide circulation in America. It would have been silly of me to pretend with false humility that my departure was not going to cause a great stir. I had to envisage the consequences of my decision as fully as possible in order to make it responsibly. I knew, then, that the news would hit the headlines and cause widespread comment. My aim was to guide the publicity and see that the truth about my position came across clearly, so that anyone who wished to comment had the facts at his disposal.

The only way I could have avoided the publicity was by falsifying my position. That is what I should have done, had I not presented my reasons and been prepared to explain them publicly and answer questions. It would have been assumed that I did not have any publicly arguable reasons for my decision, that I left the Church on purely personal, private grounds, in particular to get married, and that anything else was a cover-up. A theologian of repute cannot give doctrinal reasons for breaking with the Church of Rome, unless he is prepared to come forward to explain and defend them. For that reason I call disingenuous the objection to the publicity. Behind it lies the assumption that I am wrong to leave the Catholic Church and have no case as a believer and theologian to maintain; hence the conclusion that I should by silence try to limit the harm done by my action. However, I myself in all sincerity have acted on the conviction that I am right. I recognise the limits and imperfections of any personal conviction, but I wish to hold and discuss my present understanding of the Christian faith as openly as I professed and defended my previous Roman Catholic views. I see no reason why I should retire from the public scene. In the outburst of interest that followed the first announcement I did not whip up the publicity. I simply accepted whatever opportunities were offered me of explaining myself to people, on condition that the setting was suitable.

The same desire to answer the questions people with some reason are putting to me as a popular author and theologian drives me to write this book. I have left the Roman Catholic Church, but I have remained a Christian, while not joining any other Church. Surely, this is a paradoxical position to take. Many who have looked to me in the past have long had, as I well know, questions and doubts about the Church, about the present situation of Christians and the Christian faith. They have been deeply troubled by my decision. They want to know more about my present thinking. What I have said publicly so far is not enough. To them I owe the labour of writing a full-length account in a book.

I think it best to give here the personal statement I distributed at the meeting with the Press. It was published in full in several newspapers and used by all. But most people do not keep newspapers or cuttings, and I should like readers to have before them the reasons I publicly gave at the time for my decision. Here, then, is the statement in full:

I remain a Christian, but I have come to see that the Church as it exists and works at present is an obstacle in the lives of the committed Christians I know and admire. It is not the source of the values they cherish and promote. On the contrary, they live and work in a constant tension and opposition to it. Many can remain Roman Catholics only because they live their Christian lives on the fringe of the institutional Church and largely ignore it. I respect their position. In the present confused period people will work out their Christian commitment in different ways. But their solution was not open to me; in my position I was too involved. I had to ask bluntly whether I still believed in the Roman Catholic Church as an institution. I found that the answer was no.

For me Christian commitment is inseparable from concern for truth and concern for people. I do not find either of these represented by the official Church. There is concern for authority at the expense of truth, and I am constantly saddened by instances of the damage done to persons by workings of an impersonal and unfree system. Further, I do not think that the claim the Church makes as an institution rests upon any adequate biblical and historical basis. The Church in its existing form seems to me to be a pseudo-political structure from the past. It is now breaking up, and some other form of Christian presence in the world is under formation.

It is my intention to get married. This is not my reason for leaving the Church. To marry it would have been enough to leave the priesthood; for the reasons given I am rejecting the Church. I am marrying to rebuild my life upon a personal love I can recognise as true and real, after a life surrounded in the Church by so much that is at best irrelevant and at worst an obstacle to genuine human experience.

Rereading that statement now after several months, I realise how much in it requires further explanation and how many questions it must have raised in people's minds. Nevertheless I accept it yet as distilling the essence of my position. My intention here is to draw out its meaning, dwelling in particular upon its positive implications. I rejected the Roman Catholic Church because I wanted to be faithful to certain positive values. Moreover I do have a positive understanding of Christian faith and mission.

I gave a more detailed and more personal description of the reasons that led me to leave the Roman Catholic Church in an article in *The Observer* for 1 January 1967. This was published also in many newspapers in the United States and Canada. I do not wish to reproduce it here. While the points it makes still represent my thinking, it would by its length upset the tone and rhythm of my present exposition. Distance from the critical event itself and the spacious ease of a book make for a quieter tone and calmer pace.

Already in the article I spoke of "a peace and joy I have not known for years." The remark came out of the intense awareness I had of freedom gained after a struggle. What I find now in myself on reflection is a growing sense of steady, tranquil happiness. I should like to say a little more about this before opening the main argument of the book.

2. THROUGH DISRUPTION
TO HAPPINESS

The immediate effect of my action was to disrupt my life. The upheaval was not just mental and spiritual; I was left without a settled place to live or programme of work. Living out of a suitcase, I was separated from my books, papers and other belongings. Letters poured in upon me; packets of them were forwarded to me from place to place. Apart from their sheer quantity, I had not the environment nor the mental energy to keep abreast of them. It was good to hear from so many friends and the reaction from the general public was mostly sympathetic, but to receive a great weight of personal comment all at once is to undergo a mental battering that exhausts. And looking at the growing heap of unanswered letters, I felt crushed and unable to cope. While doing our inadequate best with the letters, Florence and I had to work out plans for our wedding and then put them into effect. We also had to find a place to live afterwards. Cambridge was chosen because of the possibility of a Visiting Fellowship at Clare College—this became a fact at the end of January. During all the demanding confusion of our practical affairs, Florence and I were feeling our way in our new relationship with each other. It was an unusual courtship. I proposed and was accepted before we had ever held hands. Our engagement was announced to the world when we were miles apart and had spent only one day together as an engaged couple. Then for several crowded weeks, while staying with various friends, together we shared the burden of a multitude of practical matters. The pressures would have tested the mutual compatibility of a couple long married, and so they offered a useful proof of our own suitability for each other. But it was a wearying and trying time. Neither of us will forget the love and help we were given in generous measure by friends. I ought here, particularly on Florence's behalf, mention Pat and Dick Mc-Carron, who helped Florence at their house in Edinburgh meet the first brunt of the publicity and who, together with Judith Hines, a tireless friend, remained afterwards constantly at our service. But no one was able to ward off from us the restless confusion of those overloaded weeks. We had at first intended to go abroad for our honeymoon, but at a certain point both of us together recognised that we could not bear to pack our suitcases once again and continue unsettled. What we wanted above all was the experience of being settled in a place of our own and establishing the normal rhythm of an ordered life together. Immediately after the wedding, then, we came quietly to the house we had rented and began our married life.

We were married on Saturday, 4 February 1967, exactly two calendar months after I, alone before God in my study at Heythrop College, had resolved to break with the Roman Catholic Church. The wedding took place at the Anglican parish church of Hasling-field, near Cambridge, where the vicar, David Isitt, and his wife, Verity, were friends of ours. (I wish I could tell all that they did for us.) Both Florence and I wanted a Christian service for our marriage; neither of us would have been happy about going to a register office. We were Christians with a Christian view of marriage, and it seemed right to celebrate our wedding in an openly Christian manner. At the same time, while acknowledging a union with all Christians, we had no intention of becoming members of a particular denomination. Fortunately, the discipline of the Church of England was sufficiently flexible for us to marry in an Anglican church as committed Christians without having to become Anglicans. The occasion was indeed no mere formality. The wedding, beautifully arranged and conducted by David Isitt and including a nuptial Eucharist, was a deep and memorable Christian experience for ourselves, for the seventy or so guests and for the parishioners of Haslingfield.

Since the day of the wedding, Florence and I have been living at the furnished house we are renting at Little Abington, eight miles south of Cambridge. We shall be elsewhere by the time this is read. We have the place only until the end of June 1967 from a don at present on leave in the United States. In this attractive and pleasantly spacious house I have resumed my intellectual work, spending as many hours as I can writing and reading. The Visiting Fellowship at Clare runs till the end of September. I am grateful for it. It has given me the hospitality of a College at Cambridge, the opportunity of meeting people with intellectual interests and, perhaps more important, the sense of having some place and status in the academic world. By the time this book is published I should have found some permanent post. I need a professional salary, but I want to continue my theological work and help interpret the Christian faith to men today. At the time of writing I am still uncertain about my future. The Fellowship at Clare, however, has provided excellently for the needs of a transitional period. I thank the Master, Sir Eric Ashby, and the Fellows, especially Dr Timothy Smiley, for their prompt thoughtfulness.

It would not be true to describe my present life as quiet. The post is still heavy enough to be a burden and constant distraction. We are receiving many social invitations. These we are accepting as far as is feasible; we need to get to know a wider circle of people than before. At the same time, there is a fair stream of guests to our house. Quite a number of people want to see us and talk. We think we should be open to as many as possible. We are keeping in touch with Roman Catholics. We want to be available, even vulnerable to others. There are, then, many interruptions. And the demands of practical living take their slice of time. Even after the wedding it was a while before we felt we were dominating the complicated affairs of our life. I am not therefore writing from the seclusion of a sheltered, undisturbed existence, but amid a tossing and distraction that often make it difficult to get any study or writing done at all. Yet, though sometimes pulled about to the point of overtiredness, there is throughout, as I have said, a growing sense of happiness.

It is perhaps dangerous to subject even strongly felt happiness to analysis. Traditional wisdom tells us that happiness should not be directly sought; it comes from a self-forgetting pursuit of the good, from a self-giving love. And happy people do not usually talk about happiness; it is the unhappy and insecure who dwell upon the theme. But one of the factors that drove me from the Catholic Church was the unhappiness I met within it, and I was caught up myself in the destructive tensions that at present mark its life. I am now like a man who has jumped off a jerky whirligig—bruised and shaken, but with a growing sense of stillness and peace. That is why I am reflexively aware of much that other people take for granted.

The unhappiness within the Roman Church reveals itself in the mutually destructive criticism Catholics indulge in both publicly and privately.

In public it seems almost impossible to hold a courteous and reasonable discussion with a conflict of opinions on a pressing or topical issue. The air is immediately filled with denunciations, cries of heresy or error, charges of disloyalty or bad faith, counter-accusations of ignorance, all punctuated with calls to charity themselves implicitly accusing the other side. The public intellectual manners current in Catholic circles show little sign of the openness and love that derive from inner freedom. Catholics in different groups have, I think, erected various defences around their faith and Church membership. They rush to the barriers at the first provocation. What makes for present confusion and quarrelling is that each group, whether conservative or progressive, has its own set of defences, so that they are excluding other Catholics as well as those outside. Were there more confidence in the truth and less anxiety, the defence mechanisms would be dispensable.

Privately there is among Catholics an endless flow of criticism and frustrated dissatisfaction with the Church. People may focus their complaints differently, but it is rare to meet joy among those who think and talk about the Church. It was wearying for me to meet this disheartened complaining at every turn among clergy and laity alike. Some of my critics thought that I went round stirring up criticism and creating dissatisfaction. But I was no glutton for punishment. Enough struggling bitterness and baffled unease broke over me without my provoking more. I wanted to meet joy not misery. I tried to give people hope and infect them with enthusiasm. Again and again

I offset the criticism, much of which had some basis, by bravely talking of renewal, although I was describing what might be rather than what was. Gradually however I began to wonder whether an institution that was cramping people to the point where love and serenity were abnormally difficult and frequently destroyed was the community of Christ.

During my editorship of *The Clergy Review* when there was a discussion on the shortage of vocations to the priesthood, a lay woman, a mother, wrote to me privately to say that in her opinion the reason for the lack of vocations was the manifest unhappiness of many priests. I know that some would want to dispute that, although the many departures from the priestly ministry do not indicate that all is well. For my part I should extend the remark to the laity. They too are often unhappy in their Church membership, and the conflict is greater in those who still care. Perhaps I was in an exposed position, like a breakwater. Certainly I experienced the Catholic Church as a sea of unhappiness, though I must admit that my own suffering was less my own than the impact upon me of what others felt.

The bishops are right in thinking unhealthy the constant criticism and mutual recrimination among Catholics. They have not however discerned the true cause, namely, the creaking inadequacy of an authoritarian system in the midst of rapid social and intellectual change. They therefore continue to exacerbate the situation by calling for submission and patient inaction under the rubric of obedience and love.

The sad fact is that the pattern of doctrine, law, ritual and government imposed upon the Roman Catholic Church no longer corresponds to the genuine and ordinary experience of people today. Even inarticulate Catholics sense this, so that a hidden tension pervades their life. For the same reason many, especially the young, leave the Church, without being able to give any precise reason for doing so. Some of the more articulate who remain have repressed their doubts, and as a result they fiercely denounce any new and disturbing idea. Others recognise the dissonance between the Church and modern experience, and they are working for change and *aggiornamento*. But they have a hopeless task. Only a revolution would now bring the Roman Church into the modern age, and there is little sign of more than marginal adjustments. Hence a constant sense of frustration, aggravated by each further instance of back-pedalling by authority and by the frequent jeremiads uttered by Rome against modern aberrations. No wonder if within the narrow space of the Roman Catholic Church the atmosphere should become highly charged. That Catholics should turn upon one another, engage in continual bickering and complaining, and calm debate be difficult is not surprising. It is the normal effect of confinement. And the excessive noise and excitement raised by the present renewal is due to the narrowness of the mental environment.

When someone asked me what it felt like to be outside the Roman Catholic Church, I found myself spontaneously answering: It is as if I had rejoined the human race. I would not here be misunderstood. I have known great love and generosity among Catholics. I have many Catholic friends, and I hope to retain their friendship. I do not consider myself as cut off from Catholics as Christian people. I am not, then, spurning Catholics as individual persons; I admire and love them too much for that. I know them as very good people, but as struggling against heavy odds. I have been talking about what happens to them when trying to cope with their Church membership and relate to one another within the confines of their Church. They are unhappy; they quarrel; they lose a sense of proportion. To leave those confines is to find a new sense of proportion by returning to the wider environment of the human race itself. The problems are vaster, but worthier of concern. The landmarks are much further apart than were the former bars, but the horizon is larger and can be increased.

When I ask myself why I have now a new sense of happiness, I find three reasons: I have taken possession of myself by a radical decision; I have accepted the risk of a wider and receding horizon; and I have joined myself in intimate love to an individual person.

3. A RADICAL DECISION

First, I have taken possession of myself by a radical decision.

Self-appropriation would seem to be fundamental to adult happiness. Happiness is not a quiescence gained by a narrowing of consciousness; it demands that a man accept the autonomy proper to him as a free person. A man has to take in hand his own becoming, decide what he is to make of himself and then carry out his decision. Just to follow what others do or say and wait passively upon events is to live a diminished personal existence. To insist in that way upon personal autonomy is, I think, compatible with belief in the working of the Spirit within us. The Spirit does not act by making us hear inner voices, but by enhancing the activity of our own intelligence and will. Nor does personal autonomy mean a refusal of external guidance or neglect of social factors and obligations. The free person is an intelligent subject, capable of recognising his social existence with its implications. But to be fully a person does mean freely to take the decisions that determine the direction and growth of one's existence.

Every reflective Christian finds himself today in a confused and problematic situation. To think with honesty he has to face doubts and questionings that go deep and affect fundamentals. The Christian faith as a living, intelligent commitment no longer fits easily into the patterns that have been used to shape and define it. The temptation in this situation is just to drift—to renounce a deliberate, personal choice and allow oneself to be carried along by what others are thinking, doing and saying. Such drifting leads many outside the Churches; not personal decision but the tide of opinion is the cause of their moving away. But a similar lack of self-determination keeps some within the Churches. People are afraid of freedom. They soon want to give it up when it becomes demanding. Continued submission to external authority is more comfortable than making personally a radical decision, and obedience can provide a respectable cover for the avoidance of personal autonomy, while verbal rebellion releases some of the tension caused by the failure to confront one's inner convictions. But the inability or refusal to be free eventually brings weariness of life, and it excludes genuine happiness. To endure the upheaval and discomfort of rending but truly personal decision is in the long run better.

I am not setting myself up as a model. In a sense I am talking to myself as I write. I am trying to weigh what I have done. Nor do I think myself more courageous than other men. The question of courage never entered my mind, until people wrote to me on that theme after I had announced my decision. What dominated my thoughts at the time was the sheer necessity for me of a personal choice. I had to confront my doubts, ask myself what I did in truth believe, and then act in harmony with my genuine convictions, whatever the consequences. Had I let things slide, balked the issue and refused to act decisively, with the vague hope that all my difficulties would eventually resolve themselves, I should have destroyed my real self and lapsed by default into a diminished existence. I felt that there could not be a second opportunity for appropriating my personal freedom.

Will Catholics reading this see it as expression of my fall by pride? This I can honestly say is not how it appears in my conscience. Vividly aware though I may be of the need to embrace freedom and not shirk its demands, I do not have the sense that I am my own, that I possess the ultimate source of my being as an intelligent subject and free person. I do not experience my free decisions as having their origin in some kind of will power, stronger in me than in others. For me freedom is bound up with seeking after the truth, with the dynamic expansion of consciousness that comes from loving the truth and following its light. It is truth that frees, and to be pursued in depth truth must be embraced with love. Here, however, in the realm of intelligent subjectivity where freedom is found, we meet what transcends ourselves. To act as intelligent and free subjects is to share in a reality greater than ourselves; for truth and love have not their ultimate source in us. The Christian names the transcendent as God and believes that God is within him. For me as a Christian personal freedom is a gift of God's grace. I did not see my personal decision, with the acceptance of freedom it demanded, as making me independent of God. What have I that I have not received? I never thought I could do more than share in his liberating truth and love. But I was convinced that God gives us that share by calling us to exercise our personal freedom and not shirk its demands.

People may opt to stay within the Roman Catholic Church by a truly free and personal decision. I am not for a moment suggesting that the only way for any Catholic to be free is to leave his Church —though I should maintain that no freedom is possible without a fair degree of inner independence from its present structure of authority. But to remain within the Roman Church was not open to me personally without surrendering my integrity and freedom.

There were two reasons for this.

First, because, as I shall explain, I was no longer able to accept the Roman Catholic profession of faith, and my situation within the Church did not allow me to hide that fact or avoid publicly following out the implications of my disbelief.

Second, the Roman Catholic doctrinal system had so taken hold of my mind and permeated its fabric that once I had begun seriously to question and doubt it I could never have attained sufficient freedom from its oppressive influence without destroying its power to grip me by a radical break with the Church. I had to throw off the many-sided claim of the Church upon my ascent in order to think freely and with straightforward honesty. The struggle to conform with its distorting effect upon my vision had to stop if my mind were to liberate itself. I knew that even were I mistaken in my assessment of the Roman Church I could personally and intelligently recognise this only by first shaking off the irrational grip and emotional conditioning caused by my envelopment since childhood in a powerful authoritative system imposed with divine sanctions. Psychologically

I could have reached a genuinely personal faith in the Roman Church only by passing through apostasy. That might seem an extreme paradox, but I think that a student of psychology would find it an understandable consequence of a system that tries to hold people back at a heteronomous stage of growth. I should perhaps add that since leaving the Roman Church I have as yet had no reason to reconsider my intellectual rejection of its claims.

I give, then, as a first cause of my present happiness the sense of a self-possession and spiritual expansion consequent upon a radical personal decision about my faith and the direction of my life.

4. A WIDER HORIZON

I am pondering on my present sense of a new tranquillity and growing happiness. The second cause I listed was my willingness to live with a wider and constantly receding horizon.

The remark is probably perplexing. I am speaking of the life of the spirit, which consists in an incessant seeking with love after the truth. Man's relation to the truth—at least in this world—is that of unwearying pursuit, not of final possession. This pursuit demands complete openness. At the origin of man's knowing is a disinterested and unrestricted drive to understand his experience and reach the truth. What renders a particular affirmation authentic in the realm of knowledge is its source in an unbiassed desire to know. Genuine love does not distort; for it seeks reality and shuns deception. True love flourishes where there is a loving concern for truth. And without an unprejudiced concern for truth genuine knowledge as well as true love is impossible. To suppress pertinent questions in order to maintain a previous position is to deprive that position of its claim to a place in intelligent thought and make adherence to it irrational. The spirit of man, the source of his intelligent knowledge and enlightened love, is an unlimited openness to reality.

While man is in constant pursuit of truth, he does not seek without ever finding. He acquires knowledge of reality; he can rightly claim objective certainties. He is not imprisoned in subjective opinions, all indifferently true because all without reference to reality as it is. Nevertheless, all man's certainties are partial and perfectible. Man cannot rest in any of them as in total truth; further questioning will carry him beyond them and lead to their completion and revision. Again, man's knowing is always from a particular standpoint; his limited view of reality is always in a given perspective. What an individual or group or age knows depends upon the particular horizon, namely the range of vision from the given standpoint. Truth as attained by man exists in human minds. It is therefore subject to the limitations proper to man as existing in history and having his being only in an historical unfolding. To isolate man's limited certainties from their historical context is to be false to human knowing. Nor can particular formulations be regarded as existing outside of history, unaffected by the standpoint and limited horizon of historical men and somehow fixed beyond revision in immutable concepts and propositions. The very objectivity of human knowing is guaranteed by the questioning dynamism of man's spirit because of which he is able constantly to review and perfect his limited certainties, correct subjective distortions and prejudices, alter his standpoint and widen his horizon. In that way man with his unceasing questioning can strive after truth and approximate his knowledge to reality as it is in itself, without however reaching a possession of total truth or escaping entirely the limitations of a human and historical perspective.

Some people, however, fear the openness that refuses no genuine questions. They are frightened lest their cherished certainties should be upset. They are anxious to avoid risk, and what they seek is reassurance and not new insights. Undoubtedly what many value in the Roman Church is the security they think it offers by claiming to possess absolute and unchanging truth about God and man. But that security has in fact been bought within the Roman system at the price of checking the dynamism of the human mind with its unceasing questioning. The openness that constitutes man's spirit was blocked, and security became rigid immobility. How far the attempt to call a halt to man's thinking by the imposition of a conceptual pattern made absolute and unchanging sets up a tension within a person depends upon both the individual strength of his drive to question and understand and the extent to which he has made the pattern his own by interiorising it. But to live within an open, pluralist society without withdrawal from its intellectual life is to experience constant threats to any security based on an exclusive claim to final, unchanging truth. The present upheaval in the Roman Church and the note of anxiety and fear continually struck in recent papal pronouncements are signs that the strain has almost reached breaking point.

I intend to return later to the question of faith and truth. I admit that we have there a very difficult problem.

Every Christian believer—at least in any generally recognised sense—gives a final, unconditional and universal place to Jesus Christ as the definitive revelation of God to man. The man Jesus is identified with the Word of God; that is, in him God opened to us his mind and purpose. And with God word and deed are one; and Christ God acted decisively in human history to achieve his purpose. Jesus Christ, therefore, calls for our absolute commitment. Faith in him is unconditional, and the Christian believer does not envisage an advance of knowledge or a change of culture that will render the Christian commitment obsolete.

At the same time, men can come to Christ only from within their human situation. Faith in Christ would not be reasonable but a violation of man's intelligence, unless inserted into the movement of the human spirit and kept within the context of a general, disinterested concern for truth. Seeking after the truth with a love beyond self-interest is man's openness to the transcendent and infinite; it is his seeking for God. When faith is given by the working of God's Spirit within us, it can only be by enhancing the dynamism of man's own spirit, not by smothering it. Faith, then, cannot be secured by a policy of suppressing the onward drive of human questioning. To remove faith from questioning is to place it outside the sphere of truth, and thus destroy it.

Nor can the absoluteness of Christian commitment be interpreted in a way that denies the historicity and consequent changeability of all man's knowing. Every formulation of Christian belief belongs to a particular historical context and represents a limited understanding from a given standpoint. Standpoints change, and the believer must constantly review the formulations he has inherited in the light of a fresh understanding. Statements of faith can be only partial and tentative. They are subject to revision. The desire for unalterable propositions and immutable concepts springs from a false view of man and leads to a distortion of the human mind, while faith should be its enhancement.

Within the Roman Catholic Church there has been fresh thinking by some theologians on the nature of truth with reference to the Christian claim as absolute and universal. These theologians, notably Schillebeeckx and Karl Rahner, are moving towards an understanding of Christian faith and dogma which fully respects what is historically conditioned, relative and changing in all formulations of Christian belief. Although this new thinking has become widespread in the theological world, it runs counter to the attitude dominant in official circles and reflected in papal teaching. Behind the official attitude are the theoretical views of a conservative group of theologians, who reject the modern, historical approach to truth. The struggles of the Second Vatican Council brought to the surface a fundamental conflict within the Roman Church on the whole question of Christian truth.

I experienced this conflict within myself. My intellectual sympathies were increasingly with the new thinking, and my own efforts at creative thought implied the same attitude to dogmatic statements. At the same time, I found it at first difficult and then impossible to reconcile the historical approach to truth with the Roman Church's teaching authority as officially interpreted and actually exercised. I have a perhaps excessive need for consistency and order in my thinking. This led me to endeavour to do full justice to all the demands of the Roman authoritative doctrinal system upon me. As a consequence I found my efforts to think creatively constantly blocked. To me it is meaningless to solve the problem of living under a doctrinal authority by simply ignoring it. So I left the Roman Church.

There is an intimate connection between institutional structures and social consciousness. The present institutional structure of the Roman Church embodies and implies a particular concept of truth. If the new understanding of Christian truth succeeds in becoming dominant, it will, in my opinion, dissolve that structure. On this point I think that the fears of the conservatives are well founded. For me the new thinking that is now abroad concerning Christian revelation and faith represents the emergence of a Christian community structured differently in its relation to Christian truth.

I have been led to anticipate some of the themes I want to deal with more fully in later chapters. At present I am chiefly concerned with recording the personal sense of release in moving out of a rigidly dogmatic Church with its insistence upon immutable formulations of faith and accepting the risk of living and thinking my Christian faith in a wider environment. Happiness, I suggest, does not lie in a security gained by anchoring the mind in fixed formulations and resisting the tidal wave of human questioning, but in allowing oneself to be carried forward towards new horizons, confident in the guidance of the Spirit as manifested in the creative thinking of Christians in communication with one another. At least, that is my present experience.

5. LOVE AND MARRIAGE

I now come finally to the third and what to people generally will be the most obvious reason for my present happiness: my union with Florence.

The general problem of priestly celibacy played no part in the questioning and thinking that eventually led me from the priesthood and the Roman Church. I did not for one moment regard my departure as a protest against the present discipline, which imposes celibacy by law on all priests of the Western Church. I saw my action in this matter as a purely personal decision, taken in the light of my own situation.

I still regard celibacy as a meaningful vocation. I see it as the free undertaking of a privation in loving dedication to Christ. The celibate surrenders the normal human fulfilment of marriage and parenthood, in order to become a sign of Christ's message of hope in a world where so many are suffering and deprived. By voluntary celibacy he makes his life an expression of his faith that privation and suffering have meaning and that man's ultimate fulfilment lies deeper than ordinary human happiness. If he is to be a meaningful sign, the celibate has to do more than remain unmarried. His dedication to Christ should in the concrete be a service of the poor, the sick, the rejected, the unhappy, so that he lives with them a life of hardship. There is no special Christian value in a comfortable bachelordom.

Clearly such a vocation is particularly appropriate for priests. It gives them a presence among the poor and suffering, and in that way reinforces their priestly work. But to be a genuine vocation celibacy must be free and must be lived positively. The mere negation of sex does not make the celibate vocation. Moreover, although there is harmony between the two, priesthood and celibacy remain two distinct vocations. The desire to serve Christ and the community as a priest does not necessarily imply that the person has the almost prophetic gift of celibacy.

With this understanding of celibacy, I do in fact disagree with the policy of the Roman Catholic Church in enforcing celibacy by law upon all priests. I think that this policy is seriously damaging celibacy as a free vocation and obscuring its meaning. Many boys and young men have a genuine desire to be priests, but without having any personal call to celibacy. They accept it because it is the law. This acceptance, though willing at the time, does not have that deep freedom that such an exacting vocation demands. Later in life the lack of a truly personal vocation makes itself felt. Many compensate the resulting frustration by material comfort, power, honours or even eccentric hobbies. Their priestly vocation itself is often eroded. The attempt to bind priesthood and celibacy together has damaged both.

That the enforcement by law is a mistaken policy has become increasingly clear in recent years, owing to advances in psychology. Further, although the tradition of priestly celibacy does embody an authentic Christian perception, the absolute insistence upon celibacy for priests is historically due to false attitudes to sex and marriage. Since these attitudes are now being gradually overcome, the call for a revision of the law of celibacy is not surprising. Where there is a right understanding of the potential holiness of sex and marriage, to allow priests to marry is no longer repugnant. Moreover, there are good arguments, theological and pastoral, for having a married ministry alongside the celibate ministry.

The Roman authorities, however, have resisted change and attempted to hold the situation by methods that show little respect for the dignity and freedom of the human person. There has been no recognition of the complexity of personal development and the rights of personal decision. Further, the authorities have not allowed the open and searching discussion necessary for the Church as a community to solve this critical problem in a truly responsible way. The attitude of the Church authorities to changes in the law of celibacy is dominated by fear. There is no confidence that the Spirit will preserve celibacy as a free and loving vocation among priests. Hence the attempt to preserve it under threat by inflexible law. What should be essentially a vocation of exquisite love is with many priests an undesired burden imposed by law.

I am, then, opposed to the present policy on priestly celibacy. Admittedly, too, my own action was inevitably an implicit comment upon that policy, insofar as I exercised a free decision about celibacy in my own case. I could not have sincerely done this without acknowledging the right of other priests to take a similar decision in their own case, if they had adequate reasons for doing so. Even in the supposition that the institutional structure of the Church requires laws and legal procedures, when these are administered in a manner that denies the essential dignity and freedom of the individual and threatens ordinary personal development, the only course for some is to act in defiance of the law to save their personality from destruction.

All the same, I myself felt no desire to lead a protest against priestly celibacy. On the contrary, my immediate reaction to the recent American writing in favour of change was to defend the meaningfulness of celibacy as a vocation. I am in truth afraid of exaggeration in this matter. I do not think that the present, undeniable *malaise* among the Catholic clergy, which is in fact leading many priests to seek dispensation to marry even at the cost of leaving their ministry, is attributable entirely to imposed celibacy. Imposed celibacy is only one feature of a whole, complex situation in which priests are today. Dedicated to the Church and immersed in its affairs, they are tied to an authoritarian structure that increasingly clashes with the social and indeed the Christian consciousness of their contemporaries. They feel frustrated in their work and in their own personal life and development. That some should seek to regain health through personal love and marriage shows how strong in man's nature is the drive towards human wholeness. But because there are many reasons for the present distress of priests, it is misleading to use it as a basis for a discussion of priestly celibacy.

Again, I also fear the danger of making marriage a panacea for all ills. Successful marriage presupposes rather than causes psychological maturity. And while a happy marriage enables a man to meet considerable stress and difficulty, it is no substitute for the absence of a meaningful role, the lack of freedom in his vocational activity and the denial of fruitful work and wider responsibility. Serious frustration in the other areas of life may indeed have a disrupting influence upon an intrinsically sound marriage. My own observation of marriages does not lead me to see in the marital state an easy solution to wider problems.

In brief, my own attitude to priestly celibacy is far from a simple advocacy of its abolition. Nor was it my direct concern to protest against the present discipline; any comment upon it was indirect and implicit. While I am in fact opposed to that discipline, I recognise that discussion about the manner of its modification will depend upon the view taken of the scope of Church authority and the need of ecclesiastical order. In making my own decision I bore no resentment against the law. I had entered into celibacy freely by a personal choice. Before committing myself I had gone over all the implications of my choice and carefully examined my willingness to shoulder the burden. I make no plea that I did not fully know what I was doing. I cannot say what psychoanalysis might reveal about my unconscious motivation, but I have no apparent cause for questioning my freedom. Consciously I chose celibacy freely, understood it as a meaningful vocation and sincerely endeavoured to live it without compromise for over twenty years.

I decided to marry because the evolution of my convictions about the Church as at the present organised seemed to demand a change to a different kind of Christian vocation. The possibilities of self-deception are here very great. However, I will try to explain the matter as frankly and objectively as I can.

I met Florence Henderson when she came to Britain from the United States some four years before my departure from the Church. A friendship between us soon formed as we worked together in planning and running ecumenical and theological gatherings. It was an open friendship, and through Florence I met a wide circle of people and made many friends—and, happily, they still remain our friends. During this time my theological thinking was increasingly concerned with the relation between theology and secular concerns and with the need to bring theology from its isolation into the creative centre of contemporary culture. It was at theological meetings and in the theology groups Florence organised and, more generally, within the wide circle of her contacts that I found an audience ready for what I was trying to say and a reaction of eager inquiry that stimulated me to further thought. My book, *God's Grace in History*, though written for the Maurice Lectures at King's College, London, owes much of its content to the work I did at Florence's suggestion. Gradually over several years I came to recognise that Florence was a person with whom I could share my life in deep personal love.

Cherchez la femme is part of the defence mechanism used by Catholics to render harmless the troublesome defections from the priesthood. But what seems a piece of earthy commonsense is in this application a coarse failure to appreciate the subtle complexity of the human makeup. While most priests on leaving the ministry marry, there are usually deeper causes and tensions at work than the chance of having fallen in love. In my own case I was not greatly disturbed by the recognition that my friendship with Florence was moving towards a more intimate love. It was a not unnatural contingency. Since we lived far apart and did not meet often, the problem raised by the new tone in our relationship did not press with dramatic urgency. I knew well enough, however, that in this area of experience drifting is virtual consent. The erotic element in our friendship would have to be checked and transcended or, if that proved impossible, we should have resolutely to draw apart. I did not wish to compromise my dedication as a celibate to Christ or to live ambiguously in any way. At the same time, I wanted to handle the situation with steadiness, not impulsively, and in particular to show due consideration for Florence in a matter that affected her so closely and was potentially destructive. Florence on her part respected my position and judgement and was prepared, if necessary, to return to America. I had time for calm reflection about the future of my relationship with Florence during the long summer vacation before my break with the Church when she was for the time being back in the States. But during that summer other problems were also pulling at me and other tensions building up their force within me. In the autumn my love for Florence became an element in a greater, more complex crisis.

I myself as well as other people have asked whether I should have left the Church if I had not loved Florence or if Forence had been unable to follow me in my decision.

The second hypothesis is easier to handle. I made my decision without consulting Florence. She was at first surprised when I told her a week after I had finally made up my mind. There was reason for keeping my struggle with the faith to myself. For her as for many others I had been a support in belief, countering difficulties and objections against the Church. I did not feel I could responsibly remove that support until my own convictions were clear enough to compel me to do so. My decision to leave the Church was therefore my own; it was not one reached jointly by discussion between us. All the same, I knew enough about Florence's own convictions and her reliance upon me in matters of faith to be pretty sure she would have no difficulty in following me and would want to do so. Had I thought that Florence would marry me just for love against her own convictions about the Church, I should not have gone ahead with the marriage. As it was, without difficulty she understood the evolution of my thought and saw that it corresponded to the direction of her own thinking. She had been searching for a new understanding of the Christian Church, which I had now argued out and was offering to her. Suppose, however, I had been mistaken, and Florence, whether willing to marry me or no, was unable sincerely to accept my conclusions about the Church. Then I think I should have still left the Church and begun a new life on my own. My situation would have been painful, indeed wretched. Perhaps I might have crumbled before the prospect facing me. But I had reached a clear conviction that I could no longer accept the Roman Catholic profession of faith, and I at least hope I should have embraced the consequences, even had they broken me.

But I must confess that in the concrete the hypothesis of Florence's not following me was so unlikely that it played no real part in the actual crisis. I counted upon her consent and confidently envisaged marriage on leaving the Church. I may have been rash to do so, but events proved my judgement correct. No one who has talked with Florence would doubt her own intellectual appreciation of my stand and her agreement with it.

What would have happened to my difficulties of faith had I never met Florence and been unable to envisage building a new life in a union of love with her? The difficulty of this first hypothesis is that emotional factors of uncertain weight would still have strongly pressed upon my intellectual judgement. I have been enveloped in the Roman Catholic system all my life; from my adolescence the Church had been for me a total framework. The emotional grip of the Catholic Church is immensely strong, even for those not completely wrapped up in it as I was. It amazes me that people in commenting upon my marriage as confusing the issue suppose that those who remain within the Church do so for unsullied motives of faith. If the only alternative to life within the Church, where I had lived since fifteen in large institutional communities, had been the harsh loneliness of a solitary existence, would I with honesty and impartial objectivity have confronted rejection of the Roman faith as a real option? I doubt it. The mind has a knack of avoiding as unthinkable what is in fact only emotionally and practically too difficult to face and live out. My problems with the Church were real. Over the years they had built up an increasing tension within me, the strength of which I now recognise since its release; mental and spiritual freedom is more palpable when it has been long denied. But my guess is that I should have continued to struggle in a state of repressed doubts until the point of mental breakdown.

Despite the elevated writing now current among Christians on marriage, when it comes to the point few apparently can consider a person marrying otherwise than for a dominant motive of sexual pleasure. Some of the letters I received were revealing enough in that respect. Now, the marriage I contemplated was not Platonic, and in other circumstances my approach would have been far less cerebral. After all, few people find it necessary to analyse their love—though when this is done with sensitivity in literature the findings do not support the crudity of those who themselves fear sex. But in my case I had compelling reasons for trying to discern my motivating desire and thus determine what I really wanted.

When I found myself turning to the thought of marriage and reflecting upon it in the middle of grappling with my doubts and difficulties against the Roman Church, I recognised that what I wanted above all was liberation. I wanted to get out. From the depths of my being I wanted to be freed from a system which was oppressing and tormenting me. I knew that if I threw away my faith, my priesthood and my peace with God for passion's sake, I should soon face disillusionment. Examining the possibility of leaving the priesthood to marry but remaining within the Church, I saw clearly that this would not serve. I might as well have remained celibate. The marriage would not have meant what I wanted it to mean. I was looking for spiritual liberation. I wanted the strength to leave the Roman Church and become myself with freedom, unafraid to face the consequences of my thinking because of the liberating power of a woman's love.

I should have turned to God, not to a woman. Yes, I, too, know the standard reply. But I did turn to God. And what I ascertained was that he sent me Florence as light and liberation. God does normally answer us through the concrete circumstances of our lives. Florence was light, because the thought of her enabled me to face my own deeper thoughts without emotional threat. Once I no longer feared to leave the Church, I faced the full implications of my objections to it. Florence was liberation, because marriage with her meant that I could go forward positively into the future and plan a new life in freedom. Even had I been able to make the break with the Church, without the positive pole provided by personal love and marriage my life would have been twisted by the sheer force of the negation, and I should have ended in unbalanced bitterness. As it is, the peace and joy of my personal life has offset the distorting power of the negation, so that I feel serene enough to work with Roman Catholics as well as other Christians for Christian renewal.

Why do people, even those most sympathetic to my personal decision to marry, regard my love for Florence as inevitably a distorting and confusing factor? Is there not a deep-seated reluctance to admit the elevating influence of a woman's love? I did not think objectively about the Church *in spite of* my love for Florence, but *because of* it. There are emotional factors other than love for a woman, many of them much stronger, operative upon the decision to believe or disbelieve, to leave the Church or remain. I did not act irrationally in counteracting the intense emotional hold of the Church of my childhood by turning to a freely embraced personal love. As for the danger of rationalising my desire to marry, there was no necessity for that. Apart from the possibility of a legal dispensation to marry, an easier and less costly rationalisation would have been to make my marriage a dramatic protest against the present law of celibacy. Some have said that such a protest would have been more widely understood. Certainly people could have been sympathetic towards me without being personally threatened. However, as I have said, to make that particular protest was not to my purpose.

In writing as I have done about my love for Florence, I can easily have given the wrong impression about ourselves and our relationship. People may think I have married not a person, but a symbol, an abstraction, an ideal. That is not true. Florence is very much an individual person, with her own distinctive background and temperament, with her own qualities of mind and heart, with her own medical history and physical makeup. Neither of us is living in a state of prolonged exaltation, but both of us are together grappling with the problem of ordinary living, trying to mesh with each other in a true partnership and having to cope with the difficulties of daily experience with its ups and downs. But I think that for both of us the happiness of our marriage, while rooted in the concrete reality of a very human and individual union, is dependent upon the power of marriage to point beyond itself. However unique in its concrete reality a mutual personal love may be, there is always in it that which transcends the immediate relationship, so that the union of the two persons exists for each as a symbol and expression of a wider desire and a deeper reality.

Our intimate love grew out of a long friendship. That friendship was based on a common appreciation of values both human and essentially Christian, a common concern for the work of the Church in relation to people, and a common desire to make Christian faith and theology relevant to men in the secular world of today. For me the marriage was the symbol and cause of a liberation from a system that I saw as opposed to the values I cherished and an obstacle to the work I was trying to promote. For Florence it was the strengthening and consistent embodiment of the values and concerns that had dominated her life as a Christian. For us both, the marriage is now the basis for a difficult and demanding Christian witness. What is the nature of Christ's presence in the modern secular world? What is the role of Christians? How should they exercise their mission today? What is the nature of Christian community and its relation to the wider society of men? These are difficult questions, but implicit in our action is the task of trying to discern the answers a little more clearly through thought, action and prayer and helping others to do the same. Our personal union must bear the needs of others and be an opening for us and them upon what transcends its immediate reality.

I have written at length of my own present happiness. Some may consider this a self-centred approach. They may also wish that I had spoken more in terms of doing the will of God and following Christ. But the reality is more important here than the language. So much religious language has lost a concrete reference and become pious formulas. I have had a surfeit of these. Love, joy and peace are among the fruits of the Spirit, and these are a better indication of the following of Christ than the dressing up of unhappiness as the will of God. Christ gave a meaning to human suffering and privation, and these are always with us. But the meaning he gave resided in the power of love to transform them. The tormenting frustration, the fear, the lack of love and the blocking of inner freedom: these defects experienced by too many within the Roman Catholic Church are no sign of Christ nor are they to be countered by exhortations to follow Christ in his suffering. The Church exists to bring and embody the transforming power of Christ's love, not to offer up its absence.

I am not afraid, then, of my present happiness. I rejoice in it as a gift from Christ and a sign of the working of his Spirit. Florence and I will have, I know, to face suffering in the future as we have both endured it in the past. There is a sense in which the scope of suffering and the impact of death are increased when personal existence is twofold, not solitary. Again, we both have to struggle against our sinful selves with the forces in us destructive of unselfish love and idealism; and no doubt we shall often fail. But I hope the peace and joy, the happiness we now have will never be destroyed but increased until we are with Christ and each other in the coming Kingdom.

PART TWO

FAITH AND THE CHURCH

A.
My Approach to the Question

1. REACTIONS TO MY DECISION

In the reaction to the news of my defection there was evident a strong element of surprise. Admittedly, it is unusual for any prominent Roman Catholic theologian to leave his Church. But the surprise was greater than the infrequency of such an event warranted, and this was due to some astonishment that I in particular should have left the fold.

Although several of the bishops, as I know, considered me dangerous and irresponsible, indeed almost heretical in my views, theirs was not a typical assessment. Most educated Catholics knew me as a moderate theologian, open to new developments but rather cautious.

Since I did not have the same power of theological thought as the great Continental theologians, I could not in any event have created a great stir by startling originality. But not all the writers and lecturers undistinguished by great originality are cautious in seizing upon and propagating new ideas. I was cautious. I liked to test the ground before moving forward. Moreover, I was irritated by the carelessness, indeed flippancy, of those who made things easier for themselves by not facing the implications of their thinking and simply ignoring the objections to their own statements. Writers, I was pained to notice, sometimes solved the problem raised by awkward, contrary statements of Pope or Council by never mentioning them. For my part I had no wish to exaggerate the bearing of authoritative

37

documents, and I did my best to determine the precise limits of their meaning and authority. But I took my acceptance of a teaching authority with deep seriousness, and the imperative need I in any case felt for consistency in my thinking made it impossible for me to elude the consequences of that acceptance. I was therefore slow in admitting new ideas and even slower to spread them before I had satisfied myself that they were compatible with the authoritative teaching of the Church.

It was this caution and the assurance it gave to others that made it possible for me to mediate between the more advanced thinkers and a large number of Catholics, especially priests and nuns. I became an interpreter of new thought to a wide public. People who wanted to move forward but did not know how to find their way amid the confusion of new ideas looked to me for guidance. They credited me with balance and moderation. They judged from my careful analyses and comments that I was not prepared to jettison orthodoxy for fashion. For some I was indeed excessively conservative. These saw me as essentially open and well intentioned, but restricted by the narrowness of my English, seminary background. They respected my theological learning and furthermore in recent years increasingly admired the boldness with which I maintained a policy of open, frank discussion in *The Clergy Review*. But, if we forget an untypical few, no one feared for my continuance in the Church. I was too much the traditional theologian for that. The news that I had decided to leave the Church came as an almost unbelievable shock.

Yet, if after the event people now reflect upon my departure, can they maintain that it is incomprehensible or even inconsistent with my past? Perhaps I can help them understand by telling what subsequent discussion with Roman Catholics has made clear to me. To put it briefly, I was led to leave the Roman Church because I had believed in it, because I took its dogmas and its teaching authority seriously, because I did not avoid tension and crisis by eluding the implications of my membership in the Roman Church or profession of the Roman Faith. The same unsophisticated attitude that made me a moderate and cautious theologian left me no alternative but to depart once that same Church had lost its credibility for me and I saw I could no longer accept its authoritative profession of faith. What has since come home to me with some force is that the reason why not a few Roman Catholics, though with the same problems about the Church as myself, do not feel any need to leave the Church is that they have not for many a day fully believed in it or taken its teaching authority seriously or paid much heed to its dogmas. Their attitude falls somewhere between half-belief and cynical detachment. In any event their relation with the Church is so loose that it is incapable of creating sufficient tension to provoke a deliberate and formal break.

Now, I am not suggesting that the many eminent theologians who remain within the Church do no believe in it. There are several arguments, worthy of close consideration, which would lead to the repudiation of my own attitude as excessively rigid. Faced with these I can only ask for a hearing. Was my break with the Church caused by a naïve and theologically unperceptive view of the Church and its teaching authority? Am I a victim of my inability to grasp the necessary distinctions in viewing the Church? Or am I not right in rejecting the proffered explanations as unsuccessful attempts to explain away? I will return to this matter. I mention it here to avoid giving the impression that I am questioning the sincere belief of those, especially the theologians, who disagree with my decision. I want first, however, to make clear my own position by placing it against the untheological expostulations I have encountered.

During the first few weeks after I had left the Church I became more than a little exasperated by the number of Roman Catholics who hastened to agree with everything I had said about the Church but went on to regret that I had not stayed to reform the Church from within. I pointed out that I could not have stayed within the Church, however desirable that might have seemed for purposes of reform, because I no longer accepted the Roman Catholic profession of faith; or, to spell it out, I no longer believed what was imposed upon my faith by the authority of the Roman Catholic Church. But those I spoke with would not take this reason seriously; they did not see it as creating an insuperable obstacle to my continued membership. I found I could not get Roman Catholics to commit themselves to any definite belief or to any interpretation of authoritative statements clear enough to form the basis of a discussion about the Roman faith. I have ceased to regard Anglicans as more elusive in their vagueness than Roman Catholics. I can at least discern some principle behind the undogmatic comprehensiveness of the Anglican faith. In contrast, many Roman Catholics seem to me simply to avoid facing the relevant issues. They have escaped from the pressures of a rigidly dogmatic Church by remaining uncommitted in regard to any definite doctrinal statement. I have failed to see any principle underlying their attitude. Its cause would seem to be that, unable to accept all the teaching of the Church, they have no clear reason for accepting any of it. They are not prepared to take their stand on any particular item of belief or, at least, not on any of the distinctively Roman dogmas.

I met with some revealing reactions. Making a point about papal infallibility, I received the answer from an intelligent and educated Roman Catholic: "But I haven't myself believed in papal infallibility for years." On one occasion I listened carefully to a brilliant exposition by a Roman Catholic on what the Christian Church was and should mean. Afterwards I said that, so far from disagreeing I could not see any important difference between what had been put forward and my own understanding of the Church. My difficulty, I added, was that as I saw it the exposition was incompatible with the Roman Catholic profession of faith, in particular with the First and Second Vatican Councils. "Well, does that really matter?" was the maddening reply. The other day a priest told me that at a gathering of Roman Catholic clergy someone put the blunt question, "Why is it that Charles Davis has left the Church but we remain within it?" The priest I was speaking with told me that he immediately replied, "Because we believe that the Catholic Church is the one, true Church of Christ." He met with an outburst of laughter.

Now, I think I am entitled to ask those who urge that I should have remained within the Church and who express bewilderment that I should have left it clearly and unambiguously to state the grounds on which they advocate continuing membership. Are these grounds of loyalty or of faith? I will later offer some observations on what I consider the harmful wrongness of loyalty without belief as a principle for the maintenance of Christian community structures. Meanwhile I simply ask my critics honestly to acknowledge the position they have adopted.

There has been a wealth of comment upon the Davis affair, especially in America. I have tried to keep up with it, but the effort has not been intellectually very rewarding. Practically no attempt has been made to answer my arguments or grapple with the implications of my assessment of the Roman Church. On the contrary, people have been only too eager to accept my evaluation of its present spirit and life. But they have then indulged in amateur psychological analyses to explain my lamentable collapse under strain and my inability to live, like themselves and so many others, with the corrupt system in the hope of reform. It has apparently never occurred to these people that their own attitude may be untenable in its inconsistency. Unless they are prepared to dispute my reasons, they have at least to show why the consequences I have drawn do not follow. The subjective causes of my decision should, I suggest, be left aside until the objective reasons I have given have been fairly weighed.

I am forced to the paradoxical conclusion that many Roman Catholics have nothing to say to me, apart from personal sympathy and regret, touched up with a few crude strokes of long-distance psychology. They have nothing to argue about, because they themselves have no definite beliefs about their Church and its distinctive doctrines, no clear grounds on which they base their faith. They retain their membership from a loyalty buttressed by a failure to conceive an alternative and from a hope of reform that will make their Church different—I should urge, essentially different—from what is actually is. Sometimes I feel I should ask my too friendly critics to request the Church authorities that I should still be admitted to the sacraments with Roman Catholics while retaining my present position, because I apparently have no greater disbelief than many practising members. The only difference is that once I did genuinely believe, so that I was led openly to avow my present disbelief.

People have even suggested that, while staying within the Church, I should have proclaimed my present convictions and waited for the Church to expel me. Since I presupposed that membership demanded acceptance of the Roman Catholic profession of faith, it never occurred to me to do this. Looking back now, I still do not think that such a course would have been feasible. The psychological pressures involved would have been enormous and probably would have broken me. Besides, the disciplinary action taken against the Dominican, Herbert McCabe, who tried to defend the Church while admitting some of my charges against it, shows that the Church authorities are not prepared to grant freedom for dissent even far milder than mine. However, let us suppose that open disbelief in currently imposed doctrine is a possible option without leaving the Church. I suggest that others, including theologians and biblicists, might try it. If everyone openly declared what he did not believe, what were the limits of his acceptance of doctrines officially regarded as authoritative, we might see more clearly where the unity of Christian faith truly lay, whether it was in fact embodied and expressed in the present hierarchically structured Church. I can at least ask that those who question my departure should make clear the sources and limits of their own belief and disbelief. I should then know on what basis to discuss my position with them.

Faced with a widespread, almost universal refusal to examine my position in terms of faith, I feel it necessary to spell out that I did not leave the Church as a matter of tactics, nor on account of a personal clash with authority. It was first and foremost a question of faith.

I did not justify my defection as a forceful means of provoking reform; I did not set out to strike a blow for the break-up of the present Churches and the promotion of a new structure for the embodiment of Christian presence in the world. Certainly I thought I could do most for Christ and Christian renewal by acting out the consequences of my sincere convictions, but for me the basis of any action of reform must be a true understanding of the Christian faith. To initiate a movement of reform without grounding it upon faith is, surely, to beat the air. Faith, therefore, had to come before action.

Again, my own relation with external authority within the Church was not of itself intolerable. No writing of mine had ever been stopped by censorship. Admittedly, I knew that action had been taken behind the scene in two dioceses to prevent my being invited to speak. But more invitations to lecture than I could possibly have accepted were pouring in upon me, so that I was sadly amused rather than troubled by the hidden ban. My various clashes with Cardinal Heenan over the editing of *The Clergy Review* did not personally threaten or worry me. I had soon made up my mind to resign if reasonable freedom were denied me, and indeed I once went so far as to do so. (The Editorial Board formed on that occasion was chosen from men I knew I could work with freely.) But I was well reconciled to that contingency and would have accepted it as an opportunity of doing other, pressing work. In fact, however, as I knew, Cardinal Heenan's policy is to go to almost any length to avoid a public conflict; he prefers the hidden hand. For my part I was and am still convinced that legitimate freedom will be wrested from the present authorities in the Church only by bringing their activities into the open and subjecting them to public scrutiny. But once I had made it clear that I had no intention of covering up my resignation with some specious reason, my position as Editor was pretty secure.

No, I did not leave the Church as a persecuted man. I had not been reduced to impotence, so that I had to leave the Church in order to speak or publish at all. Indeed, apart from some minor harassment I was left alone. The most troublesome censor the system imposed upon me was internal; my own drive to think consistently did more to restrict me than any threat or action by authority against myself. Nevertheless, my relation with authority did contribute much to my leaving the Church. Neither the Holy See nor the bishops directly blocked my activities, but they helped considerably in destroying my faith. What they helped to destroy for me was the credibility of the Church.

I will come back to this point shortly. What I want at the moment to stress is that my personal crisis was a crisis of faith, not the sorry outcome of a particular conflict with authority. Everything, including my own personal experience with authority, converged upon the question of the credibility of the Roman Catholic Church as the Church of Christ. I have not and do not wish to conceal the personal factors, both of internal temperament and of external circumstances, which do much to explain why to confront my doubts about the Church became not only possible but also ineluctable. I have tried to allow for subjective distortion. Whether I have succeeded or not, others can judge by testing the strength of my objective reasons. At any rate, the conclusion I reached was that the Roman Church lacked credibility as the Church of Christ.

To put my position, then, bluntly and briefly: I left the Church because I had ceased to believe in it. Placed in the Church where my profession of its faith was publicly implied in my situation, I could not with integrity and truth remain when I no longer accepted that faith.

I do not accept the Roman Catholic faith. That is the straightforward, indeed some may think naïve, reason why I did not stay within the Church to work for its reform. Roman Catholics who stay within the Church but do not in fact accept its authoritative profession of faith may, I grant, be personally most sincere. All the same, the subtle explanations must be on their side. Granted the same lack of assent to Roman claims, it is for them to justify their remaining more than for me to defend my departure.

That being said, I still have the task of explaining how the Roman Church lost its credibility for me.

2. FAITH AND CREDIBILITY

I should, however, first say something about how I understand credibility in relation to faith. There is nothing original in my view of the matter, but a few words on the subject will help readers to enter into my thinking.

The pivotal moment in the process of faith is the acknowledgement or judgement by the prospective believer that he can and should believe. It is this judgement that makes the leap of faith both possible and obligatory as a human and intelligent action. Faith is a leap because it is a commitment beyond what can be proved or verified, but it is a leap intelligently and deliberately made, not the result of a blind, irrational impulse. Guiding the leap is the judgement I have mentioned, which is usually called the judgement of credibility. It ensures that faith is a genuine commitment to God, not a superstitious credulity nor a bigoted obscurantism nor an unreasonable and immoral refusal of truth. The judgement in question is both a declaration and an imperative. By it the person declares the possibility of faith and affirms his obligation to believe. In other words, the judgement is the acknowledgement of the duty to believe in a particular instance. The free commitment of faith should follow upon it, although, since free, faith may in fact be refused.

For someone to recognise that faith is demanded as the only appropriate response when confronted in the concrete with a claim that God is present in a self-revelation he must have reasons for doing so. He requires, in other words, evidence of credibility for the supposed revelation. He needs signs or motives of credibility to ground his judgement that he can and should believe in God as here present in his revealing word.

The reasons grounding the judgement of credibility will not demonstrate God's presence beyond the possibility of doubt nor provide a rational proof for the content of his self-revelation; otherwise, faith would not be faith. Faith as a free commitment to the transcendent is inevitably a leap into what lies beyond the understanding, reasoning and critical judgement of man. We may rightly think of it as an ecstatic trust, not in the sense of an abnormal trance, but as implying a going out of ourselves in loving reliance upon an unknown darkly present. Faith cannot be confined to the category of human knowing, even when this is at the interpersonal level. It demands a passing beyond the sphere of reality proportionate to man in a transition in which the believer breaks out of the world where things, persons and relations are tested and judged in the scale of reason alone.

But the grounds for believing the inquirer seeks should be sufficient to form a clear invitation to believe, a call to faith. He will not ask that God should manifest himself in dazzling light nor that God should prove the truth of his Word. He·is prepared for the darkness of faith, for the free commitment to the presence that lies beyond the furthest point of his understanding grasp. But he does and should want to know that faith is in the concrete context an appropriate response, that his free commitment is not superstition or idolatry but a reasonable service, the fulfilment of a sufficiently perceived duty. In brief, the signs claiming his attention should be enough to ground a judgement of credibility.

The signs or motives of credibility are many and various. They are classified and analysed in treatises of apologetics. But the signs as perceived in the concrete by each individual differ in their selection, combination and force. No precise procedure can be laid down for coming to faith. The concrete situations in which belief may take place are too many to enumerate. The signs actually available to each according to his own background and situation are not the same. The workings of the mind in grasping, weighing and ordering the complex data of a particular, concrete claim upon his belief are bewilderingly subtle and often impossible to analyse and formulate.

Previous intellectual formation and moral factors will strongly influence a man engaged in an inquiry intended to lead to a personal commitment determining his fundamental attitude to reality and his whole manner of living. Signs that are analysed in the abstract in apologetics are operative in the concrete where the personal equation cannot be ignored. There are many roads to faith. No single set of reasons will serve to formulate and explain how God calls men to believe in him through Christ and the Church. Enough to state that for faith as an intelligent and free commitment a man must in some way have sufficient grounds for judging that here and now to believe is the only appropriate response.

I would not give the impression that faith is a human work; it is a gift of God. God does not reveal himself and then leave us on our own to make our response. That response is itself the effect of his Spirit acting within us. But what the Spirit works in us is a personal, free and intelligent commitment, not an irresistible impulse from within nor the constraint of an external force. We should always see the Spirit as enhancing not replacing our activity as men.

I should, then, see the Spirit as working already in and through the judgement of credibility, not just in the final commitment of faith itself. No doubt the signs pointing to God's Word, which are formulated in the arguments of apologetics, can be handled by reason. It does not require the light of the Spirit to learn about them, study and discuss them, argue about them and appreciate the answers to particular difficulties. A preliminary inquiry conducted strictly within the limits of reasoning is sometimes necessary to open the road to faith. But reason alone can never bring a man to the conviction that he ought to believe. What he cannot grasp without light given by the Spirit is the sufficiency of the evidence to ground a judgement that he can and should believe. Admittedly, this statement depends less on psychological analysis than on Christian teaching that faith is a gift. But suppose, for example, a man can find no fault with the rational arguments urging him to believe. He can still say that the arguments would be fine if they did not lead to nonsense or that no amount of evidence attainable by man can justify commitment to an unknown beyond man's grasp. Faith is a going out of ourselves in a commitment to what lies beyond our grasp. Even the conviction that we ought to believe depends upon a power to appreciate the signs of

God's self-revealing, a power greater than reason's own. In short, the interior call to faith, which in the concrete is the light enabling us to grasp that we can and should believe, is itself a gift.

Granted now the uniqueness and complexity of each individual's approach to faith under the working of the Spirit, it is still possible to delineate some fundamental traits in the character of those who are open to faith. To do this will enable us to grasp the working of the Spirit better. The Spirit leads a man to faith by bringing about in him the basic attitude necessary for genuine faith.

Faith first implies an openness to truth. Truth must be seen as a universal and absolute value, which is to be pursued even when it transcends the mind of the individual, group or age.

There are two kinds of people: open people and closed people. This is not a distinction of temperament or emotional character, but of spiritual stance.

Open people are those who are open to all reality. They are prepared to go beyond themselves. They are open to all questions, including ultimate questions. They reject the obscurantism that would turn away from the beckoning of transcendent truth. They are, therefore, open to the Word of God, to the call to go beyond the comfortable limits of knowledge proportionate to man's own understanding and embrace the disconcerting demand to accept mysteries and enter into the darkness of a new, transcendent relation with God.

Closed people are those who refuse to go beyond themselves. They call a halt and stop at some stage in the process that draws them on beyond the familiar. They remain perhaps within the comfortable, tangible world of sense. Or they refuse to step outside what they can prove for themselves. They find even belief in other men difficult and jib at the mutual trust and readiness to commit oneself to others it involves. They prefer cynicism and remain distrustful and sceptical wherever they are not the masters. The call to go beyond truth proportionate to men and accept what they cannot understand or prove from a God who remains hidden and demands commitment in the darkness of faith strikes them as intellectual suicide. If God wants them to believe, let him come within their world so that they can number, measure and weigh his words by the light of their own mind. "The Rationalist," said Newman, "makes himself his own centre, not his Maker; he does not go to God, but he implies that God must come to him." Thus they remain enclosed within themselves, within the narrow sphere of their own intellects.

Here it is important to notice that a genuine openness to truth cannot be limited to an openness to the transcendent in itself and a readiness to believe in God. On the contrary, we reach out towards the unlimited transcendent and do not rest in and idolatrise our own limited concepts and formulations only if we recognise truth as an absolute and universal value to be sought unconditionally wherever it may be found, even in secondary and everyday matters. Concern for truth is necessarily as universal as truth; otherwise, a supposed concern for truth in particular instances is only specious and is in reality a concern for something else, such as security or authority. And true belief can exist only in the context of an unconditional pursuit of truth. Without this context there is nothing to distinguish belief in the true God from belief in false gods, and faith is corrupted into idolatry and superstition. True believers must be concerned with the truth of their beliefs. Consequently, they must be prepared to disbelieve if ever their belief should be shown to conflict with the truth. As Leslie Dewart puts it: "A genuine and lived concern with truth means a hypothetical willingness to disbelieve should the truth require one to do so."[1]

This, as I understand it, does not imply any doubt about one's belief. Nor does it mean the abandonment of belief at the first sign of apparent conflict with other truths. What it does describe is the fundamental attitude of the true believer. He believes and does not doubt because he acknowledges truth as an absolute value and is prepared to hold to what surpasses his own understanding, provided truth demands that he should do this. Faith is not genuine faith but the projection of fears or desires and the pursuit of self-made idols where it is not inserted into the movement of man towards truth. Concern for truth is man's basic openness. When it is made active by the Spirit of truth, it becomes the source and context of true faith.

The distinction, then, between open and closed people applies to believers as well as to unbelievers. A declared belief in God or Christ or the Church is not necessarily the sign of an untainted faith.

[1] Dewart, *The Future of Belief: Theism in a World Come of Age* (Herder and Herder, New York, 1966), p. 73.

Prejudice, clinging to the familiar, and similar mental attitudes may easily be confused with faith. True faith demands openness. The extent to which a person is closed to truth or lacking in concern for truth is the measure in which his faith has suffered corruption.

The point I am stressing is made so well by Leslie Dewart in regard to belief in God that I feel obliged to quote this long passage from the book I have already mentioned:

Thus, belief in the *true* God means not simply belief in a god which, (logically enough), we must *presuppose* to be true, under pain of otherwise not being able to believe at all. It means belief in God precisely *as true*. It would not be inexact, therefore, to say that belief in God really means to have an ultimate commitment to the truth; I mean, to all truth, totally and universally—not particularly to a transcendent, subsistent Truth, that is, not to the presumed Truth of God's self-identity, which is a hellenization of the Christian experience, but to the transcendent truth which is immanent and manifested in every truth. I am talking about the truth which evokes the attitudes of honesty and truthfulness—I mean, that precise sort of openness which is apt to earn self-respect. I refer to that truth which calls for fidelity to the truth wherever and whatever it might be. Religious *dishonesty*, the disposition to advance the cause of God through insincerity, uncandidness, lack of forthrightness (if not through outright deception, both of others and of ourselves), is one of the consequences of disregarding the need to condition the Christian faith in God upon the truth. Conversely, the hallmark of the commitment to God *as true* is a certain conditioning of one's belief by the willingness to admit the real possibility of disbelief—both by another and by oneself.[2]

Now, while I have my own reservations about the author's views on the Hellenization of Christian experience—in any case, too large a subject to enter into here—I am completely at one with him in maintaining that all genuine faith demands an ultimate commitment to truth wherever and whatever it might be. Religious dishonesty is the corruption of faith.

Faith further demands an openness to love. When we examine this closely, we find it implies the priority of the personal and, in the concrete, a concern for persons.

[2] *Ibid.*, p. 74 (author's italics).

Among men, to believe another is to enter into a personal relationship with him. The interpersonal element in belief may seem pretty slight in many examples of belief between men. But even so, it is there. To accept the word of another is to respect him in some degree as a person. And social collaboration among men rests upon a common willingness to trust one another and accept one another's word. Such mutual trust is impossible without a measure of respect, which is at least an initial love. Where, for example, racial prejudice denies others their value and dignity as persons, there is no mutual trust and no genuine social collaboration. In short, belief in its most general form depends upon the context of social relationships, with the mutual trust, respect, acceptance and commitment these involve.

Then there is belief in a higher sense, which even as between men is called faith. It is the mutual commitment, total at least in intention, between people bound together in a self-giving love deeper than respect and esteem. Here, accepting the word of the other becomes an element in a profound relationship where mutual fidelity and trust arise from a union of personal love. Believing the word of a friend, a parent, a husband or wife is clearly a function of a mutual commitment as persons. In such a relationship, when adequately realised, what is primary is faith in each other as persons, a personal commitment going beyond the mutual respect required for general social living and collaboration.

It is well to note that neither human belief in the general sense nor faith in a person who is loved, conflicts, when rightly understood with an unrestricted openness to truth. Truth is not reached by the individual in isolation; man becomes himself and attains truth only in relationship with others. Man pursues and gains knowledge in collaboration with others, and such social collaboration depends upon mutual trust and a willingness to believe. Again, two people bound together in love accept each other's word because of the insight love gives into the character and mind of the person loved— an insight incommunicable to someone who does not share the same relationship. Truth exists in the hearts and minds of persons, not coldly packaged in some impersonal realm. The cynic or misanthropist, who is unable to open himself to others in love and trust, cuts himself off from all except superficial truth. To commit oneself in faith to another and accept the insight love gives is as a person to pursue truth in close relation with another person. If all knowledge depends upon social collaboration, the perception of deeper, human values comes from those who have been able to relate themselves to others in faith and love. No doubt, a man may be deceived and have his faith in another shattered by experience. Human life is in any event imperfect. All the same, the man who cynically refuses faith in any other person closes himself off from truth.

When we turn now to faith in the transcendent, faith as the response to God in his self-revelation, we find that it demands a personal commitment in love. The model of our commitment to God in faith is the mutual personal commitment binding together two persons in faith rooted in love.

There are two reasons for this.

Genuine commitment to the transcendent is by its intrinsic tendency total, affecting our whole being as persons and embracing our whole life. "And you shall love the Lord your God with all your heart, and with all your soul, and with all your might" (Deut. 6:4). Partial commitment to the transcendent is a contradiction; it is a refusal to acknowledge God, the transcendent, for what he is. The response to absolute Truth includes love without reserve, because the response must come from our whole being. No doubt faith without love is a possibility. The imperfection of man allows inconsistency. But such dead faith is a limit case; it puts a man in contradiction with himself. Eventually the tension will be resolved either by the complete cessation of faith or by its expansion into love. The basic attitude demanded by faith as a response to God when he reveals himself is a personal commitment total in its striving and without any deliberate limitation. When we look for a model of such total commitment, we find it best in the demands of personal love.

Again, faith in the transcendent inevitably implies a going out of ourselves in trust. A surrender is involved, a surrender of our own self-sufficiency as we commit ourselves to what lies beyond our own understanding and rational control. There is a leap of ecstatic trust in answering God's call and entering into union with the transcendent. We no longer enclose ourselves in a cherished autonomy, but give ourselves freely to a presence that draws us. Such self-giving finds its counterpart among men only in the self-giving of personal love. Commitment to the absolute Truth in faith is not reflected best

in the unremitting pursuit of impersonal knowledge, but in that
yearning for truth implicit in the dynamism of personal love. Truth
found in and through self-giving is the pattern of faith. And a person
who has never learnt to go out of himself in love will draw back
before the demands of faith as exorbitant, seeing them as a destruction of his enclosed self.

Thus, the structure of faith in God is that of a personal commitment in love. And the God whose self-revelation is recorded in the
Bible addresses us as a person and calls us into a personal union.
Our commitment is to the God of the covenant, who enters into
relations with men, whose truth is described in personal terms as a
fidelity evoking trust, and whose love for men is compared to that of
a bridegroom for his bride. The New Testament takes us further.
God now presents himself as the Father of Jesus Christ. God's word
to us, his presence and self-revelation in history, is now manifestly
personal, incarnate in the person of his Son, the man Jesus. Christian faith is a commitment to God as disclosed and encountered in
the person of Jesus Christ. Christ is not just an outstanding prophet
bearing witness to God's revelation. He is God's Word made flesh.
To believe in Christ is to believe in God. Thus we give to Christ the
same total and unreserved commitment that we give to God. By faith
a Christian personally commits himself to Christ as the Word of
God, and through that commitment to Christ commits himself to
God as revealed in Christ.

No reader of the New Testament could doubt that by faith in
Christ is meant a relation of personal communion with him. The
texts of Scripture repeatedly refer to the interpersonal communion
between ourselves and Christ. The union consists in mutual knowledge and love as found between persons.

"I am the good shepherd; I know my own and my own know me"
(John 10:14). Christ not only knows his own, but he also loves
them, makes them his friends, and through that relationship makes
known the Father: "Greater love has no man than this, that a man
lay down his life for his friends. You are my friends if you do what I
command you. No longer do I call you servants, for the servant does
not know what his master is doing; but I have called you friends, for
all that I have heard from my Father I have made known to you"
(John 15:13-15). Paul wrote: "I have been crucified with Christ; it

is no longer I who live, but Christ who lives in me; and the life I now live in the flesh I live by faith in the Son of God, who loved me and gave himself for me" (Gal. 2:20). He asked for the Ephesians "that Christ may dwell in your hearts through faith; that you, being rooted and grounded in love, may have power to comprehend with all the saints what is the breadth and length and height and depth, and to know the love of Christ which surpasses knowledge, that you may be filled with all the fullness of God" (Eph. 3:17-19). He told the Corinthians: "For the love of Christ controls us, because we are convinced that one has died for all; therefore all have died. And he died for all, that those who live might live no longer for themselves but for him who for their sake died and was raised" (II Cor. 5:14-15).

In brief: Christ knows and loves us; we in return believe in him and love him. As a consequence there is a mutual indwelling. Christ said, "Abide in me and I in you" (John 15:4). According to Paul, we are in Christ and Christ is in us. Between Christ and ourselves there is an interpersonal communion.

Union with Christ in faith and love is made possible for us today, twenty centuries after Christ walked on earth, by the gift of the Spirit, namely, the inner power and presence of God coming to us through the risen Christ. The departure of Christ from this earth was in fact his coming to us in the Spirit. Christ had to go away from us as regards his visible, bodily presence on earth and be removed by the resurrection from the conditions of existence in this world, in order to come closer to us in a personal presence. He said: "And I, when I am lifted up from the earth, will draw all men to myself" (John 12:32). The resurrection established Christ as universally accessible. Faith in him is commitment to a living person.

However, if this union with Christ is interpreted in an individualistic way, it simply dissolves into fantasy. Love in general is only too easily narcissism. The narcissistic orientation experiences and judges as real only what fits in with one's uncriticised interests, needs and fears. Reality is not distinguished from the delusory picture formed and cherished by one's own fears or desires. Persons and events are seen as distorted by the dreams of a self unable to escape from the dominance of its own self-regard and self-concern. All genuine love demands the overcoming of one's narcissism and the grounding of one's love upon an undistorted view of reality. Many people are in fact only in love with their own desires or protecting themselves against their own fears when they claim to be loving the real person before them. The danger of deception is particularly great in any supposed love of Christ or proclaimed union with the transcendent God. Too much religion is merely the projection of psychic needs and an illusionary wish-fulfilment.

While a continual struggle against self-love and self-deception is inevitable as men strive towards freedom and maturity, Christians have at least been given a clear test of the genuineness of their commitment to Christ: an unselfish love of their fellow men. And this test is not an extrinsic criterion; it arises from the intrinsic nature of the gift of the Spirit.

By the gift of the Spirit, men in being united to Christ are united in a new way with one another. The texts are familiar. "For just as the body is one and has many members, and all the members of the body, though many, are one body, so it is with Christ. For by one Spirit we were all baptized into one body—Jews or Greeks, slaves or free—and all were made to drink of one Spirit" (I Cor. 12:12-13). "There is neither Jew nor Greek, there is neither slave nor free, there is neither male nor female; for you are all one in Christ Jesus" (Gal. 3:28). "There is one body and one Spirit, just as you were called to the one hope that belongs to your call, one Lord, one faith, one baptism, one God and Father of us all, who is above all and through all and in all" (Eph. 4:4-6).

Such texts could be multiplied. Essential to faith in Christ is the acceptance of a new community amongst men. Christ was sent to all men, and died for all. The Spirit was given to the disciples of Christ as a community gathered by him to form the nucleus of a new mankind. Although the gift of the Spirit comes to each personally, provided he does not wilfully refuse to follow Christ, it is given to him insofar as he accepts, in one way or other, the new community of which Christ is the Head. The Spirit is thus the principle of a new unity among men, a unity that transcends all distinctions of nation, race, class or sex. To refuse that unity, which is a genuine community of persons bound together in love, is to cut oneself off from Christ and from the gift of the Spirit. As John makes very clear in his First Epistle, if we do not love one another, we do not love God and God does not abide in us.

It follows that Christian faith has necessarily a social dimension.

Faith in Christ is the basis for a social collaboration potentially universal as embracing all men. It establishes a network of personal relations binding men together in love. And this social collaboration and communion is the context in which faith in Christ is preserved and transmitted from age to age. The faith of each individual originates and develops only in and through the new community initiated and sustained by Christ and his Spirit.

The visible body of Christians, the Church, is that new community precisely as made manifest both in its nature and in its origin and continuous dependence upon Christ. The Christian Church is thus the context in which an explicit faith in Christ originates in successive generations, and is preserved and developed. As a community of faith and love, open to all men without distinction, it stands as the visible expression or sign of the universal presence of Christ in the world and history. Likewise, it is the visible model and witness of that interpersonal communion amongst men which is the salvation he brings. And the visible community of Christians, the Church, continues the mission of Christ to the world. It functions as a means extending and strengthening the new unity among men, which was the purpose of Christ's own mission. The Christian Church is intended as a dynamic force at the service of mankind, an avant-garde leading its true advance towards a unity grounded upon God through Christ. In its task of renewal, in its overcoming of obstacles, in its struggle against evil and in its healing of divisions, it finds itself working with all those forces of true development which are present throughout mankind because of the universal latent activity of Christ and his Spirit. The new community of Christ is not confined to the visible Church but extends beyond it wherever the same values and aims are recognised and cherished, even if only implicitly. What the Christian Church does is to render visible the nature of the unity towards which mankind is being drawn and by explicit faith to acknowledge its basis in Christ. In doing so, it serves as a means for the promotion of that unity.

The structure of the visible Church and the relation of the Church to the wider community of mankind in Christ will receive more attention later in this book. At the moment I am concerned with making clear the basic attitude necessary for genuine faith.

Faith, I have been arguing, demands an openness to love. Taken by itself the statement is too vague, especially since genuine love is not always distinguished from its counterfeits. All that I have said converges upon the conclusion that the openness to love required for faith implies the acceptance of all persons irrespective of race, class or sex and a willingness to enter into an interpersonal communion with them. Certainly our union with others will be realised in different degrees of intensity on account of the limitations of human existence. No man can achieve an intimate relationship with more than a few. But our attitude to all men must be one that acknowledges their dignity as persons, accepts their worth as potential friends, loves them as Christ did, and is vulnerable to their needs. That is the attitude presupposed by Christian faith. Faith is a personal commitment and, in the concrete, a commitment to other persons. It is the acceptance of a new community of all men in Christ.

The point made previously with regard to openness to truth also applies to openness to love. A genuine openness to truth cannot be limited to an openness to the transcendent in itself and a readiness to believe in God; it demands an ultimate commitment to truth wherever and whatever it might be. Similarly, the openness to love presupposed by faith cannot be limited to the love of God or the love of Christ. Unless it is an openness in love to all persons whoever they may be and whatever their condition, it is not genuine love of God or Christ. A lack of concern for persons is a corruption of faith, and to damage or destroy persons in the name of faith in God is an ugly perversion.

3. LOSS OF CREDIBILITY

I have dwelt upon credibility and faith in general at what some may think excessive length because the understanding I have tried to convey forms the positive background for my rejection of the Roman Catholic Church. I now have to take up the question how that Church ceased for me to be credible as the Church of Christ.

My objections to it are concerned not directly with people as individuals, but with structures. By structures I mean ordered systems of social relationships, institutions that embody these relationships, the self-understanding of the structured community as formulated in its public, official documents, and the attitudes and actions that result from the structured relationships, institutions, doctrines and laws. In brief, I am concerned with the Church as an identifiable social entity. My concern, then, is not, as some have wrongly thought, exclusively with the ecclesiastical hierarchy. The mistake of my critics is perhaps understandable. The Roman Church as it exists at present is in fact an authoritarian structure, dominated by hierarchical power. Any criticism of it is bound to insist upon that distinctive feature. Nevertheless, my assessment of its credibility does rest upon a consideration of the Church as a whole—the Church as including priests as well as bishops, laity as well as clergy. What is true, however, is that I do for that purpose consider Church members precisely insofar as they are related to one another in the structure of the Church and have their attitudes and actions determined

58

by its institutions, doctrines and laws. To ask whether the Roman Catholic Church is credible as the Church of Christ is to ask whether a particular, identifiable structured community is thus credible. Only insofar as the attitudes and actions of the individuals take their origin or colouring from that community are they relevant to an assessment of its Christian truth and value.

Structures do not exist apart from people; living institutions are the way in which people are related to one another; language, doctrines and laws are an expression of the thought of people; attitudes and actions are found only in people. How, then, can I say that my objections are concerned not directly with people as individuals, but with structures? Am I making a false distinction or attacking an abstraction? No, I do not think so. No single social structure, even one so comprehensive in scope as the Roman Church, exhausts the lives of individuals. Particularly in the modern world, people live in the framework of a diversity of institutions and are subject to many influences. The question, therefore, arises whether Catholics who are fighting for particular Christian values are doing so because of their Church or in spite of it. Further, some distinction can be made between an individual and the society in which he lives; otherwise, social reform would be impossible.

Perhaps I can drive home the point I am making by means of an example. The social structure of South Africa as a community is dominated by *apartheid*. This structure establishes the people of South Africa in a set of social relationships involving segregation. *Apartheid* determines all the social institutions; it is formulated as a doctrine; it is supported by laws; it gives rise to attitudes and actions characteristic of South African social life. Individuals are moulded by the social structure. I have heard it said by someone who worked in South Africa that it takes approximately three months for even a well-intentioned person from abroad to fall in line with the system so universally pervasive and enforced as it is. Now, I should condemn that social structure as evil. In doing so, I recognize that I am condemning the deliberate work of men and that it would be meaningless to say that no one is responsible. At the same time, I do not find it necessary to apportion blame or condemn individuals. Certainly, the individual evil actions resulting from the system must be denounced for what they are. Individuals cannot escape their responsibility and condone the system. But it must be acknowledged that the evil of such a system can overwhelm the individual and be beyond his power fully to counteract and successfully to resist. It is not for others to judge those who are faced with a demand for heroism. Even less would I deny the goodness and love, the genuine values and truth, undoubtedly found among the people of South Africa insofar as the system does not embrace the whole of human life and thought or is not fully effective. Further, I should readily admit the presence in South Africa of forces contrary to the dominant system, which at least tend to its dissolution or overthrow.

To use that example may perhaps suggest a stronger condemnation of the Roman Catholic Church than I should personally be willing to support. I do not think its social structure is as bad as *apartheid*, even though its institutional corruption is bad enough to lead it to compromise with that and similar social evils. But the point I am making here is that I am criticising a structure, not individuals as such. I do not find the Roman Catholic Church sufficiently credible as a structure embodying Christian truth and values. I think that its present structure establishes wrong relationships and leads to unchristian attitudes and actions. That does not mean that I deny the immense goodness and unselfish zeal, the Christian faith and love, found within the compass of the Roman Catholic community. Nor do I want to engage in the sterile occupation of apportioning blame for the present situation, which in any case has complicated historical roots. Individual examples of wrong attitudes and actions must be given to illustrate what is being denounced, but the responsibility of individual persons is an affair between them and God. Finally, without hesitation I admit as an evident fact that there are forces within the Roman Church contrary to its present structure, which are tending to the dissolution or overthrow of existing institutions. What I reject as no longer an embodiment of Christian truth and value is the Roman Catholic Church in its present form as a structured community. And, as far as my theological understanding goes, the key features of that structure are authoritatively imposed upon the faith of all its members under pain of anathema.

The Roman Church lost its credibility for me from two different points of view. This double loss corresponds to the two lines of argument used in apologetics to establish the credibility of the Church. The first line of argument is biblical and historical. Using biblical texts as a basis and tradition and history for interpretation and confirmation, it sets out to show that Christ instituted a visible Church, that he gave his Church an hierarchical constitution, that he established Peter as its visible head and the apostles as its rulers, that he intended Peter and the apostles to have permanent successors in pope and bishops. The Roman Church alone, it is thus maintained, has kept the structure of the Church as instituted by Christ and is alone in unbroken continuity with the first apostolic community. The signs or motives of credibility are the biblical and historical testimony. The second line of argument starts from the Catholic Church as it exists at present. The Church, it is argued, is a perennial sign of its own divine origin. By its universal unity, by the sublimity and holiness of its teaching and by the inexhaustible fruitfulness of the Christian life within it, it manifests that it comes from God and forms of itself a sufficient motive of credibility to lead men to faith and to sustain the faith of its members. These two sets of argument are capable of much elaboration. I am not, however, writing a book of apologetics, nor trying to compose a detailed refutation of Roman claims. My purpose is to indicate the course of my own thinking and offer some explanation for my decision to leave the Roman Church. I simply point therefore to the familiar arguments and pass on to tell why they cease to convince me. For the same reason I will start with the second line of approach, because that order will give readers a better insight into the evolution of my thought.

The Church,
the Sign of Christ

1. THE GENERAL ARGUMENT

To argue that the Church in its existing structure and life is of itself a sign sufficient for faith comes to asserting this: the Church is the visible embodiment of Christian faith, hope and love, and as such draws men to itself.

Faith, hope and love are the fundamental elements of the Christian outlook and life. They mark that outlook and life as transcendent in origin and nature. They distinguish Christianity as a cultural form. They indicate the presence of Christ in the Church.

All the other features of the Church that serve as signs of credibility are reducible to faith, hope and love as visibly embodied. Consider the four traditional marks of the Church, namely, universality, unity, holiness and apostolicity. Mere numbers and geographical extension are no sign of divine origin, so that universality as a motive of credibility is the expression of a common faith and the effectual dynamism of a universal love that knows no exclusive distinctions. Unity may have different causes, and the unity, for example, of a totalitarian State does not indicate that the regime comes from God. Unity as a sign of Christ is a unity based upon a free personal faith and love. Holiness and fruitfulness of life is another way of describing the exercise of faith, hope and love. The Church remains apostolic by preserving and fostering the faith of the apostles and by being like the apostolic community an embodiment of Christian hope and love.

Is, then, the present Roman Catholic Church as a social structure a credible embodiment of Christian faith, hope and love? That it was not was the conviction I gradually reached. I came to see the Roman Church as inimical to Christian faith, because it had become a zone of untruth, pervaded by a lack of concern for truth. It was, I came to realise, an obstacle to Christian love, because it had forgotten that authority and institutions were at the service of the freedom and communion of persons, so that people were being damaged and destroyed to preserve an antiquated system no longer in harmony with their needs. Stifling for the truth and unlovingly repressive, the atmosphere created within it was crushing people into anxiety and fear rather than freeing them for hope and happiness. And by making its institutional form an end not a means, it was going counter to Christian hope, even to the extent of compromising its mission to mankind when institutional advantage seemed to demand this.

How can I convey an assessment reached by a cumulative experience built up over many years? A difficult task. There is, however, no need for me to formulate a cogent proof of my contentions. All that is necessary is to draw people's attention to a situation they can observe and judge for themselves. I am not asking others to accept my word. My purpose is to provoke people to look at the reality around them. As a matter of fact agreement with my criticisms of the Roman Church has been surprisingly widespread. Even I expected more Catholics to come forward and say that I was wrong about the Church—not just wrong in my final decision, but wrong in my assessment of its present state. Apparently few articulate Catholics were sufficiently happy about the Church to say confidently that the Church as I described it was not the Church they knew. But the many who hastened to agree with my criticisms have not given them the same decisive value as I have done. Perhaps the account I have given of the meaning of faith and credibility will help people understand why these criticisms, if true, as I maintain, are for me of the utmost importance.

2. THE CHURCH AND TRUTH

The Roman Catholic Church contradicts my Christian faith because I experience it as a zone of untruth, pervaded by a disregard for truth.

In his book, *The Grave of God*, Fr Adolfs, the Dutch theologian, takes from Josef Pieper, the German Catholic philosopher, the idea of a zone of truth. He writes:

Plato brought many different charges against the Sophists, and all of them apply strictly to our contemporary situation. One of his accusations was their "corruption of the word" [*Korrumpierung des Wortes*]. An element of human existence is contained in the word, and, if the word is corrupted, human existence cannot remain inviolate. The Sophists, Plato maintained, corrupted the word, which, in their teaching, no longer had the function of communicating truth, but was simply manipulated for the purpose of making an impression, without regard for truth. This resulted in the other person ceasing to be a real partner in dialogue and becoming merely an object—human *material*—to be used by the speaker. The word thus lost its communicative character and became a means of power, a weapon.[1]

Both Pieper and Adolfs apply the charge of corrupting the word to our contemporary society. Pieper himself suggested that the university should be in contrast a zone of truth, but Adolfs goes on to say:

[1] Robert Adolfs, O.S.A., *The Grave of God: Has the Church a Future?* (Harper & Row, New York, 1967), p. 143 (author's italics).

Without wishing to dispute this, I should like to suggest that the Church should primarily show the deeper dimension of her service and ministry as the sacrament of salvation in our society by being the *zone of truth*. I am also convinced that the Church can carry out this function only very imperfectly in her imperial form of power because, in a situation of power, her own prestige is always at stake.[2]

Now, to be a zone of truth is, as I see it, essential to the Church of Christ, because of the nature of Christian faith, which presupposes an ultimate commitment to all truth. If a social body has ceased to be a zone of truth, it is no longer credible as the Church of Christ. Further, for me it is the first passage I have quoted that only too vividly expresses the attitude and practice I found dominant in the Roman Church. Words were used not to communicate truth, but as a means of preserving authority without regard for truth. Words were manipulated as a means of power.

I should like a literary expert to make a critical study of ecclesiastical language, which is, in my opinion, corrupt. He would need, I suggest, to pay special attention to papal encyclicals and documents from Roman Congregations, although the pastoral letters of bishops, their official pronouncements, and even many ordinary parochial sermons, all reflect a similar corruption. The words are not alive. They are not at the service of living minds, but in slavery to a fixed, unalterable pattern. Clichés abound; after all, they are safe and do not smack of innovation. Hyperbole in support of the established order and accepted doctrines or in fear-provoking condemnation of vaguely adumbrated errors is greatly encouraged. Plain statements are at a premium; they are apt to connect with uncomfortable reality or draw a clear refutation from unintimidated opponents. Ambiguity is thus frequent, and is used to ease the manipulation of any statements that might later prove awkward or to harmonise what is now being said with the different statements of the past. Any suggestion of questioning or lack of knowledge or humble searching after truth not yet possessed is carefully avoided. Above all, there is never an admission of past error or a frank avowal that present statements contradict past teaching.

Occasionally the manipulation of language to hide truth and protect the prestige of authority reaches the point of absurdity. Mon-

---

[2] *Ibid.*, p. 144 (author's italics).

signor Vallainc, the head of the Vatican Press Office, when asked how the Pope could say there was no doubt about the official teaching on birth control despite the fact that a Commission had been appointed to study the question said, as widely reported in the Press, that the Church was in a state of certainty, but that when the Pope made his decision the Church would pass from one state of certainty to another. Usually the practice is more skilful, but the principles behind it remain the same. Someone has wittily remarked that when the Church changes its teaching on birth control the document announcing the new doctrine will begin: "As the Church has always taught. . . ." The quip, I am afraid, is very near the truth. Official documents as an habitual rule cover over changes of attitude and teaching with specious claims to continuity with illustrious predecessors. This has been done with reference to relations with the Eastern Churches, the ecumenical movement, the liturgy, biblical criticism and social teaching, especially in regard to the attitude on freedom.

It is perhaps unfortunate that the general effect of the mandarin and involuted style of official documents upon the Church at large is soporific. They should receive more critical attention. The blame for their wordy, unclear style is often laid at the door of the Italian manner, but I understand that educated Italians from a secular *milieu* would disown it. What I think we are dealing with is the corrupt style of a decadent system. Plain, unambiguous statements, absence of hyperbole and honorific rhetoric, openness to new questions and an honest facing of difficulties—these are not to be found in an absolutist structure turned in upon itself, anxious about its authority and prestige, worried about precedents, fearful of anything likely to disturb the *status quo*, still trying to live on its past glory and keep its hold but having lost its real power. Fresh, living language is the expression of a social structure open to truth.

The insistence upon Latin is not surprising. It is no longer a vehicle of living thought and is in every respect that matters a dead language. All fresh Christian thinking, even among Roman Catholics, has long been done in the vernacular. Actually, in the intellectual history of Europe, the emergence of the various vernaculars and the struggle against the dominance of Latin has been part of the effort to win freedom of thought and to shake off the oppression of hierarchical authority and the grip of clerical power. Hierarchical power still sees Latin as a useful instrument for its purposes. The appeal to the practical necessity of a universal language does not explain why Latin was imposed upon the Second Vatican Council and again upon the Synod of Bishops. The chief purpose was the same as that of the similar insistence upon secrecy: to check new ideas and to hamper free, open communication. Admittedly, that purpose was partly frustrated in the Second Vatican Council by the skill of some bishops and theologians in using Latin as a secondary, translation medium for their thinking and by the determined efforts, especially on the part of the Press but supported by a number of bishops, to break down the secrecy barrier. But some success was achieved in preventing the Council coming to full self-consciousness and gaining control of itself over against the Roman Curia. In any case, what is most relevant here is the spirit behind the attempt, not the degree in which a particular manifestation was successful. That spirit still remains, and it spreads its corrupting influence throughout the Church, even where the vernacular is used. The insistence upon Latin is an example of the use of language not to discover and communicate truth, but as a means of hierarchical power and thought control. In that respect it is significant that *Veterum sapientia*, the notorious document attempting to enforce the restoration of Latin in the seminaries, is an egregious example of a document pervaded by rhetorical untruth.

The degradation of language, which has been debased to obscure rather than reveal truth, reflects the present arcane complexity in the workings of papal authority. What is aimed at with the general public is to have an aura of supreme, unquestionable authority around all documents from the Holy See, so that, whether infallible or not, whether important or secondary, they are all regarded as the voice of the Holy Spirit. What happens behind the scenes is not a patient search to discern the mind of the Church and give due weight to the signs of the Spirit in the whole Church, but the intrigues of differing groups of officials, countering or supporting hidden pressures from various circles abroad. Secrecy, the common weapon of absolutist power, is essential to the process, though leaks too have their part to play in the power game. Groups achieve their aims by the insertion of suitable paragraphs or clauses, by modifying statements during the process of their translation into Latin, or even by successfully fathering whole speeches or documents. What is done by one group is sometimes nullified in a similar way by another group. Thus, a seemingly clear statement is subsequently given a hitherto unsuspected interpretation. No wonder the ordinary reader, whether Catholic or not, has largely given up the attempt to interpret Roman documents and decrees. Even the theologian often does not know what to make of a statement or how seriously to take it, until he receives information about the hidden state of affairs from someone in the know at Rome. As I suggested in my article in *The Observer*, there is need for a new science of Vaticanology, in order to provide expert guidance on which pressure groups have succeeded in getting their way and to interpret documents, especially their more cryptic references, in the light of the current Roman background.

The Vatican paper, *L'Osservatore Romano*, fits in well with the Roman scene. The ambiguity of its standing, "authoritative" yet not strictly official in its comments, corresponds to the present ambiguity in the working of papal authority, and it serves as the medium for much of the palace politics. At the time of writing, a typical instance of the confusion of truth by hidden pressures and counter-pressures has just occurred, centring on the "authoritative" article in *L'Osservatore Romano* which restrictively "interprets" the evasively encouraging remark on birth control in the recent papal encyclical, *Populorum progressio*, on world poverty. Needless to say, the Vatican paper in general reflects the corruption of language to which I have been referring.

One of the effects upon me of attending the Second Vatican Council was that I could no longer take papal documents, such as *Mysterium fidei* on the Eucharist, with any seriousness. I was not aware of this effect at the time, but my subsequent reactions revealed to me that exposure to the inner workings of the Roman system had destroyed my respect for papal authority. This change of attitude was not due to the clash of opinion at the Council. Far from it. I welcomed the clash as healthy and found myself more in sympathy though not agreement with some conservatives than with many of the middle-of-the-road progressives. No, what repelled me was the methods used to assert and exercise papal power. These were not methods that showed any respect for the truth, any humility before it, any respectable theology of the workings of the Holy Spirit in the

Church. They were methods of power, which distorted doctrine into prejudice and defended fixed positions by any means available. The reformers at the Council won some victories, but it has yet to be shown that they dealt any mortal blow to the system of Roman power dominating the Church. Despite the wide opposition from episcopal conferences in the last session of the Council, the theologically backward "reform" of indulgences was issued shortly after the bishops were safely back in their dioceses. Nor have the reformers convincingly demonstrated that the power structure of the Holy See is not a simple implication of the universal jurisdiction granted definitively to the Pope in the First Vatican Council and reiterated again and again in the Constitution on the Church of the Second Vatican Council. As for myself, far from experiencing the papal authority as a living doctrinal centre, focussing, representing and sanctioning the mind of the Church, I am compelled to the admission that the Pope is enmeshed in an antiquated court system, where truth is handled politically, free discussion always suspect and doctrinal declarations won by manoeuvering.

Some readers may feel that I have attributed too much importance to the Roman bureaucracy. I should dispute that. If we look at the social structure of the Roman Church as it exists, not in the minds of some progressive theologians, but in concrete reality, then we cannot deny that it is still dominated by papal authority. That authority affects the whole life of the Church, even to the attitude and actions of individuals. One has only to examine even progressive Catholic newspapers and periodicals to ascertain that. And Pope Paul continues to urge his authority without intermission or qualification. Not unfairly have some detected in the tone of his recent call for a year of faith a desire and demand that theologians and scholars should suspend their questionings and judgements until he, the Pope, has personally managed to solve every problem now facing the Church. The life of the community is being universally hampered by a resolute refusal to allow the papacy to suffer diminution in the excessive authority it exercises in practice over the Church.

But I am less concerned with abuses in themselves than with the attitude to truth these manifest. This is for me the nub of the question of credibility. And I find the spirit that subordinates truth to authority and power throughout the ecclesiastical structure. I have looked in vain for a joyful sense of the value and power of truth as truth.

I often wished that my own relations with local authority were more Christian. With all my heart I wanted frank and open mutual co-operation. I had no desire to counter secret pressure with an appeal to publicity. But for me the question was the very possibility of my continuing my theological and editorial work with integrity. Had I followed the suggestion of Cardinal Heenan that I should take up ordinary parochial duties, my dilemma would have been resolved. But was it the will of God that I should bury my theological talents? Because that in effect is what would have been involved, despite assurances to the contrary, as anyone with experience of the demands of theological work will easily recognise. Whether rightly or wrongly—the element of personal incompatibility is always difficult to assess—I had the conviction that to submit to the mind of Cardinal Heenan as distinct from obeying his explicit orders was to surrender my reverence and pursuit of truth. The basis of a shared attitude to truth was lacking. Truth understood in any other way than as the confident possession of a fixed body of conceptualised doctrines with the consequent avoidance of any questions or discussions that disturbed the *status quo* was regarded as simply irrelevant. Indeed, even that is too positive a statement. There was no inkling of any other possible approach to truth. To speak of truth in other terms was like talking of colour to the colour-blind.

To those complaining of such a situation, which is by no means uncommon and in a far worse form, people often cite the example of Teilhard de Chardin. Here was a man, they say, who obeyed unreservedly. He did not live to see his work come to fruit, but, under the Spirit guiding the Church in spite of human failing, his obedience has had its reward in the present spread and impact of his writings. Now, apart from the fact that Teilhard did take steps to ensure the hidden circulation of his works during his lifetime and their survival after his death, there is a deeper objection to that attempt to whitewash the destructive effects of suppression. As Professor Donald MacKinnon of Cambridge pointed out in a talk on the BBC Third Programme in March 1967, the visionary Teilhard was unquestionably damaged intellectually by the decision to inhibit publication of his writings during his lifetime and to prevent him taking an academic post in France. He was deprived of the kind of criticism his ideas badly needed. "The history of his development," he went on to say, "reveals how he was driven in upon himself and in consequence was encouraged by isolation to adopt eccentric and unbalanced attitudes." In other words, we have been deprived of the Teilhard we might have had, had he been allowed to develop and modify his thought in constant interaction with the criticisms and suggestions of an open intellectual environment. The work of other thinkers, such as that of the great Dominican biblical scholar, Lagrange, has been likewise stunted. Speaking of the recantation forced upon Galileo in an earlier century, Friedrich Heer writes: "Descartes hurriedly destroyed his Copernican *Traité du monde* and the Catholic world passed the pre-eminence in research to the Protestant."[3] So, while the Holy Spirit may be rightly held to counteract the destructive effect of human failure, appeal cannot be made to his intervention as a *Deus ex machina*. Unless hierarchical authority is regarded as an unquestionable absolute in every instance, a thinker threatened with abusive suppression or hindrance has to choose in conscience between the damaging or destruction of his work and submission. To submit may sometimes on balance be right; it is sometimes immoral. Christian obedience does not mean that one must be the submissive tool of forces suppressing truth. When the hierarchy acts as the enemy of the communal faith of the Church, the work of the Spirit is to foster resistance.

The fundamental question, I repeat, is the attitude to truth in the Church as a social structure. Is the Church a zone of truth and thus the embodiment of faith? I do not think that it is. The characteristic reaction of the Church as at present constituted towards the questioning of living thought is suppression. But questioning is the dynamism of the human mind in its relation to truth. When held by suppression of relevant and genuine questions, doctrine is turned into prejudice. It may by coincidence be true, but it is not held as truth. It has been removed from the dynamic context in which alone truth can be attained as truth by the human mind. A statement may happen to be true while existing for a social group not according to its quality as truth but as degraded into prejudice and held as the

[3] *The Intellectual History of Europe* (Weidenfeld and Nicolson, London, 1966), p. 308.

result of unreasoning bias. When this occurs, the statement itself is almost inevitably distorted in its content and implications. Truth for man is a function of the open dynamism of human questioning. Faith, as I have argued earlier, does not destroy but enhances that dynamic openness.

That the typical reaction of the Church to questioning is suppression emerges clearly from the lamentable history of the last few centuries. The Church has repeatedly opposed advances in human knowledge. Freedom of thought in the secular sphere has been won in the teeth of opposition from the Church. No wonder that European intellectuals fear and distrust the Church. They are hardly to be consoled if the Church welcomes and uses what it can no longer suppress. And the same attitude prevails even more strongly in its own doctrinal sphere. The history of the biblical movement within the Church is of a long, bitter struggle against a refusal to face relevant questions. The fumbling errors of Modernism were met by hysterical fear and blind prejudice, which denied the real problems raised and mowed down Catholic intellectual life in an irrational attempt to prevent any new growth of living thought with its questioning. True, thought is not so easily stifled, and suppression by Church authority is less and less effectual in the environment of secular society. Under the moderate Pope Benedict XV, the Church managed to shake off the evil dominance of the integralists, namely, the extreme antimodernist group, which, encouraged by authority, established a secret espionage network and terrorized the Catholic intellectual world. But the spirit of suppression is still pervasive and, if in a less blatant form, remains more typical of the Catholic social structure than openness to truth and freedom. The upheaval surrounding *la théologie nouvelle* in France after the Second World War produced its sorry count of books suppressed and of people removed from their position or hindered in their work. The tone of Pius XII's encyclical, *Humani generis*, issued on that occasion, is that of a closed and arrogant possession of truth rather than that of a humble openness to a development in the understanding and conceptualization of the faith, with the questioning this presupposes. The story of the ecumenical movement within the Church has been of a struggle for survival against the suppressive force of papal and local authority and, if there has now been a breakthrough, it is accompanied by a characteristic unwillingness to confess radical change. It would be difficult to find a theologian so immersed in tradition and reverent towards it as Yves Congar, the Dominican, but because his very knowledge of tradition enabled him to transcend the narrowness of the existing official line, he was persecuted for his views without the opportunity of a reasonable defence. De Lubac, Chénu, Karl Rahner, John Courtney Murray have all suffered restriction in differing degrees. Here, what we are confronted with is not a reasonable exercise of authority against error, but a refusal to listen, a fear of new ideas, a denial of new problems, a determined effort to suppress any questioning of fixed positions— in other words, the defence of what is held as prejudice against the movement of believing minds holding doctrines in the dynamic context of truth.

Admittedly, Pope John XXIII and the Second Vatican Council mark a partial breakthrough. Pope John XXIII, whatever the limitations of his own conservative piety, had a fundamental openness of mind. And it is openness of mind that counts rather than the particular views a man holds. In his wonderful opening speech at the First Session of the Council, Pope John made this remarkable statement:

The salient point of this Council is not, therefore, a discussion of one article or another of the fundamental doctrine of the Church which has repeatedly been taught by the Fathers and by ancient and modern theologians, and which is presumed to be well known and familiar to all. For this a Council was not necessary. But from the renewed, serene, and tranquil adherence to all the teaching of the Church in its entirety and preciseness, as it still shines forth in the Acts of the Council of Trent and First Vatican Council, the Christian, Catholic, and apostolic spirit of the whole world expects a step forward toward a doctrinal penetration and a formation of consciousness in faithful and perfect conformity to the authentic doctrine, which, however, should be studied and expounded through the methods of research and through the literary forms of modern thought. The substance of the ancient doctrine of the deposit of faith is one thing, and the way in which it is presented is another. And it is the latter that must be taken into great consideration with patience if necessary, everything being measured in the forms and proportions of a magisterium which is predominantly pastoral in character.[4]

[4] Walter M. Abbott, S.J. (ed.), *The Documents of Vatican II* (Guild Press, America Press, Association Press, and Herder and Herder, New York, copyright © 1966 by The America Press), p. 715. Used by permission.

Despite its caution, this statement together with the rest of the speech does delineate a new attitude, a new openness. Certainly, few theologians would have so boldly stated the distinction between the substance of a doctrine and its presentation (which must include its formulation), after the warnings of Pius XII in *Humani generis*.

And then a new spirit breathes through many passages in the Council documents. Let this noble passage from the Pastoral Constitution on the Church in the Modern World stand for the rest:

. . . . let it be recognized that all the faithful, clerical and lay, possess a lawful freedom of inquiry and of thought, and the freedom to express their minds humbly and courageously about those matters in which they enjoy competence.[5]

I have no desire to minimise the forces at work in the Roman Catholic Church which are endeavouring to counteract and overcome the suppressive tendencies I have been denouncing. I do not, however, find their presence sufficient to save the credibility of the social structure. First, to date the freedom they proclaim represents an aspiration rather than a fact, except where seized against the will of authority. Second, despite its limited victories, the Council, taken in its entire course including the Fourth Session, did not succeed in gaining free discussion for itself, let alone for the whole Church. Third, events and attitudes subsequent to the Council confirm the judgement that for the forces of freedom and openness to succeed in the Church the present structures will have to be broken.

I should like to stress that the spirit inimical to the openness of living faith is not confined to the Holy See nor to the ecclesiastical hierarchy. It exerts its corrupting influence upon the whole social structure of the Church. I will pass over the activity of the Delegates of the Holy See in various countries since they are an extension of papal power, but it should be noticed that their hampering effect upon the life of the local Church is sometimes considerable. Again, I will not dwell upon the minor despotism of local bishops, who by manipulating censorship, by disciplinary action, usually private, against individuals, by refusal of permissions and by off-the-record telephone calls to Catholic newspapers and periodicals often try to

[5] *Ibid.*, p. 270, n. 62.

prevent the emergence of disturbing new ideas or questioning within their dioceses. What chiefly concerns me is the attitude of compromise forced upon Catholic biblicists, theologians and thinkers.

Catholic writers who keep a measure of interior independence become adept at knowing how much they can get away with. There is often a contrast between what they write publicly and what they say privately or even venture to express in unpublished lectures. They do not write with a simple concern for truth nor even with an understandable care over the difficulties inherent in the acceptance of a communal faith with a long, venerable tradition, but with an anxiety to avoid trouble with an authority they personally regard as misguided. Under such conditions, open discussion is seriously hampered, and mere honesty and straightforwardness become difficult to achieve. Further, the situation leads to the avoidance of many urgent questions, the postponement of pressing but tricky problems, the failure to meet the demands upon Christian thought in the changing world of today. New questions are rarely safe; they are by their nature disturbing. Sometimes the raising of such questions outside the Roman Catholic Church allows Catholic thinkers to make an indirect comment. But to break new ground and lead the way in Christian thinking is a dangerous business without the assurance of strong protection or the untouchability of great prestige. No wonder that many draw back before the probable personal cost. The crisis over birth control would be less acute had theologians honestly expressed their minds at an earlier date. How many biblical scholars escaped into the minutiae of erudition to avoid confronting authority upon the major issues? It is surprising how quickly wide theological support is gained for a new position when a matter once regarded as inviolate is forced under questioning by the determined effort of one or two. Is it unreasonable to regard the previous consensus as suspect?

Writers of lesser calibre become victims of the system. It is sad to go through popular Catholic writing of the past few decades and read the earnest but biassed arguments used to defend the indefensible. The starting-point is a position held as a prejudice outside the dynamic context of a search for truth. Arguments are valued not for their power to reveal the truth, but for their apparent usefulness in supporting the official line. All sources are drawn upon with this purpose in view. Great writers are not studied to learn from their distinctive contribution to the advance of thought, but plundered for detachable insights and apt quotations. Or, if unusable, dismissed briefly for their errors. At this time when the Roman Catholic Church has abandoned many previously held positions, the dishonesty with which those positions were defended is glaringly obvious. Notice that the point is not the inevitable worthlessness of much popular writing nor the mere fact of error. The question is what attitude to truth is manifested as prevalent in the Church. It seems to me that truth is used, not respected or sought; doctrine is held in the manner of a prejudice not as truth; words and arguments are not handled to discover and communicate truth but manipulated as a means of power to support an authoritative system: in brief, that truth is subordinated to authority, not authority put at the service of truth.

I experienced the distorting influence of the social structure of the Roman Catholic Church upon myself. As I have said before, I was not much troubled in my work by external interference from ecclesiastical authority. My difficulties came chiefly from the internal pressure of trying to meet the demands the Church made upon me. With all sincerity I wanted to take the teaching authority of the Church seriously. Apart from a desire to live out my faith, the need I felt for consistency and order in my thinking would not allow me to profess adherence to a teaching authority in theory while ignoring it in practice. But a growing experience gradually prevented me from retaining a respect for the workings of Church authority sufficient to support my believing conviction. I saw that in fact it conflicted with the exigencies of truth. This problem merged with another. I strove for a complete openness and fidelity to truth. This led me to recognise the existence of many problems about traditional doctrines in their present received formulation. I wanted to discuss these problems in open communication with others. I have no desire to think in proud isolation as a solitary individual; I want to think in community, to share in a communal enterprise, to subordinate my thought to the mind of the Christian Church. I did need, however, to discuss the problems openly. But I found discussion within the Church always limited by reasons of expediency, by consideration of what the present régime would take. Problems had to be shelved for the time being, not because there was as yet no reasonable way of reinterpreting tradition, but because any questions of those matters would raise a storm about one's ears. People possess varying degrees of psychological strength. I, too, began to calculate how far I could go without openly challenging authority. I see now how twisted and inhibited my mind became in trying to conform, partly from a sincere desire to accept authority, partly from the pressure exerted by an authority prepared to suppress dissentients. Some may say that, had I felt like that, I should have struggled for interior freedom and stayed within the Church to become a witness to the truth. But each one has to take the road to freedom that is open to him. I knew I could win interior freedom only by leaving the social structure of the Roman Church and shaking off the grip of the system that was oppressing me. Besides, when I eventually faced up to the implications of my desire for truth, I found that the Roman Church no longer had sufficient credibility to hold me.

Thus, I reached the conviction that the Roman Church is not a zone of truth but, rather, of untruth, and so is no longer credible for me as the embodiment of Christian faith. I say this conscious of the genuine love and zeal for truth found in many of its members. I would not do them an injustice. But my judgement concerns structures, together with the attitude and actions typical of those structures, not the noble achievement of individuals who successfully resist the dominant influence. Further, I do not find my conviction weakened by the necessity of admitting that a similar untruth is prevalent in many areas of our contemporary society. I do not think I am blind or naïve about this. But I hold that the Christian faith is the liberation of man for truth, and I am not prepared to acknowledge it as credibly embodied in a social structure that I cannot experience as a zone of truth.

3. THE CHURCH AND LOVE

I am explaining why the Roman Catholic Church ceased for me to be a credible embodiment of Christian faith, hope and love. I will now turn to the question of Christian love and the social structure of the Church. Let me repeat that I am concerned with Church structure, with the attitudes and actions it embodies and provokes, not with people as individuals. What I am going to say does not therefore deny the immense love found in many within the Church. My contention is that the present structure of the Church is an obstacle to that Christian love.

I will return later to the general problem of the relation between structures or institutions and persons. This will give me the opportunity of explaining more fully why the present Church structure is stifling Christian love. But I should here at once say that I see no essential opposition between institutions and personal freedom. On the contrary, a person becomes a person only in relation with others; he attains personal maturity and freedom only in and through community; and human community is embodied in institutional structures. For man as a social being institutions are necessary, as the body is necessary for human life or as language is necessary for social communication. Institutions are the medium for mutual presence, the embodiment of common thought and the means for comon action. And they alone provide the environment required for the emergence and development of each person as a person.

My objection, therefore, is not against institutions as such. It does not arise from a prejudice that all institutions are impersonal and inimical to persons. What I hold is that the present social structure of the Church is no longer a living institution, inasmuch as it no longer adequately embodies Christian experience. It is an antiquated structure out of harmony with the thinking, needs and desires of active Christians today. It clashes with the contemporary Christian consciousness and cannot serve as the expression and vehicle of Christian commitment in the modern world. Since it survives as an empty shell from a past age, the attempt to keep it in being is inevitably inimical to persons. Defence of this institution, with insistence upon an authority structure no longer appropriate, does in fact mean the subordination of persons to an impersonal, because dead, system. Concern to maintain the structure against the mounting forces of disintegration has led to an increasing lack of concern for persons. The inadequacy of the structure to the present situation and the growing signs of a breakdown of authority within the Church itself are causing fear, insecurity and anxiety, with a consequent intolerance and lack of love. People are being deprived of the social structure they need; many are being damaged and destroyed as persons by the efforts to preserve an institutional structure from the past, which, inadequate in itself and unreasonably defended, has become an impersonal, unfree and inhuman system.

To anyone who acknowledges, rightly as I think, the fundamental importance in personal development of a complete openness and fidelity to truth, what I have previously said about the Church and truth will be sufficient to show the crippling effect upon persons of the present institutional set-up. The constant frustration of man's dynamic movement towards truth prevents personal expansion and blocks the source of personal freedom. And all genuine love rests upon truth. Christian love is no exception. It rests upon faith as an entry into the truth of God and a liberation of man for all truth. Christians for whom doctrine is distorted into prejudice and who are rendered tense and fearful by the suppression of questioning cannot love as they should. They are without the full basis of Christian truth for their love. They fear the freedom that would liberate them for love. They are too repressed and anxious to meet others with joy and tolerance. Prisoners of a narrow, intolerant system, they, too, be-

come narrow and intolerant. Only those who shake off the pressure
of the institution and manage largely to ignore it are able to release
the full expansive dynamism of Christian love. They may not
themselves realise what they are doing, but others will remark that
they are not institution men.

I spoke previously of the unhappiness I met among people within
the Church. Unhappiness is no basis for lovingness. Suffering indeed
may serve as a purifying influence and lead to a greater capacity for
love. But a loving person will have a core of deep happiness, despite
difficulty, suffering and external failure. Unfortunately, so many in
the Church are at war with themselves. The teaching they hear has
no purchase upon their minds; the laws of the Church do not fit their
lives; the liturgy has ceased to be meaningful for them; they sometimes come into conflict with the clerical administration of the
Church. Something, they recognise, is wrong. Is it themselves? But
they cannot change their experience as modern men. I think they
would be happy enough if the problem of Christian faith in the
modern world were frankly and honestly tackled in a community
that genuinely engaged their lives. Problems even of faith are not of
themselves personally destructive. Why should a believer fear truth?
People are, however, held by an institution in which they have no
real part or say and in which they cannot be themselves. They are
reluctant to release themselves from it because they see no alternative and instinctively they want some social structure in which to live
as Christians. But the more earnest they are the greater the tension
of living under a structure that simply does not correspond to their
experience and needs. Recent changes have increased the tension by
raising hopes without fulfilling them, and their chief effect has been
to show that tinkering with the present structure is no solution. Man
cannot develop or confront his problems outside a social environment adapted to his needs. No wonder, then, Catholics are unhappy,
deprived of a suitable structure for their Christian faith and experience and saddled with a vast, complex system against which they
dash themselves in vain. With authority increasingly anxious and
subjects increasingly resentful, there is little room for love.

Christian love, unselfish and concerned with others, is nevertheless an outflow of a personality unfolded and fulfilled. Not indeed
that it is the result of a narcissistic self-cultivation, but that it is the

outgoing radiance of a person freed for love of others by sufficient self-possession, with the security and confidence afforded by adequate personal development. That this development is seen by Christians as taking place under the saving influence of Christ does not remove the need for it nor imply that ordinary human factors may be ignored. Granted that a person's worth before God is not measured by achievement and that the psychologically handicapped are not to be blamed for their defects, it remains true that people stunted in their personal development, immature, fearful and insecure, will not be capable of actually giving themselves to others in an outpouring of unselfish love. The present social structure of the Church is, however, having the effect of stunting the development of people and is thus hindering the expansion of Christian love.

It is not easy to document such a statement. I can give only a personal assessment, though this is based upon a long and extensive experience. Some, I know, will repudiate my conclusion. I write, however, confident that only too many in the Church know what I am referring to and can confirm it from their own experience.

Occasionally an occurrence or a publication illuminates the situation I have been trying to describe and draws attention to it. Such an instance was the article of Robert Blair Kaiser on "The Nuns That Quit," published in the American magazine, *Ladies' Home Journal*, for April 1967. His starting-point was the reliable estimate that at least 3,600 American nuns, not novices or postulants but professed sisters, left the religious life in 1966. Now, American nuns in general give the impression of an openness unusual among religious women, and I am not alone in regarding them as the most dynamic element in American Catholic life. Yet the article, written after interviews with dozens of former sisters, reveals a story of women frustrated in their personal development as Christians by the rigidity of an inadequate social structure. Some of the remarks recorded go straight to the point:

I just thought I'd be more of a Christian if I left. I simply had to have freedom to make mistakes. And it wasn't a question of turning my back on Christ. Instead of saying that I want what Christ wants, I began to feel that the good things I want might be the same as what Christ wants.

I left to be free, to be able to live my own rhythm.

I had to leave the convent to do what I entered it to do—live for others.

Being a sister is great when you are young. But once you start observing the older sisters, you begin to see where it all leads. I started to wonder how long it would take me to become as bitter as some of them.

Now I am available, I can be of service wherever the opportunity presents itself. In the convent it was all so abstract. Love was a forbidden word. Literally. We signed our letters "charity."

But the Church is caught up with the status quo. Those in charge believe in the institution rather than in the people it should try to serve.

I know that some will want to dismiss that report with contempt as a piece of popular journalism. But there is an extensive enough literature on the renewal of the religious life from which the same criticisms can be drawn, though they are usually wrapped up more carefully. And the increase in the numbers leaving the religious life and the decline in religious vocations are facts too well known for denial. That the key factor in this trend is not lack of generosity but the failure to adapt the religious life to contemporary consciousness and needs is generally accepted. It is worth noticing that the refusal to change leads to unchristian results. An archaic institution because destructive in its effects becomes an heretical structure.

In this respect attention should be paid to the latent as distinct from the manifest function of many practices imposed upon religious. The uniform religious habit, the change of name, the public confession of faults in community, the denunciation of one another's faults, the exclusion of particular friendships, the opening of letters, various penitential practices of an humiliating kind: all these are presented as part of a total surrender to Christ. But their latent function is the abolition of personal identity and the complete subordination of the person to the system. A lack of psychological awareness in an earlier age rendered these practices both more excusable and less harmful. Again, in the past the institution did correspond to the general level of personal development and contemporary psychic

needs. Today, however, the structure of religious life clashes with
the self-understanding common to most people, so that the attempt
to maintain that structure becomes a crushing of persons to fit the
system.

Am I forgetting the renewal that is in fact going on? No, I
acknowledge that many changes have taken place. But my estimate
of what is happening differs from the accepted version.

What has struck me in reading the books on the renewal of the
religious life is that the forces of change do not originate within the
social structure of the Church. They come from outside, mediated by
those who have had the opportunity of secular experience and secular studies. The Church is slowly being compelled against its own
resistance to admit elementary principles of psychological, social
and even physical health long taken for granted in the secular world.
Now, that Christians should learn from the secular study of man is
perfectly normal. It corresponds to the manner in which the understanding of Christian faith and life has developed from the beginning. But that the Church, far from welcoming and promoting the
advances made by human and social studies, should lag behind until
the threat of a breakdown necessitates concessions indicates that
something is very wrong with its structure. Do not Christians claim
to offer men liberation through Christ? Is this claim credible when
Church authority has to be dragged with an immense expenditure of
energy into allowing what is ordinarily recognised by men at large as
reasonable conditions for personal development to the members dedicated to its service in the religious life? My belief in the liberation
brought by Christ has led me to the conclusion that this liberation is
not represented and embodied in the present structure of the Church.

Thus, the movement of reform has not reconciled me to the existing institutional structure of the Church, but underlined its hindering
irrelevance. While the reform of the religious life has had to struggle
against an inertia within the religious orders themselves, particularly
among the older religious, the chief obstacle is the reluctance of
ecclesiastical authority to allow radical change. There is great talk of
renewal, couched in high-flown spiritual language, but when the first
tentative reforms begin to have practical effects, the authorities draw
back, uttering warnings and issuing new restrictions. They are frightened of the confusion and untidiness of growth. The plain fact is that

the present system cannot take more than superficial adjustments. I do not want to give the impression of disparaging the noble efforts of those working for reform. I admire their aims and determination. But it seems to me they cannot fully succeed within the present framework of the institutional Church. They are asking for more freedom than it can allow while retaining its present identity. I think that some of the more clear-sighted reformers are beginning to perceive that.

Possibly I have been unfair in taking religious orders of women as an example of what happens to people within the Church. Women, lay as well as religious, have notoriously a raw deal in the Church. One of the clearest signs that the structure of the Church is antiquated is the attitude to women it embodies and enforces. Apart from being one of the signs of a wrong and unhealthy approach to sex, this attitude makes the Church a quaint survival from a past social order. But perhaps the refusal of adulthood to women is an exceptional case, which should not be used as a general criticism of the Church's social structure. There may be some truth in this. On the other hand, it can be argued that religious women are those most fully absorbed into the social structure of the Church, so that its typical effects can in them be seen in purest form. Others, including priests, can at least partly escape from the impact of the Church into the freer environment of the secular world.

At the same time, the lives of seminarians and priests reveal the same story of a frustration of personal development, with a consequent blocking of the expansion of Christian love.

The abundant writing on seminary renewal catalogues similar defects to those found in religious orders of women. I doubt whether anyone who has worked in a seminary will deny that it is often the better student with greater maturity and personal independence who leaves. And it is instructive to follow up some of those who leave or who have been dismissed and find how, seemingly immature in the seminary, they have found their personal identity in responsible work. What is saddening is to observe how far the seminary system is out of accord with the educational, psychological and sociological understanding long since operative in institutions outside the Church. A wry example of this is the way that faults and virtues of students are discussed without any awareness that often both are simply the reaction of different temperaments to the pressures of a closed environment. The study of the effects of so-called total institutions upon their inmates is valuable here. Again, I wish seminary reformers every success, but my own view is that seminaries, more or less in their present form, are necessary to prolong the existence of the present social structure of the Church outside its original context, namely, Christendom. Either radical reform will be successfully resisted or that structure will collapse.

Priests are not allowed to be vocal in the Church, although some more recently have broken their silence. But the conditions of priestly life are well known. They are hardly a model for those seeking a responsible and satisfying task with reasonable personal freedom. The uncompromising judgement of priestly life by the young is certainly a factor in the decline of vocations. And I have met more than one priest who admitted to me that they would never encourage a young man to be a priest, so unwilling were they to expose others to the experience they themselves had endured. Assistant priests are a depressed class, deprived often for years of any responsibility. Not all are so unfortunate as the priest who lamented to me that in sixteen years of priesthood he had not once had the opportunity of making a responsible, personal decision in his priestly work. The lucky few, like myself, gain independence through a special job. Again, conditions vary from diocese to diocese. But the numbers queuing up for laicization show how much is wrong and constitute a silent rebellion. It is too facile to explain this as a failure to resist temptations against celibacy. Granted that the imposition of celibacy by law creates its own problems, other causes are also at work here. And it is understandable enough that a priest looking for human wholeness after a life of frustration should turn to marriage, dangerous as this approach to marriage might prove for himself and his partner.

Alan Lynn did not leave the priesthood to marry, but on account of the Church's defective attitude to modern war and birth control. He has become a student social worker. This is how he describes the contrast with his priestly life in *The Scotsman* for Wednesday, March 8, 1967:

My subsequent life as a student social worker has been illuminating: to be treated as a person and called by one's first name; to be trusted in mixed company and not subjected to an 11 P.M. curfew; to be allowed to use one's room as a home and to have visitors; to enjoy spontaneous intelligent discussions as a normal everyday experience; to be a member of an institution which is not obsessed by a seniority-juniority complex.

The very triviality of the points highlights the petty restrictions which hedged about his life as an ordained minister of Christ.

It is not surprising that men kept in short trousers for years should be incapable of authority and responsibility when thrust upon them as parish priests in middle age. I cannot blame the parish priest who browbeats his assistants, works off the tension of administrative worry by haranguing the people incessantly about money, supports his ego by a building spree, and in general acts like a petty tyrant in his parochial domain. Men such as that are victims of a system that destroys persons.

I know young priests who suffer a much greater agony than I have described. They imbibe the insights of modern theology and a high ideal of the Church from a seminary professor or from reading. They endure the seminary as a transitional phase in their lives. They come out resolved to spend themselves for Christ. And then they find themselves compelled to live a life that contradicts their Christian convictions. There is a barrier between themselves and the poor or even the ordinary working class. The presbytery is a castle from which the laity are excluded, apart from an occasional interview in the parlour. It is not a focus for the Christian community, a place where parishioners can be invited for a meal and, feeling at home, meet and talk with the priests and one another. The assistant priests themselves are often more like lodgers than fellow workers in the ministry. With no fellowship among the priests, no genuine sharing of life, no working as a team, no common prayer, how can the zealous young priest with any sincerity preach that the Christian Church is a community? And wanting to share his life with the people whom he was sent to serve, he finds himself drawn into a style of living that keeps him apart, remote, with money but no responsibility or struggling to make ends meet, forced to live in a material environment that goes against the witness he is trying to give to Christ. Surrounded perhaps with social or racial problems, the priest wants to speak unambiguously and act effectually. More often than not, he is prevented from doing so. Any action that has bite gets him into trouble with his superiors. Imaginative initiative even in less ticklish matters than social or racial injustice is quickly squelched. He is under pressure to become a smoothly running sacramental machine and an obedient functionary for the administration of the propertied corporation that goes under the name of Christ's Church. His reward will be a comfortable bachelordom with eventual promotion within the system. Sympathy with the poor and the oppressed is indeed the official line, provided it stops at paternalistic compassion and spiritual exhortation; to want to espouse their cause or share their lives is imprudent extremism. Preaching the Gospel is a duty laid upon him, but it is not expected to disturb or imply any changes in the *status quo*, whether of Church or of State. I am afraid that many an idealistic young priest succumbs and learns to close his eyes to the glaring irrelevancy and his mind to the blatant contradiction in what is supposed to constitute his priestly ministry. Some hold out within the system itself. But there are others who ask themselves whether they should not leave to avoid betraying Christ.

Reform of the priesthood raises the whole question of the social structure appropriated to the Church in a secular world. What should be the shape of the ordained ministry? Is not a more diverse distribution of functions called for? Need the ministry be a permanent state of life? What is the relation of the Christian minister to secular society and secular commitment? Why should worker-priests be exceptional? Should not the imposition of celibacy go? To answer these and other similar questions requires a rethinking of the relation of the ministry to the Christian community and of the Christian community to the secular world. These questions go deep. For that reason the Decree on the Ministry and Life of Priests, issued by the Second Vatican Council, is too platitudinous to be very helpful. It is in fact a typical example of that avoidance of the real problems by an escape into the spiritual which has been the trap for many a reform. Not an idealization of the established order, but a questioning of it will alone serve to meet the present situation.

In complaining of the defects of religious and priests it is only fair to remember that they are victims of the system under which they live. The same must be said of bishops and of the Pope himself.

These are good men. Not always outstanding, but upright men trying to do the will of God. Outside their official duties they are often kindly and loving, wanting to give and receive human friendship. In their official capacity they are personally affable; they try to be sympathetic and helpful; they certainly act from a sincere conviction that they are serving others for Christ. This is not said as a matter of form or to heighten the effect of the criticism I am going to make. I got to know a fair number of bishops at the Vatican Council and the men I met do not correspond to the figures railed at by the more exasperated among the clergy and laity. There are, I know, exceptions, but it would be difficult to find another body of men in high position of such personal humility, goodness and integrity. But except a few, such as the late, deeply mourned Bishop Bekkers of 's Hertogenbosch in Holland, they are servants of a system. They have been chosen for the most part because of their institutional conformity. Despite the many brave words in the Council, when it comes to the push, they submit to the system. How many have acted independently, even in a tentative fashion, to relieve the distress of their people in the present intolerable situation over birth control? In defence of the institution they can be ruthless and inconsiderate, overriding personal freedom and indifferent to personal rights and needs. As I said in my article in *The Observer*: "Even good people in a position of authority become victims of the system and cease to act towards others in a normally human way."

Let me take an example from the article of Alan Lynn I have already quoted:

The Church's concern for the individual person is well illustrated by the fact that I have not yet had any reply whatsoever to my application to leave the priesthood. I have not had even an acknowledgement, much less a decision. I wrote by recorded delivery to my bishop in December, pointing out that nine months was a long time—even for Rome. I asked him to confirm that he had forwarded the application, and that no reply had been received. That, too, has elicited no reply. The Church, which claims to represent Christ, fails to give the elementary courtesy expected of any secular business firm.

A failure to answer letters may seem a minor fault, but in this instance it manifests the utter lack of concern for a person who has dared to go against the institution. The treatment of priests who leave or who "cause trouble" is in general a fair example of the unchristian writing off or crushing of those who fail to conform. The dominance of a legalistic morality and the slow grinding of a complex canon law, especially in matrimonial matters, produces its own crop of personal tragedies among the laity. But the paramount concern to preserve the system leads to a bureaucratic insensitivity to people and their suffering. Then there is intolerance towards dissent, whether the dissent is doctrinal or practical, and the evident desire to suppress all criticism and questioning of authority. Fortunately, Church authority is ultimately impotent in a secular society against a man with the strength to stick to his sincere convictions, but the spirit that reveals itself in the actions that are taken within the range of power available is not reassuring for those anxious about personal rights and freedom. Few would care to be under the untrammelled power of the present Church. It is surely anomalous to be protected against the Church of Christ and assured of some freedom and justice from it by the restraining force of secular society. Am I to accept such a Church as the embodiment of Christian love?

In varying measure the laity escape from the influence of the social structure of the Church. This does not mean, I hasten to add, that I am identifying the Church with the ecclesiastical hierarchy. But I am, as I have explained, dealing with its social structure. This structure is in fact hierarchical in form, so that the Church is governed by Pope and bishops and in many of its everyday activities directed by the local clergy. It does, however, include the laity. All the same, the recent attempts to restore lay people to their proper place within the Church and see that they fully exercise their role show that their lives are not sufficiently engaged by the Church to which they belong. The lives of many are only marginally influenced by their membership of the Church, and even among those of deep Christian conviction there are some who are working out their Christian commitment chiefly under influences coming to them from outside the Church. In assessing the credibility of the present structure of the Church as the embodiment of Christ, it is necessary, then, to try to discern the attitudes and actions it brings about in its members or at least allows to flow back into itself for the development of the common social consciousness. Not all that the laity do or say as individuals can be attributed to the Church as a social entity and used to characterise its structure and life. Admittedly, this is likewise true of individual bishops and priests; but their lives are in general more fully absorbed and determined by their Church membership.

The first relevant fact in assessing the Church as a social structure is the number of people who have left it. Catholics sometimes talk as if the multitude of the dechristianised came from another planet, instead of acknowledging that it is made up of people or their children whom the Church could not hold. I do not wish to be supercilious, but I cannot forebear a sad smile when it is without a second thought urged against me that a disintegration of the present structure of the Church would lead to a great loss of faith among ordinary people. After all, what has already happened? The present structure has been insistently maintained, but *pari passu* a vast loss of faith has occurred among the masses of Europe. No doubt complex causes have been at work. I am not suggesting that the Church is entirely to blame nor forgetting that evil forces will always threaten Christ's Church and lead many to apostasy. But historically it is highly improbable to explain the loss of faith and the present rejection of the Church by so many of good will by external forces attacking a Church adequate in its structure and happily adapted to contemporary man and his experience. Apart from other objections, this would not explain the difficulties against the present form of the Church felt by those who remain within. And even a little experience with the young, who are leaving the Church in great numbers, would make one hesitate to exonerate the Church. I suggest that it is a reasonable hypothesis that the Church has failed to adapt itself to the changes that have taken place in human consciousness, both individual and social, so that it no longer serves as an appropriate institutional expression for modern man: and, further, that this is an important factor in the decline of Christian faith and Church membership. This hypothesis is at least worthy of consideration and should be closely examined before an attempt is made to preserve what faith is left by a continued insistence upon the present social structure of the Church. Otherwise, there is a possibility that the cause of the disease will be advocated as its remedy.

In considering the laity I turn next to the large number of educated people who have been called *emigrés de l'interieur* in their relation to the Church. These continue their sacramental practice and are sometimes devout Christians to the limited extent in which the Christian life may be understood in terms of personal piety. But beyond that they do not have and under present conditions do not want anything further to do with the life and work of the Church. They do not participate in any common activity among Catholics, except for the liturgy, and they avoid any involvement in Church affairs. Some have tried to work as Christians within the structure of the Church, but as professional and educated people they have found it impossible to endure their exclusion from the decision-making process and their treatment as minors by bishop and priest. Those who have attempted to assume the kind of relationship and role they take for granted in their secular lives have only too often been rebuffed and seen their initiatives squashed. Many have sensed the situation from the outset and preferred to have as little as possible to do with an organisation that has no place for people like themselves. Now, I do not mean to imply that the mission of lay people is confined to work within Church groups or even chiefly exercised in that form. The layman will carry out his mission as a Christian and as a member of the Church principally in his secular environment, namely in and through his ordinary work in the world. But I am speaking of those who are partly alienated from the Church and do not experience it as a Christian community that engages their lives and integrated their Christian endeavour with that of other members for a common purpose. They find the social structure of the Church offensive and out of accord with their needs, so that it does not provide a framework for strengthening their Christian work, an opportunity for discussion and mutual support. They use the Church like a filling station to get the sacraments. Any further involvement would be stifling.

There are indeed many earnest lay people, though their number in proportion to the total membership is probably small, who are working as Christians openly in relation with the Church. Some belong to professedly Catholic or, more recently, ecumenical groups and organisations. Others use their talents as writers and journalists to take part in the mission of the Church. Then there are those who in their professions or trade unions are known as Catholics and take a Christian stand where this is called for or simply work with others at human problems but openly from the Christian convictions they have as Catholics. Some join with others of no Christian conviction in striving against social or racial injustice, but do so as bearers of a witness in these matters they think the Catholic Church and its members should give. All these people would want what they do to be counted as the work of the Church, which they rightly refuse to identify with the ecclesiastical hierarchy.

But how far does all this admirable Christian work serve to establish the credibility of the present Church as a social embodiment of Christ and Christian love? I have no desire to overstate my case. I am trying to discern the truth. I admit that this activity of lay people, supported by a number of priests and particularly prominent in recent years, is the most powerful argument I know for belief in the Roman Catholic Church. But in the end it has failed to convince me, because reflection has led me to the conclusion that, were the implications of this witness to Christ and Christian love followed through, the result would be a Church essentially different in structure from the Catholic Church as it at present exists.

I have no need to exaggerate. I readily acknowledge that many Catholics working in the manner I have described are happy about the Church and glory in their membership. But is it not true that the groupings of active Christians correspond less and less to the boundaries, divisions and structures of the existing Churches? Catholics find themselves more closely united, in both deep spiritual conviction and common work, with other Christians or even some non-Christians, than with some members of their own Church or with many priests and most bishops. Membership of a particular Church ceases to matter much in their work and sometimes seems quite irrelevant. And increasingly for active Catholics the attempt to remain close to the Church and relate their work to it produces tension, caused by frequent clashes not only with authority but with the established set-up and mentality generally and by growing impatience with the institutional expression allowed. A sign of the loosening relation with the present structure of the Church is the recourse to experimental liturgies which ignore both existing rubrics and denominational restrictions on participation. This is done in defiance of authority, not I think from irresponsible rebellion but from an imperative need in people to find an appropriate expression for their Christian experience. Opposition to the existing institution occurs again and again over both aims and methods. I have a fairly wide experience of active lay Christians in both Great Britain and America. The impression I have received is that the Church as an institutional structure is constantly in their way as an obstacle to effective Christian action. Some indeed spend a considerable part of their time and energy in battling with it; others have found release by largely ignoring it.

And from where do the more active Christians draw their motivating beliefs and values? Do the attitudes that mark them arise from within the social structure of an hierarchically constituted Church? All the key Christian movements of today—biblical, doctrinal, liturgical, ecumenical, social—cross all the denominations and are creating new unities among Christians that do not follow the existing divisions. These movements have little to do with present Christian social structures; they have spread by open communication, more often than not in opposition to the established institutions. While, admittedly, bishops are not expected to originate new ideas, in any theology of the episcopate they must be given a meaningful role in fostering, co-ordinating, discerning and sanctioning the Christian insights on which members of the Church base their lives. But how many are the active lay Catholics who have long since ceased to look to the bishops for any doctrinal or practical guidance and support? They have no sense that the beliefs and values that motivate them are dependent upon the episcopate, and they have resigned themselves to working without leadership from the bishops, grateful if they can escape interference. The bishops in the Second Vatican Council certainly recovered some lost ground and took a step forward in sanctioning some of the new ideas. I do not think, however, that I am being ungenerous in saying that, viewed in the light of continuing and increasingly rapid developments, what they did was too little and too late. And that brings me to the observation that the ideas now being put forward by the reforming element within the Church are diverging more and more from official teaching. Particularly in Holland and America, there is an upsurge of thinking and writing that cannot be reconciled with the doctrinal stance of the Roman Church nor assimilated, I think, into its present structure. And that, I might add, is also the judgement of Pope Paul and most bishops.

I suggest that there are two possible ways of interpreting what is happening.

The first is to regard the unrest and deviations as a temporary disorder, inevitable after a Council and in a time of renewal, which will, however, be eventually overcome. When the excitement is over, people will be brought back to submission to authority and into conformity with the established order. There will be some adjustments, but the existing structure and official teaching will remain essentially unchanged. This is the attitude naïvely summed up by Archbishop Cardinale, the Apostolic Delegate in Britain, in an interview with George Scott: "Everyone will line up at the end when an admirable obedience to the decisions of a Council is generally witnessed."[1]

The second is to recognise that we are observing the disintegration of the existing institutional Churches and the struggling emergence of new forms of Christian presence in the secular world of today. This, in my opinion, is the more likely interpretation. The first view does not do justice to the dimensions of the present crisis. It presupposes a trend towards conformity of which there is no sign; on the contrary, the dissent is increasing. Further, it whitewashes the spiritual and intellectual bankruptcy of existing authority and the established order. Whatever the confusion of ideas among the dissidents, these are at least tackling the real problems and coming up with promising lies of thought and action.

Those are the reasons why I do not find the admirable Christian work of the lay people striving for Christian renewal an ultimately convincing argument for the Roman Catholic Church. For me it is not a proof that the existing social structure is a credible embodiment of an active Christian love, but the delineation of a new structure gradually emerging.

I have now to consider the multitude of ordinary Catholics, those the bishops constantly refer to as the simple faithful, the fear of scandalising whom is used to justify their attempted suppression of anything likely to disturb the *status quo*.

As a matter of fact I myself have never found the simple faithful as simple as all that. Some I have met of no formal education worth mentioning have been quite capable of making penetrating remarks upon the Church and the present situation. Particularly noticeable is that in this world of modern communication they are not content

[1] George Scott, *The RCs: A Report on Roman Catholics in Britain Today* (Hutchinson, London, 1967), p. 275.

with the evasion of questions. I have also discovered how much they welcome solid doctrinal nourishment when this is given them in ordinary language. "Why has no one told us this before?" is a remark I have heard more than once after a sermon or talk.

But what depresses me when I think of the multitude of ordinary Catholics is the spiritual impoverishment in which they have been left and the distortion of personality to which they have been subjected.

I know Catholics, naturally intelligent and teachable though not highly educated, who have been to Catholic schools and attended Mass faithfully for years, hearing countless sermons. They are docile to the Church, eager to follow its guidance and laws. But what formation have they been given as Christians? Their religion is a projection of psychic needs, expressed in a variety of secondary and sometimes odd devotions. They have little understanding of the fundamental Christian truths. Their personal consciences are unformed. They have not passed the heteronomous stage of personal development and, stunted by legalism, they are incapable of a truly personal moral decision. Their confessions are childish and sometimes a compulsive spiritual cleansing similar to a compulsion to wash one's hands. Confession is also used as a means of avoiding any confrontation with the deeper issues of the moral life or of lessening the pressure towards a genuine conversion. To confess one's sin repeatedly can be a way of coming to terms with it. Their religion is shot through with fear and anxiety, particularly about sex but also about anything that seems to threaten salvation. It is hardly a religion of love and of joy, of salvation received, not held out in the future under stringent and apparently arbitrary conditions. Mortal sin and its avoidance would seem to dominate their lives.

Some accused me of an almost hysterical imbalance when I spoke in my article in *The Observer* of a collective neurosis in the Church and suggested an investigation of the pathology of the present Church. I had in mind all the effects of the perpetual dominance of a dead system over the person: the fear, anxiety and insecurity manifested by authority; the tension and unhappiness among earnest and active Catholics; the immaturity, distortion of personality and frustrated development observable among the general faithful. Perhaps these words of a Catholic psychiatrist, who wrote to me after my decision to leave the Church, express better than I could something of what I am trying to say:

Since I understand only too well the neurosis you refer to in the article I am always available to any fellow Catholic or Christian to help in any possible way. This neurosis is essentially the setting up of the Church as a massive supportive entity, which offered security at the price of personal impoverishment and frequently annihilation. The institutional Church is terrified to lose this so-called strength because it has yet to find the strength in love which the Lord gave us and which exists in pockets within the Church. There is as yet little understanding that the massive structure erected is conditioned by the social structure of the past but serving primarily psychological needs of dependency and immaturity. One major explanation of the Papacy is the need to have someone to lean on and the pathetic attempts to preserve this structure in the terror of being abandoned. We have yet to find the support of Christ in our interpersonal adult relationships. But the Church must be seen as a developing entity in terms of thousands of years and one hopes that yours and the sacrifice of others will help to achieve this.

I should recall at this point that the basis for my present examination of the Roman Catholic Church is the conviction that the Church of Christ should be an embodiment of truth and love. Unless, despite inevitable abuses and failures, a social entity retains sufficient signs that it is in reality such an embodiment, it is no longer credible as the Church of Christ. The points I have been making are diverse and some of them banally familiar, but they have been given because they converge for me upon the conclusion that the Roman Catholic Church as a distinct social entity with a particular social structure is not credible as an embodiment in this world of the truth and love of Christ.

4. THE POPE AND BIRTH CONTROL

In the process of my reaching this conclusion and taking the consequent decision to leave the Church, the papal statement, made on 29 October 1966, postponing a decisive pronouncement on birth control had the effect of an igniting spark. But the blaze it kindled in my mind had the accumulated material of years of experience and reflection to work upon. People have exaggerated the role of the birth-control issue in my decision. The papal statement came as a climactic incident, but I did not leave the Church merely or even chiefly on account of its attitude to birth control.

Let me, however, try to explain why the papal statement had such a violent effect upon me. With piercing clarity it focussed the lack of concern for truth and the lack of concern for persons that in so many ways I had been finding characteristic of the Roman Church. In a striking manner it illustrated the subordination of truth to the prestige of authority and the sacrifice of persons to the preservation of an out-of-date institution, which have been typical marks of ecclesiastical policy and behaviour.

First, the papal statement was dishonest. It was a diplomatic lie, covering over an awkward but plain fact.

Pope Paul in that Address, it will be remembered, stated that the existing norm in the matter of contraception must still be followed and said that it should not be considered as not binding "as if the teaching authority of the Church were now in a state of doubt, whereas it is in a period of study and reflection." *Non dubium sed studium*, as the Pope is alleged to have summed up his statement to a visiting bishop.

Now, it is evident even to the world at large that the teaching authority of the Catholic Church, namely, the Pope and bishops, is (at the time of writing no decision has yet been given, and what is relevant here is the time when Pope Paul made his delaying statement) in a state of bewildered and anxious doubt concerning the previously strongly affirmed stand against contraception. The failure to issue a clear statement after widespread questioning and years of study is sufficient enough proof of that. As I wrote in my editorial in *The Clergy Review* for December 1966:

In view of the serious and open challenge to that teaching and the urgent pastoral necessity of clarifying the position with a decisive pronouncement, the fact of an indefinite postponement of such a pronouncement is of itself cogent evidence that doctrinally a cloud of doubt hangs over the matter. The present Address is, in fact, carefully worded to avoid predetermining the future decision; nothing is said to exclude a change in the existing norms. Certainly, there must be some reason for a failure after three years of study expressly to reaffirm the previous teaching. The presence of such an inhibiting reason is in ordinary parlance called a doubt.

Defenders of the Pope against my charge in *The Observer* article that, in order to save the authority of the Holy See, he told a lie by dishonestly evading the truth and denying a plain fact have not themselves attempted to deny that there is a state of doubt concerning the teaching on birth control. They see that as too evident a fact for denial. But they consider that I have misinterpreted the bearing of the Pope's words.

The most powerful presentation of this case is by John T. Noonan, Jr., in his article "The Pope's Conscience" in *Commonweal* for 17 February 1967. He argues that, considering the knowledge and attitude of the Pope himself and the language of recent official pronouncements, we should take it as admitted that there is a doubt whether the existing norms constitute divine law. What is not in doubt is the governing norms themselves as law binding the faithful and requiring their generous obedience. In brief, the Pope in effect said that the existing norms are undoubtedly still binding, although he implied that they might change in the future and therefore were not beyond doubt divine law. This roughly corresponds to the attempted explanation I myself gave in the editorial I have quoted, in which I went on to say that the Pope should be understood as excluding a state of doubt only in a juridical and practical sense. However, I now see that I was covering over the unpleasant fact in order to avoid publicly attacking the Pope. This was one of the instances when with a jolt I realised the effect that the Church system was having on my own honesty and sincerity.

I do not think that the explanation of Dr Noonan will pass muster.

First, the Pope did not say what in this explanation he is alleged to have said. To accuse, as Dr Noonan does, those who make this objection, of being guilty of "fundamental literalism" is disingenuous. The *magisterium* or teaching authority of the Church has taught with an insistence that barely falls short of an *ex cathedra* definition that contraception is against the natural and divine law. To declare that the teaching authority—note, the *magisterium*, not the legislative or jurisdictional authority—is not in a state of doubt but only in a period of study is reasonably understood as meaning that it does not doubt its previous teaching that contraception is against the natural and divine law. An argument from the knowledge and attitude of the Pope and the language of previous pronouncements is an argument that, in the absence of further, adequate support from the text itself, concludes to what the Pope should have said, not to what he did say. In the light of the general handling of the birth-control issue (including the fight behind the scenes at the Council to prevent the virtual closing of the question by a papal modification of the text of the Constitution on the Church in the Modern World), it is not unreasonable to suspect papal vacillation and an attempt to have it both ways when inconsistencies in the Pope's words and actions are observed. Such an attempt to allow for future change without, however, admitting doubt is indeed illustrated with beautiful absurdity by the Vatican Press Officer in the statement already quoted that the Church was not in a state of doubt, but that when the Pope issued his decision it would pass from one state of certainty to another.

Next, the change from norms binding by divine law to norms of ecclesiastical law is itself so momentous that for it to be made as an implication of an ambiguous statement is already a dishonest evasion of the truth. This change is in itself a very great shift of position. The Pope is not acting straightforwardly unless in a matter of such practical urgency he speaks clearly in describing the present situation. The Church has insisted so strongly upon the natural and divine law against contraception and intervened for that reason so considerably in people's lives that it cannot in justice and truth allow a doubt about the grounds of its teaching to be inferred from scattered hints, while the Pope without qualification continues to say that the teaching authority must not be understood as being in a state of doubt. I should myself consider it a sufficient indictment of the papal attitude to truth that in restricting the liberty of the faithful in a matter intimately and sometimes disastrously affecting their lives he has not spoken clearly about the uncertainty of the grounds on which this is done. Surely, it is already intolerable, if not tragically ridiculous, that there should be room for debate about what he meant. And in view of the general puzzlement the statement provoked it can hardly be maintained that there is no room for such debate.

Further, Dr Noonan's interpretation would have practical consequences that the Pope himself and most of the bishops do not admit. Ecclesiastical laws do not bind in the same way as natural and divine law. That is why I described the change from one binding force to the other as momentous. Ecclesiastical laws do not bind a person's conscience when there are grave reasons militating against their observance. An ecclesiastical law never has an absolute force in conscience; as a positive law it can be left aside where there are serious enough contrary reasons. If, then, the existing prohibition of contraception is not grounded upon natural and divine law because the extent and bearing of such law is uncertain, it becomes an obligation of ecclesiastical law. According to Dr Noonan, an insistence upon its continued force as ecclesiastical law was the meaning of the papal exclusion of doubt. But in that case it is not absolutely binding, and people faced with weighty enough reasons for not observing it can in good conscience consider themselves justified in breaking it. What reasons are weighty enough would no doubt be discussed by moralists, were they openly able to accept Dr Noonan's interpretation of the papal statement. People would also be entitled to public guidance from the bishops along those lines, at least an admission that some circumstances might excuse observance. Although I have not seen their statement, I am told that the Dutch bishops have given pastoral guidance to the effect that the prohibition against contraception is not absolute. But I think it is true to say that most bishops have not dared to do more than leave well alone and hope that the Pope would soon make up his mind. They have not acted on the assumption that the prohibition is one of ecclesiastical law, not binding where there are serious contrary reasons. And they have had no encouragement from the Pope to do so. He insists in his statement upon the continued binding force of the existing norm. He excludes a state of doubt precisely to prevent anyone supposing the contrary. No indication is given that the binding force has changed or lessened. And Fr de Riedmatten, the secretary of the papal Commission on birth control, as reported in the *St Louis Review* for 18 November 1966, said shortly after the papal statement in question: "As long as the Church has given no new pronouncement—and this pronouncement can only be in profound continuity with her previous pronouncements—all must hold rigorously to the norms thus far laid down." If, as Dr Noonan argues, the Pope in denying a state of doubt is in fact admitting a state of doubt, it would not seem, to judge from Vatican interpreters, that he is granting the practical consequences of doubt.

I am sorry to burden readers with such a lengthy argument about the meaning of a papal statement. Perhaps, however, it may provide a useful illustration of the obfuscation frequently caused by documents from the Holy See. Despite the offence I have given in saying so, I remain convinced that, according to the straightforward interpretation of his statement, the Pope denied the plain fact of a state of doubt concerning the teaching on birth control. He made a false statement to protect the authority of the Holy See and out of fear of the consequences, both theoretical and practical, of admitting that the teaching authority of the Church was uncertain in such a matter.

The impact upon myself of this dishonesty of the Pope may be best conveyed by the remark I made in *The Observer*: "One who claims to be the moral leader of mankind should not tell lies."

The second reason why the papal statement so vehemently upset me is the callous disregard it showed of persons and their present distress. By "callous" I mean unfeeling, and my charge is that the Pope in his Address acted with insensitivity towards the sufferings of people.

That the unyielding stand of the Church against contraception has caused great hardship and personal suffering is a fact well known to priests in their pastoral ministry, observed by social workers and of common knowledge and experience among lay people themselves. I should myself contend that much of this suffering would never have occurred had Church authority not suppressed free communication and discussion on moral questions. The supposition was that any new problem could be settled by authoritative decrees from the Holy See, which once issued were regarded as unquestionable. The system did not work, but insistence upon it meant that narrow, unsuitable and even untrue moral norms were imposed upon people because of the inability of an authoritarian structure to adapt to social change. Had there been open discussion in the Church over birth control, the moral teaching on the subject would have gradually evolved. Instead, an acute crisis has been provoked, because Church authority has resisted change to the breaking-point. Meanwhile, the cost in human suffering has steadily mounted. Admittedly, we should make allowance for inevitable human failure and error in those who guide the Church. But people have at least the right to expect a careful concern and sensitivity over suffering and distress that Church authority has itself largely caused.

The present confused situation has brought release to many people. They have been free enough to make their own decision in the matter, seizing the opportunity of the vacillation of authority. But those who most need help are those most dependent upon the Church. Any insistence upon the existing norms falls with an unrelieved impact upon those who have been trained to look to the Church and priest for every moral decision. Particularly in sexual matters they are unable to free themselves, because the Church's prohibitions have fitted into the taboos already rampant in that area.

But what help does the Pope give in his statement? Confronted with confusion and doubt, he offers no pastoral guidance adapted to the reality of the present situation in which the grounds of the Church's prohibition are uncertain. All that he does is woodenly to insist upon observance of the existing norms. His dominant concern is to keep the authority of the Holy See intact by rigorously holding the Church to the previous authoritative rules until he replaces them by another set of authoritative rules. Whether this is just to people whose lives may well be disrupted or even ruined by following norms that are not certainly divine and that might change in the future did not apparently enter into consideration; or if it did, the need to preserve authority was allowed to override any such hesitation. The unofficial leniency of priests in dealing with people personally, with the refusal of many of them to insist upon the prohibition against contraception, shows that a similar insensitivity is more difficult when persons, not abstract authority, dominate the horizon.

In describing the papal statement as callous dishonesty in my article in *The Observer* I was not attacking the personal character of the Pope himself. Apart from not regarding myself as entitled to judge the man, I have no difficulty whatever in accepting the evidence that he is most conscientiously trying to reach a decision over birth control. Dr Noonan misses the point in urging the intelligence and conscientious character of Pope Paul. What is in question for me is the social structure of the Church, together with the distorted attitudes and actions it imposes upon even very good men who try to preserve it or conform to it. Because Pope Paul is acting upon the archaic absolutist conception that he personally for the whole Church must decide so intricate an issue and come up with a solution, because he thinks that the faithful must be directed even in the intimacies of their married life by authoritative laws promulgated by the Church, because he is acutely anxious that the authority of the Holy See and its teaching should not in any way be lessened, he was led to issue a statement that evaded the truth with a diplomatic lie and failed to show justice and love to people suffering under the existing norms.

In brief, I did not leave the Church because I thought Pope Paul was a sinner and dishonest man. Even if he were, the fact would have been as indecisive in itself as the evident personal goodness of Pope John XXIII. His statement was a factor in my departure because it so vividly illustrated the defects of the social structure of the Church and its lack of credibility as the embodiment of Christian faith and love.

5. THE CHURCH AND HOPE

In considering the credibility of the Church as a sufficiently manifest embodiment of Christian faith, hope and love, I have left to the
end reflection upon the Church and Christian hope. There are two
reasons for this: first, the failure of the existing institution in this
respect is more easily seen as a consequence of the defects noted
under faith and love; second, the points to be made under this head
had a confirmatory rather than a motivating influence upon my own
decision. However, I will take this opportunity of explaining how I
understand the relation of the Church to the mission of Christ.

The Church of Christ should free the Christian for hope and
happiness.

Christian hope is not the expectation of a reward after a life
essentially different from what is to come. It is a trusting assurance
that the life in Christ we now enjoy will prevail over every contrary
force, including death itself. We have already been liberated, and our
hope is the confidence that the new life we have been given is indeed
eternal and will endure despite all afflictions and even beyond death.
United to Christ we have the Spirit with us who brings truth, joy,
love and peace as the pledge that nothing can separate us from
Christ and that Christ will keep us safe for the final Kingdom, the
fulfilment of the salvation we have now received.

Christian hope, therefore, is the joyful confidence of men who are
free and who are experiencing the freedom brought by Christ. What

does Christ offer us? A freedom from sin: "We know that our old self was crucified with him so that the sinful body might be destroyed, and we might no longer be enslaved to sin. For he who has died is freed from sin. But if we have died with Christ, we believe that we shall also live with him. . . . So you also must consider yourselves dead to sin and alive to God in Christ Jesus" (Rom. 6:6-8, 11). A freedom from the slavery of law: "For freedom Christ has set us free; stand fast therefore, and do not submit again to a yoke of slavery" (Gal. 5:1). A freedom through truth: "If you continue in my word, you are truly my disciples, and you will know the truth, and the truth will make you free. . . . So if the Son makes you free, you will be free indeed" (John 8:32, 38). A freedom from the fear of death: "Since therefore the children share in flesh and blood, he himself likewise partook of the same nature, that through death he might destroy him who has the power of death, that is, the devil, and deliver all those who through fear of death were subject to lifelong bondage" (Heb. 2:14-15). A freedom manifested through mutual love from the evil, hatred and negation of life, all aspects of unredeemed death: "We know that we have passed out of death into life, because we love the brethren. He who does not love remains in death" (I John 3:14).

And this freedom gives rise to our hope, to the assurance that, being transformed into the likeness of Christ, we shall share his glory forever: "Where the Spirit of the Lord is, there is freedom. And we all, with unveiled face, beholding the glory of the Lord, are being changed into his likeness from one degree of glory to another; for this comes from the Lord who is the Spirit" (II Cor. 3:17-18).

The first Christians experienced entry into the Christian community as a liberation. They saw life in the Church and life in pagan society as a contrast between freedom and slavery. By becoming Christians they entered a new environment—out of a world of darkness, despair, fear, anxiety and mutual domination into a community of light, love, hope, joy and mutual service. Is this how Catholics today experience their life within the Church?

Could it not be said that the contrast between the Church and the world runs in the opposite direction? We live in an open, secular, pluralist society. It is still very imperfect and has dangerous defects. But there is an accepted tolerance, with freedom of thought and

expression. There is also a deep social concern among many, resulting in disinterested work for the socially deprived and constant
efforts to promote justice and peace. But a sense of narrowness and
restriction pervades the Church. We meet with a suspicion of individual initiative, an anxious fear of new ideas even before they have
been examined, a reluctance to discuss reasonably and a pressure to
conform. Where is the joy and confidence in the truth which should
be the mark of those freed by Christ? Is a Church that fears truth in
the way I have previously described a likely environment for Christian hope? The social concern of the more active Catholics constantly comes up against an ecclesiastical adherence to the *status
quo*. In contrast to the tolerant understanding of the complex causes
of human failure and the unwillingness to judge others now characteristic of social workers and reformers, churchmen thunder out their
condemnations and, unaware of their own hidden aggression and
repressions, adopt a judgemental attitude to "sinners." The Church
is indeed oppressed by a fear of sin, aggravated by a legalism which
reflects the teaching of the Pharisees more than that of Christ. Where
is the freedom from sin and law? I have already analysed how the
present social structure of the Church hinders love and prevents
personal development. The Church is frustrating people and crushing them into anxiety and fear, not freeing them for hope and joy
and love. And fear of death and the threat of damnation are more
dominant for many than the confident assurance that Christ is with
us and will keep us safe.

Is it surprising that men have thrown off the yoke of the Church
as an unbearable oppression? They are looking for freedom; they
want to be themselves. They find no signs of a liberation in a life
within the Church. And not a few Catholics today if they dared to
formulate their thought would say, "Thank God we live in a secular
society where ecclesiastical writs do not run far and our freedom and
personal development are guaranteed by factors outside the Church."

But this also means that the Church is leaving many men to their
despair. It is Christ who frees us for hope. Where the vast social
structures that claim to represent Christ do not embody his truth,
love and freedom, they serve as a sign against Christ and prevent
men knowing him. There is another side to modern society besides
the openness, tolerance and work for human development I have

contrasted with the attitude prevalent in the Church. Much secularism contains an element of despair, and despair is a frequent theme in modern writing. Is not this despair a measure of the failure of the existing institutional Churches to embody the hope of Christ? Be that as it may, what is observable is that the inadequacy of the social structure of the Churches is driving many Christians to despair, not in the loose, jocular sense of the word, but in its strict sense. I have met many Catholics reduced almost to despair, troubled about their faith, uncertain about their Christian life, because they are deprived of a community support and institutional expression in harmony with their real experience. And the sense that the Church has no room for people like themselves, does not understand their outlook and their needs, and is not going to change in a radical way leaves them hopeless, unable to live much longer within the present Church but seeing no alternative other than abandoning any Christian faith. I suggest, too, that much of the wildly unorthodox thinking and writing by Christians is a despairing gesture by those who want to keep faith in Christ but have found no possibility of reconciling contemporary experience with the present institutional expression of Christianity.

But the Roman Catholic Church does not only fail to embody Christian hope. It contradicts it by making itself an end not a means and compromising its mission to preserve and strengthen its institutional position.

At the origin of the Christian Church is the sending of his disciples by Christ to preach the Gospel and bear testimony to his redemptive action. Through this sending of the disciples Christ continues his own mission to men. "As the Father has sent me, even so I send you" (John 20:21). "And Jesus came and said to them, 'All authority in heaven and earth has been given to me. Go therefore and make disciples of all nations, baptizing them in the name of the Father and of the Son and of the Holy Spirit, teaching them to observe all that I have commanded you; and lo, I am with you always, to the close of the age' " (Matt. 28:18-20).

This mission of the disciples is made possible by the Spirit. The Spirit is the power and active presence of God. They receive the Spirit from the risen Christ, and it is by sending the Spirit from the Father that Christ remains with them and works through them. In sending his disciples out into the world to be his witnesses, Christ gave them the Spirit. After the words of Christ, "As the Father has sent me, even so I send you," the text of John continues: "And when he had said this, he breathed on them, and said to them, 'Receive the Holy Spirit'" (John 20:22). And according to Acts, Christ said to his disciples before his ascension: "But you shall receive power when the Holy Spirit has come upon you; and you shall be my witnesses in Jerusalem and in all Judea and Samaria and to the end of the earth" (Acts 1:8).

The fundamental shape of the Church, namely, of the permanent community of Christ's disciples, is determined by its mission, which is its purpose or *raison d'être*. The mission of bringing the Good News of Christ to men is not a function added to the Church, which it can neglect while remaining essentially intact as the Church of Christ. It determines its essence, so that the Church is by definition the body of men who are the visible witnesses of Christ in the world. The Church is mission; it is the visible embodiment of the movement of Christ, the representative Head of mankind, to take up the men he represented into himself and unite them to his saving power.

That movement of the One to the Many is achieved by the sending of the Spirit. The mission of the Church was launched and is sustained by the mission of the Spirit. The visible Church is the embodiment of that mission in a community with its social structures. The Church arises out of the sending of the Spirit, and all its institutions and structures are to be seen as serving as the shape and form, the vehicle and embodiment, of the action of Spirit. And that action is the movement outwards from Christ to embrace all men. In that movement, which is the dynamism of the Church's mission, the Church as a social structure is at the disposal of the Spirit, not the Spirit at the disposal of the institutional Church.

The goal of that movement is the final Kingdom. The Church is essentially in tension towards the future and cannot rest in any intermediate stage. The Church of Christ is a people on the move, so much so that if it settles down and refuses to go further it ceases to be the Church. Any attempt of the Church to make its temporal form an end denies its own mission and purpose, prevents its being the vehicle of the Spirit and excludes the active presence of Christ. In other words, if the Church as a social structure becomes an end in itself to which its activity is directed and subordinated, it no longer exists as the embodiment of Christian hope, which is an active tending towards the final fulfilment. And a characteristic effect of the Spirit is hope.

It is true, as I have already said, that Christian hope arises from a present possession of salvation, an enjoyment here and now of the liberation brought by Christ. The final fulfilment will be in continuity with the life we already have as Christians, not a reward replacing that life by another essentially different from it. We have been given the first-fruits of the Spirit. For that reason the Church as the community of Christ is the initial presence of the final Kingdom. The final order or, as it is known theologically, the eschatological reality, is not simply in the future nor, on the other hand, is it fully realised in the present. It is with us, but as still being realised; with us, but in an essential tension towards a future fulfilment. With that in mind, we should not regard the visible Church as a mere instrument of the Spirit, but as an achievement of the Spirit; not as a mere means of the Christian mission, but as a provisional result of that mission.

However, the word "provisional" is here most important. The Christian life, which is already eternal life itself, can exist only as embodied in social structures, but no particular embodiment is as yet more than transitory. We await the final resurrection of the body. The Christian life is lived only in and through our present bodies, but our bodily existence will be transformed into a state so different that it lies beyond description. The social structures in which we live as Christians correspond to the present conditions of bodily existence. They have no claim to permanence, and they share the mutability proper to man's present historical mode of being. To cling to particular structures as permanent is not only to go contrary to the forces of man's historical development, but also to forget that we who have the first-fruits of the Spirit are still waiting in hope for the definitive resurrection. "We ourselves, who have the first fruits of the Spirit, groan inwardly as we wait for adoption as sons, the redemption of our bodies. For in this hope we were saved" (Rom. 8:23-24).

As a matter of fact, the present possession of the Spirit and the joy in the initial realisation of God's Kingdom, far from diminishing the tension towards the future and lessening the force of Christian hope increases that tension and that hope. Dr Berkhof puts this well:

We can best make this clear by a comparison with what often happens in our daily life. Someone who is ill can acquiesce in that situation as long as he is convinced that his disease is incurable; but, if a medical authority tells him that he can recover after a shorter or longer treatment, a new period of restlessness and longing begins. The more signs of recovery the patient discovers, the more his restlessness and longing grow. That is the paradoxical situation of God's children in the world. That they hope is not primarily due to what they miss, but to what they have already received. The joy and peace which are granted by the Holy Spirit make us abound in hope (Rom. 15:13). We have a hope which does not disappoint us, because God's love has been poured out in our hearts through the Holy Spirit which has been given to us (Rom. 5:5). Faith and love produce hope. In the light of what God has given, we discover how much the present situation of our world clashes with God's gifts in Christ and in the Spirit. That makes us look forward eagerly to a world which is re-created according to the gifts already bestowed upon us. In faith and hope we revolt against the status quo. The joy in what we possess evokes the groaning about what we do not yet possess. The experience of having and lacking keep pace with one another.[1]

These reflections help us to understand what the Church of Christ should be like as the embodiment of Christian hope. It should be a Church in a permanent state of mission, its structure shaped and determined by the needs of its mission, since that mission is the very purpose of its existence. It should be a Church in a constant tension towards the future, never resting in any particular historical realisation of itself but recognising that, although it already has the new life brought by Christ, it has this in a transitory embodiment subject to the mutability of all historical forms. Indeed, an important function of the Church as the bearer of Christian hope is to make men dissatisfied with all established orders here on this earth, so that, refusing to be enclosed in the sinfulness and inadequacy of any temporal

[1] Hendrikus Berkhof, *The Doctrine of the Holy Spirit: The Annie Kinkead Warfield Lectures, 1963–64.* (The Epworth Press, London), pp. 107-108.

order, they strive after the perfect and final order promised by
Christ. Further, the mission of the Church of Christ, because of the
revolutionary force of Christian values, will inevitably bring that
Church into conflict with the powers of this world, with those whose
interest is the maintenance of the injustice and oppression of the
status quo. When such conflict arises, the Church has to remain true
to its mission, confident that the forces of evil will never finally
prevail against it. It has to be prepared to face the destruction of its
institutions, the suppression of its social structures and the loss of all
property and privilege rather than compromise its testimony to
Christ and Christian truth and values. Here it follows the example of
Christ himself, who faced death to rise again and thus saved mankind. The Church will often have to undergo death in embracing its
own apparent destruction, but it does so with an unshaken hope
in the resurrection, confident that God will not allow the mission
it bears to be finally frustrated. To the extent that a Christian body
betrays its mission to save its institutional position or existence,
it ceases to be the Church of Christ. It has lost its Christian *raison
d'être*.

Granted that the Church will always in this world be imperfect
and subject to partial failure on account of the sins and weaknesses
of Christian men, it must reflect the ideal I have sketched at least in
sufficient measure to remain credible as an embodiment of Christian
hope.

I do not think that the Roman Catholic Church in its present
social structure has sufficient credibility in that respect.

From the Constantinian era onwards, the Church gradually developed a kingly and imperial structure of power. This structural form
of the Church reached its full expansion in the Middle Ages with the
growth of the universal papal monarchy in the West. Here we find an
hierocratic structure of jurisdictional power centred on the kingly
and priestly government of the Pope as universal monarch. How far
that structure was an inevitable development for the Church and one
adapted to the needs of its mission in those centuries does not concern me here. Certainly, it can be said that it played an important
part in the social and political formation of Western Europe. At the
same time it had dangerous defects from the point of view of the
Christian faith and mission. It led to an exaggerated identification of

the Church with the Kingdom of God on earth, which caused an absolute and permanent value to be given to merely transitory structures. It weakened and distorted the missionary force of the Church. Apart from the comparative neglect in the high Middle Ages of the unevangelised outside Christendom, there was the use of political means and physical force to compel adherence to the Christian faith. Again, the Church supposed that becoming a Christian meant acceptance of the sacral, politico-ecclesiastical order of Christendom. This supposition in a less blatant form still distorted later missionary effort. The legacy of the attempt to impose Western customs and structures upon other peoples is perhaps going to prove too great to be offset by the belated efforts of a more purified Christian zeal. In short, whatever the original Christian dynamism behind the formation of Christendom, the Church settled down in it as an established order to be defended at all costs as the Kingdom of Christ, ruled by his vicar on earth, the Pope. In doing so, it tended to subordinate its mission to itself as a social structure rather than itself to its mission, and lost much of the dynamic adaptability of Christian hope.

However, such defects may well be regarded as only a partial failure that left the medieval Church still sufficiently credible as the Church of Christ. The essential failure of the hierocratic and monarchical structure of power as an embodiment of Christian hope and vehicle of Christian mission came with the attempt to keep it in being after the collapse of Christendom.

The French Revolution may be taken as dramatically marking the end of Christendom. Clearly, any such statement is a crude simplification. Historians would trace the forces of disintegration much further back and, moreover, the death throes of the old order lasted well beyond the blow it then received. But despite the long drawn out efforts to revive it, the old order was in fact finished, and Europe was irretrievably launched upon the transition from Christendom to the modern secular States.

The Church now had to pursue its mission in a new setting, requiring new structures. It was not simply that the political order had changed, but that there had been a shift in the social and political consciousness of men, which made the restoration of Christendom impossible. In the new situation that gradually unfolded there were unchristian elements, which the Church had to oppose; but there were also values deeply in accord with Christian faith, and these the Church should have discerned, welcomed and fostered.

Unfortunately, the Church authorities neither recognised nor accepted the radically new situation, with its stimulus to a revival and restructuring of Christian mission. The genuinely human and Christian values present in the new social and political consciousness were ignored, indeed opposed and condemned because they threatened the *status quo*. Haunted by an illusory hope of a restored Christendom, incapable of accepting a different situation for Christian mission, the papacy embarked on the spiritually sterile policy of trying to contain the secular, liberal forces of modern Europe by political influence and arrangements. This was the policy that has been called political Catholicism, the adoption of which blocked the alternative Christian policy of meeting the new situation with a spiritual renewal and structural reform of the Church and a confident and fruitful encounter with emergent, modern culture.

Political Catholicism was not just a practical failure; it ensured the break between the Church and the modern world. The Catholic Church had reached a nadir of spiritual and intellectual decadence in the eighteenth century. What was urgently needed was a renewal that returned to the original, creative power of the Christian spirit, with its ability to leave aside transitory elements from the past and confront the present and future with hope. Instead, the popes placed their trust in princes and in political alliances, careless of the support they gave to an establishment associated with injustice and unfreedom. But what in fact did most harm both inside and outside the Church was not the political manoeuvrings and alignments, the excessive claims and intolerance, but the spiritual and intellectual barrenness that lay behind Church policy and was made worse by it. The tentative efforts of the Catholic liberals in France was stifled. An incipient Catholic revival, which emerged in Germany in connection with the romantic movement, was checked and died away as the dominant papal policy invaded the German scene. In general, the cleavage between the Church and the culturally conscious and intellectually active was driven ever deeper. Refusing mutual penetration and discriminating interchange with the modern world, the Church retreated into an attitude of undiscerning opposition. Catholics became isolated in a cultural and intellectual ghetto, and a rigid authoritarianism, linked with political reaction, was preferred to the living progress of Catholic thought. The Syllabus of 1864, with its unperceptive condemnation of modern ideas and ideals, may stand as the charter and symbol of the spiritually sterile and politically reactionary papal policy. It may be explained, but it cannot be excused by its failure to distinguish between truth and error in modern thought and by its myopia in judging the universal situation in the light of the anticlericalism of the Italian *Risorgimento*. The ultramontane movement, which led to the definition of papal primacy and infallibility at the First Vatican Council, was a continuation of the antirevolutionary appeal to authority. Its irrelevance, indeed futility, in relation to the new situation of the Church and Christian mission was illustrated by the dispersal of that Council because of the outbreak of the Franco-Prussian War with the consequent Italian invasion and annexation of the papal States. The claim that the spiritual authority of the papacy was never greater than after the loss of the papal States is only a partial truth. Spiritual prestige could soar, because it no longer implied any effective engagement in the political, social and cultural development of modern Europe. The spiritual exaltation of the papacy in fact marked its removal from the real scene and covered over the achieved disjunction between Christianity and the forces that were moulding the modern world. One ounce of effective Christian influence on social, political and cultural developments is worth a vanload of papal declarations. The papacy lost its former role and retained nothing more than the right to issue politely received Christian interpretations and exhortations, together with a peripheral diplomatic function, which had a place on the international scene similar to that of the Red Cross. Meanwhile, the restructuring of the Church for an effective Christian mission in the modern secular world was largely hindered.

A spiritual and intellectual renewal has begun and is still going on within the Church. After the First World War the forces that had been held in check during the nineteenth century achieved a partial breakthrough. These forces were more radical than the neo-Thomism encouraged by Leo XIII and the still paternalistic social teaching of the same Pope. The thinkers of the earlier, romantic revival in Germany were drawn upon for the development of a new theology of the Church. The biblical, liturgical and ecumenical movements got under way. Between the two world wars much was done to give the laity an active share in Christian mission, though mostly under the aegis of the clericalist concept, Catholic Action. During the first part of this period, the forces of renewal were severely trammelled by the phrenetic antimodernism that racked the Church. The situation eased, but all through the interwar years the movements of renewal had to contend with constant opposition, not least from Church authorities. However, political Catholicism was checked by the condemnation of the rightwing *Action française* in 1926, and this opened the way to a more positive relation to the social and political forces of the modern world. After the upheaval of the Second World War the reforming movements shot forward with great rapidity and, despite the initial alarm and resistance of authority, continued to move onwards to the Second Vatican Council, where the extent of their influence was revealed to the consternation of many, including the Roman Curia.

On the papal throne itself, Pope John XXIII, who called the Second Vatican Council, brought a revolutionary change of attitude, which has not subsequently been adequately sustained. As Mr Hales points out in his book, *Pope John and His Revolution*, John broke the long sequence of papal protests against the modern world which "go back far behind Gregory XVI to the days of Pius VI (1775–99) to whom had fallen the duty of denouncing the great French revolution itself. Not until we get back as far as the reign of Pius VI's predecessor, Clement XIV, do we find a pope who was by way of sending cheerful letters out to the world".[2] The difference between John and his predecessors "was that he *accepted* and *welcomed* the modern world (as a working partnership, not in the sense of accepting its beliefs) and they did not, they mostly censured and rebuked it, frequently, and even sometimes angrily."[3] In other words, with Pope John we return at long last to Christian hope and a call to the Church confidently to reassume its mission to the modern world. As he told us himself in his opening speech at the Council, he did not share the attitude of the "prophets of gloom" who surrounded him.

[2] E. E. Y. Hales, *Pope John and His Revolution* (Doubleday & Company, New York, 1965), p. 39.
[3] *Ibid.*, p. 5 (author's italics).

Pope John's remark in that speech was in line with his general attitude. Mr Hales writes:

Deliberately turning his back upon the tradition of reproach and censure, he appealed in his encyclicals to "all men of good will" to go forward, in confidence, building afresh, and building better; to all Christians, united by virtue of their common baptism, all men of good will, united by their common recognition of the natural law, given by God, Whose sons they were, whether they recognized Him or no. Picking up the liberal Catholic tradition, with its acceptance of the new liberties, and its confidence in a better future, founded on freedom, he deliberately turned his eyes (as Archbishop Darboy had urged Pio Nono to turn his) towards what his epoch held that was honourable and good and he "sustained her in her generous efforts."[4]

Mr Hales, who is an historian of the nineteenth-century papacy, shows in detail in his book that this attitude of Pope John was a reversal of the attitude of previous Popes, including Leo XIII and Pius XII.

Paradoxically, Pius XII, for all his acceptance of modern science and technology, his exceptional intellect and his great interest in modern problems, was fundamentally a less modern man than Pope John with his Garden-of-the-Soul piety. In his first encyclical, *Summi pontificatus*, Pope Pius is still harking back to Christendom, conceived idealistically. He sees the world as having gone disastrously astray at the Reformation. That great act of infidelity, the breaking of allegiance to Rome, is the source of the evil which has led to secularism, to laicist liberalism and to atheistic socialism on the one hand, and to monopoly capitalism on the other. The dark solemnity of *Summi pontificatus* was maintained by Pius XII throughout his reign in his many writings. He was always warning the world, pointing out its errors, exposing its philosophical mistakes and lamenting the bleak historical consequences of its infidelity.

That Pius XII, unlike Pope John, fundamentally worked from within a close system of thought is, *malgré lui*, shown by Fr William Purdy in his book, *The Church on the Move*, the conscious purpose of which is to establish the continuity between the policies of the two Popes. He writes:

4 *Ibid.*, p. 38.

Pius, in considering anything, never went far without asking, and, answering, the question: is this accommodated easily within the existing total Catholic scheme of things. No one could have been more ready and anxious to be aware of what was stirring in the world, but always it was to be judged by Catholic standards which were at once fixed and very comprehensive. There was little notion of Catholics and others beginning a modest exploration from common ground. Thus an attitude of mind possibly appropriate in the field of strict dogma was often extended into fields where a more empirical mood was called for, in which it would have been more encouraging and relevant, to the outsider at least, to say "*we* are all feeling our way together towards common solutions" than "*you* are feeling your way towards solutions to which *we* can perhaps award a *nihil obstat*." Thus utterances which were in fact remarkably positive and encouraging towards modern movements (compared say with the rather self-regarding jeremiads of the mid-nineteenth century papacy) could sometimes fail to strike the sparks of sympathy for which Pius XII so passionately hoped.

John XXIII, by contrast, seemed disposed by nature to meet men, to search out and come down on to common ground, without fearing that the *magisterium* would be thereby compromised.[5]

Pope John was turned outwards to the world. He was concerned with all men and their problems. As Mr Hales remarks, he was "less preoccupied with the visible Church than with the world as a whole. . . . He was not directly trying to get the world 'back in.' He was going out into the world, to help the world, in whatever way the world was willing to be helped."[6] His concern for Christian unity was part of a wider concern for the unity of mankind. He welcomed co-operation with all, including the Communists. He certainly regarded Communism as false, but he saw that men, movements and countries could not be identified with their ideologies. Men were always changing, and Catholics and Communists should collaborate where they had the same objectives. Pope John was modern in having a sense of the concrete, changing reality of men involved in the ambiguity and complexity of history. He did not allow himself to be imprisoned in the clear-cut, static opposition of fixed doctrinal systems.

In short, Pope John manifested the true spirit of Christian mission

[5] William Purdy, *The Church on the Move* (John Day Company, New York, 1966), pp. 140-141 (author's italics).

[6] *Op. cit.*, pp. 82-83.

and hope. He wanted to turn the Church outwards, to open the Church to the world, to initiate co-operation with all men of good will in solving human problems, and thus to make the Church a light to lead mankind towards unity, peace, justice and freedom.

It is the inspiration of Pope John that lies behind the Pastoral Constitution on the Church in the Modern World, issued by the Second Vatican Council. Less in its detailed contents, which are defective in many respects, than in its symbolic value in sanctioning a positive approach to the world and an involvement in human problems, this document marks a new stage in the understanding by Catholics of Christian mission. Alongside it we should place the Declaration on Religious Freedom, likewise issued by the Council. Not only because its acknowledgement of freedom of conscience is the essential condition for the Christian mission to the world as urged by Pope John, but also because it is the belated burial of political Catholicism. The Church, in opposition to the policy of the nineteenth-century Popes, has formally recognised that political pressure is inappropriate as a means of securing the preservation and progress of Christian faith.

I have dwelt at length upon the present revival within the Roman Catholic Church, because I want to do full justice to the new vision of Christian faith and mission now operative among Catholics and reflected in the documents of the Second Vatican Council. But now that enthusiasm for the renewal has become more sober, further questions press upon any thoughtful Catholic: To what is the present renewal leading? How far does the renewal render credible the existing social structure of the Church as an appropriate embodiment of Christian mission in the world today?

I suggest that, if we look at what is happening from the standpoint of a general history of ideas, then we shall judge that the Catholic Church is being compelled to acknowledge truths that have been gained and developed outside itself. It is the fortunate fact that Catholic thinkers have not the social structure of the Church as their total environment and are strongly affected by influences from other Christians and from secular writers, which has enabled them to transcend the tradition they have received within the Church. How much that is original have they derived from their life within the Church? They have related the new thought to the sources of Catholic tradition and endeavoured to show its compatibility, often defending a continuity in Catholic teaching that others cannot perceive. But is the Roman Catholic Church with the tradition that animates it an element to be reconciled and fitted in or the fundamental source of their thinking? Little in the Pastoral Constitution on the Church in the Modern World would be regarded as strikingly new by Christians outside the Roman Church who have been thinking and writing on Christian mission. The important point for them is that the Church of Rome is now saying these things. And the Declaration on Religious Freedom is in fact an overdue acceptance by the Church of values long cherished in the secular world as well as by other Christians. Concerning Pope John himself, Mr Hales writes pointedly:

If the world had followed the political advice of Pius IX, instead of the political advice of Mazzini, there could have been no free peoples for Pope John to welcome or instruct. Roncalli could not realize it, because he had not been seriously educated in modern history, but in fact his world had been made by Mazzini and the other liberals. Without them the progress, the liberalism, and the modern civilization which he welcomed, and which Pius IX had castigated, were not imaginable. In the historical order Roncalli was the heir not of Pius IX but of Mazzini.[7]

Again, what progress has been made where the Roman Catholic Church is the dominant and almost exclusive environment? It is true, I think, that the main impetus towards reform has come from areas where Catholics are most subject to influences from outside the Church. Further, while one does not expect bishops to be pioneers, a living hierarchical authority should make some meaningful contribution. It is difficult to see that its intervention, even in the Council, has done more than weaken and obscure teaching that would otherwise have been expressed more clearly and powerfully. And it is a diminishing number today who are going to be more influenced by a Council document than by insights and truths spread through open, unauthoritative communication.

The Roman Catholic Church as an identifiable social entity is given its specific form by an hierarchical structure of power, centred

[7] *Op. cit.*, p. 165.

on the papal monarchy. That social structure, a legacy of Christendom, ceased to be a credible embodiment of Christian mission from after the French Revolution at least, if not earlier. The question is whether the present renewal in the Church is resuscitating the hierarchical form of Church structure and rendering it once more a living and credible expression and vehicle of Christian mission. Does the upsurge of new forces within the Church go to show that the existing social structure is still appropriate for Christian mission in a secular world, merely requiring some adaptations that will leave its form essentially the same? I do not think that this is so.

The structure of hierarchical authority has had little to do with the present renewal. Indeed, it has largely proved an obstacle to its development. While the strength of the reforming forces within the Church secured a limited sanctioning of the new thinking by the Second Vatican Council, there is little sign that the movement for reform is basing itself upon the restricted formulations of that Council. Rather, it is already sweeping beyond them, much to the bewilderment of the bishops, who have not yet fully assimilated what they agreed to at the Council. Even in the comparatively minor matter of the language of the liturgy, the cautiously worded concessions of the Constitution on the Sacred Liturgy now seem out of date. No, the forces of renewal do not arise from nor can they be contained within the existing social structure of the Church. They are driving onwards towards a Church structure that will no longer be built around hierarchical power and papal universal jurisdiction. The hierocratic and monarchical system developed in the Middle Ages is inappropriate today. Little will be achieved by the timid recognition of episcopal collegiality, carefully formulated to leave intact papal primacy as defined in the First Vatican Council. Both the secularisation of the West and the need to envisage a Christian mission genuinely adapted to all the peoples of the world require a questioning of Church structures far more radical than the limited questioning of the Protestant Reformation conditioned as that questioning was by a past historical situation. I think that such radical questioning is increasingly found among Christians of all denominations. Either the Catholic revival will be halted and lose its force or it will go on to break the shackles of the existing hierarchical structure. Whichever happens, I cannot conclude that it establishes the credibility of that structure as the embodiment of Christian mission.

Pope John was indeed a prophet in the See of Rome. His position as Pope enabled him to have a great impact upon the Church and the world. It gave him the authority to call a Council and release the forces of renewal throughout the Church. But granted that he acted within the context of his historical situation, does his action suffice to offset the other objections to the system of hierarchical and papal power? His success had little to do with the infallibility and jurisdictional primacy assigned to the Pope in the First Vatican Council. It was another form of leadership, which could equally well have been accommodated in a different kind of Church. Insofar as he himself was restricted by the system, for example as Patriarch of Venice or in the routine business of papal administration, his own actions are open to serious criticism. And there were grounds for the feeling of Curial officials that papal government could not survive a series of popes like John. With Pope Paul the Holy See has returned to more normal functioning. The result is a constant stress upon authority, mounting anxiety about the present situation with its threat to the existing structure, frequent warnings about doctrinal aberrations, timid progress that does not measure up to the Spirit of the Second Vatican Council itself, and a general inability to cope with the problems now facing the Church. The prophetic voice has gone. Now we can see the regular functioning of the social structure.

No, let me be fair. Allowance must be made for the personality of Pope Paul. The papacy could function much better than at present. But my main contention stands. Pope John cannot be taken as a typical pope nor an assessment of the papacy be based upon his prophetic quality.

I will examine later the general question of Church structures and develop the reasons why I think that an hierarchical structure is inappropriate for Christian mission today. I want, however, to conclude this account of how the Roman Catholic Church lost its credibility for me as an embodiment of Christian hope and mission by pointing to the frequent compromising of Christian mission by efforts to maintain and work through the present institutional structure. If we prevent our gaze from being riveted upon the movement of renewal, a broader observation reveals a Church that is constantly failing to bear witness to Christian truth and values because it is concerned with itself, with its own property and privileges, with its institutional stability, safety and progress. What also comes into view is the inability of the Church in its present form to act effectually in promoting Christian values in the present situation.

Concern over its institutional privileges, with a clinging to the papal States and a past political role, led the papacy to betray its Christian mission to emergent modern Europe. It not only failed to meet the challenge of secularism, but gave a great fillip to it by positively blocking the necessary development in the understanding and application of Christian truths and values. Such a betrayal has been repeated ever since in various parts of the Church.

The most glaring example is the failure of the Church in Germany to resist the evil of Nazism. The dominant concern of the German Church was not to bear witness to Christian values at all cost, but to keep its institutional structure intact. And despite the beautiful theological constructs now in circulation, there is little sign that the German Church in the concrete is better adapted now for the needs of Christian mission or freer from compromise with the political *status quo*.

Fear of risking its institutional position by a clash with the régime has led the Church in South Africa to a series of compromises with the unchristian policy of *apartheid*. A similar compromise with racial discrimination has marked the history of the Church in the south of the United States, though this is now being offset (not without some dragging of feet by bishops and priests afraid of upsetting the establishment) by the Catholics who have joined the general struggle for racial justice.

The Church as a social structure, with both clergy and laity, is deeply implicated in the social injustice that characterises so much of South America.

Then there is the general involvement of the Church in the capitalist establishment of the West, owing to its large investments and considerable holdings of real estate. The Church in the United States for example is a vast property owner and is at the same time dependent upon contributions from big business for the financing of its many enterprises. How far does this leave the Church free for a fearless Christian witness to social justice? Is not the perennially necessary Christian opposition to social evils muted in order to avoid giving offence and provoking the cutting off of financial support? Again, apart from the danger of blatant compromise, the sheer deadweight of material plant and investment is a great obstacle to the adoption of a radically new policy and new methods. The inertia it creates is enormous. The Church has all the inflexibility of an overgrown industrial enterprise without sufficient liquid capital for change. Buildings by their existence, location and design determine a way of life; financial considerations strongly influence policy. The Church is committed to lines of action no longer in keeping with the real needs of Christian mission, committed simply because so much capital has been sunk into pursuing a particular policy.

The institutional privileges and undesirable political involvements of the Church in Eastern Europe aggravated the clash with Communism and obscured the real point of conflict between Christians and Communists. Defence of antiquated institutional structures is proving an obstacle to an effectual Christian mission in the new situation, and some observers think that the only fruitful Christian work is being done by people on the fringes of the present Churches.

No doubt these are only scattered remarks. I do not myself offer them in isolation as a decisive argument. But in the context of convergent indications against the existing form of Church structure they have a confirmatory value. In trying to assess the credibility of the Roman Catholic Church as a vehicle of Christian mission, I find numerous instances of failure and compromise, attributable not to malice but to the inadequacy and inappropriateness of the present social structure. To offset these instances, I find no example of the Church as a social body courageously entering into conflict with established authority to bear witness to Christ, even at the cost of its institutional position. There are, I am glad to note, many examples of energetic and selfless action by Catholics in the cause of Christian values, but so often these people are working against the established order of the Church itself rather than drawing inspiration and support from it.

The sheer inability of the Church as at present constituted to bring Christian values to bear upon contemporary problems is well illustrated by its attitude to the war in Vietnam. No clear Christian guidance is forthcoming from the American hierarchy. Some bishops, like Cardinal Spellman, are fully committed to the official government policy and offer the familiar scandal of unqualified Church support for the political establishment. Others, while worried about what is happening, do not wish to disturb the consciences of their flocks and associate themselves with socially unpopular and politically dangerous protest. They take refuge in the usual excuses: that the situation is complicated; that government policy must be given the benefit of any doubt; that simple condemnation is uncalled for; and that political disobedience should not be encouraged. Meanwhile, the Pope is working earnestly for peace behind the scenes, but uttering public exhortations that fall short of full clarity and so can be welcomed by all parties with little practical effect.

Is not what emerges this: the inappropriateness of hierarchical authority for meeting a situation of that kind? The only effective Christian action will come through the awakening of the consciences of American Catholics. This cannot be done by authoritative declarations. If these are blunt and clear, they simply do violence to unformed consciences not yet ready for them. Besides, the ambiguities and complexities of any concrete social or political situation require tentative judgements, leading to immediate but provisional and constantly modified action. Hierarchical authority is too weighty and clumsy an instrument to be used in that way. Afraid of committing their authority whenever repercussions are to be expected in the practical order, Pope and bishops have recourse to generalities or silence. And the Church structured on hierarchical authority remains inactive and content to go along with the dominant political policy, even to the betrayal of Christian values, the consciences of people quieted by the public acquiescence of Church authority. Effective Christian protest comes only from those no longer dependent for their Christian life upon guidance from the hierarchy. The conclusion, it seems to me, follows that an hierarchically structured Church has ceased to be an appropriate vehicle for Christian mission. Any effectual Christian action depends upon freeing Christians from any reliance upon the existing Church structure and helping them to learn to work through open, unauthoritative communication among themselves. This will lead them to form whatever structures they need for interchange and mutual support and for common action. I do not see that the present hierarchical structure is now serving any purpose in relation to the needs of Christian mission. It is simply getting in the way.

Those are the reflections which, when I was grappling chiefly with the failure of the Church to embody faith and love, drove home its lack of credibility by making me see that I could not accept it as a sufficiently credible embodiment of hope and Christian mission. The Roman Catholic Church does not correspond to what the Church of Christ should be as a Church shaped for mission, moving under the action of the Spirit through the transitory structures of this world, applying the teaching of Christ to every new situation, and leading men in hope towards the final Kingdom. It gives the impression of a rigid structure settled in a past age and now, in more senses than one, hopelessly trying to maintain itself.

C.

The Church in
the Bible and History

1. THE ROMAN CLAIM

I have said that the Roman Church lost its credibility for me from
two different points of view, corresponding to the double line of
argument commonly used in apologetics to establish the credibility
of the Church. I have now at some length explained one side of that
loss of credibility. I do not perceive, so my argument has run, sufficient signs within the Roman Catholic Church to support belief in its
claim as the Church of Christ to be a visible embodiment of faith,
love and hope. Indeed, there are weighty indications militating
against any belief that it is such an embodiment. My objection has
been directed against that Church as a social structure, because it is
as a visible social entity that the Roman Church makes its claim.

Now I must turn to the second line of approach to credibility,
which is biblical and historical. The Roman Catholic Church does
not merely offer its own existing reality as a perennially sufficient
sign of the credibility of its claims, but it also appeals to the biblical
and historical data. These are said adequately to establish its credibility as the one, true Church, instituted by Christ and alone in
unbroken continuity with the first apostolic community.

Do the biblical and historical data support the Roman claim?
These data are said to establish the following points: that Christ

instituted a visible Church; that he intended this Church to have an hierarchical structure, namely to be ruled by successors of the apostles having an authority and priesthood not possessed by the rest of the community; that in Peter he established a permanent primacy of jurisdiction over the whole Church, linked with a further prerogative of infallibility; that the Bishop of Rome as the successor of Peter is the divinely instituted visible head of the Church, with a supremacy of jurisdiction over the whole Church and in respect of every member and with a promise of infallibility for his definitive teaching; that the Roman Catholic Church as alone retaining the structure instituted by Christ is, unlike other Christian bodies, in the full sense the one, true Church of Christ, without substantial defect, and alone in complete and unbroken continuity with the first apostolic community.

It will be seen that, if in truth the biblical and historical data establish these points, then the social structure of the Roman Catholic Church in its essential lines as an hierarchical structure centred on the papal primacy of jurisdiction is unalterable and a matter of Christian faith. This is indeed the faith of the Church of Rome, imposed upon all its members.

That acceptance of the Church structure as described is part of the Roman Catholic profession of faith is so clear that it would seem unnecessary to labour the point. Since, however, I have found some Roman Catholics reluctant to face up to the fact, I must insist upon it. The scope of this book does not allow me to cite the many official documents that repeat or reflect this teaching. I will take, however, the papal primacy as a key element in the general thesis, give the definition of that primacy as formulated by the First Vatican Council, and then add some further clarifications from the documents of the Second Vatican Council.

On 18 July 1870 the First Vatican Council solemnly defined the primacy of the Roman Pontiff in the following canons:

Therefore, if anyone says that the blessed Apostle Peter was not constituted by Christ the Lord as the Prince of all the Apostles and the visible head of the whole Church militant, or that he received immediately and directly from Jesus Christ our Lord only a primacy of honor and not a true and proper primacy of jurisdiction: let him be anathema.

Therefore, if anyone says that it is not according to the institution of Christ our Lord himself, that is, by divine law, that St. Peter has perpetual successors in the primacy over the whole Church; or if anyone says the Roman Pontiff is not the successor of St. Peter in the same primacy: let him be anathema.

And so, if anyone says that the Roman Pontiff has only the office of inspection or direction, but not the full and supreme power of jurisdiction over the whole Church, not only in matters that pertain to faith and morals, but also in matters that pertain to the discipline and government of the Church throughout the whole world; or if anyone says that he has only a more important part and not the complete fullness of this supreme power; or if anyone says that this power is not ordinary and immediate either over each and every church or over each and every shepherd and faithful member: let him be anathema.[1]

Thus, the papal primacy of jurisdiction as a structural element of divine law, coming from Christ himself, is an indisputable part of the Roman Catholic faith.

Let me notice in passing that the implications of this primacy for the concrete mode of government in the Church cannot be so easily evaded as some think. It is now a commonplace in theology to say that papal primacy does not involve administrative centralisation such as we have now. But when authors point to the early Church as proof of this, they commit the fallacy of supposing that the early Church recognised the papal primacy in the sense defined in the First Vatican Council. Even if the difficulty that the early Church did not is avoided by appealing to a development of doctrine, it remains true that the practical consequences of an explicit acknowledgement of a papal supremacy of jurisdiction will necessarily differ from those of a merely implicit awareness. Now, if one starts with the primacy as defined by the First Vatican Council, it can hardly be denied that a fair measure of administrative centralisation is implied, unless the declaration is to be rendered meaningless in practice. While some decentralisation is possible in comparison with the present, what is

---

[1] The English translation is from *The Church Teaches: Documents of the Church in English Translation*, edited by John F. Clarkson, S.J., and others (B. Herder Book Co., St. Louis, 1955). The canons, which come at the end of expository chapters, are given in nos. 203, 205 and 211. The Latin text will be found in Denzinger-Bannwart, *Enchiridion*, nos. 1823, 1825 and 1831.

defined is government by a single head with fulness of supreme power; and, presumably, effective government is intended. This necessarily implies some form of centralised administration.

Insofar as the Pope himself is subject to divine revelation and law, papal power is not absolute. Likewise, as we shall see, the Pope cannot abolish or render nugatory the body of bishops, who also have their place in the hierarchical structure by divine institution. Nevertheless, the form of government laid down in the definition may be described as having the general characteristics of an absolute monarchy, which in historical fact is usually subject to various checks and limitations. I should like those Catholics who are pressing for a radical reform of the papacy to come clean at the outset about how far they accept the terms of the First Vatican Council's definition. Then it would be possible to judge whether they are in fact advocating a papal primacy different in kind from that defined.

Papal primacy cannot be understood except as an element in an hierarchically structured Church. Belief in the primacy, therefore, carries with it belief that the social structure of the Church is unalterably hierarchical. Indeed, according to the intention of the First Vatican Council itself, the papal primacy leaves intact the authority of the bishops as the divinely appointed rulers and teachers in the Church. The Second Vatican Council, as is well known, developed the teaching on the episcopate and formulated the relation of the college of bishops, namely the bishops as a corporate unity, to the Pope. With a footnote reference to earlier documents, the Constitution on the Church declares the divine institution of the episcopate:

Just as the role that the Lord gave individually to Peter, the first among the apostles, is permanent and was meant to be transmitted to his successors, so also the apostles' office of nurturing the Church is permanent, and was meant to be exercised without interruption by the sacred order of bishops. Therefore, this sacred Synod teaches that by divine institution bishops have succeeded to the place of the apostles as shepherds of the Church, and that he who hears them, hears Christ, while he who rejects them, rejects Christ and Him who sent Christ (cf. Lk. 10:16).[2]

[2] Walter M. Abbott, S.J., (ed.), *The Documents of Vatican II*, p. 40; Constitution on the Church, n. 20.

From the treatment of the college of bishops, the following passage may be selected as stating most clearly its relation with the Pope:

> But the college or body of bishops has no authority unless it is simultaneously conceived of in terms of its head, the Roman Pontiff, Peter's successor, and without any lessening of his power of primacy over all, pastors as well as the general faithful. For in virtue of his office, that is, as Vicar of Christ and pastor of the whole Church, the Roman Pontiff has full, supreme, and universal power over the Church. And he can always exercise this power freely.
>
> The order of bishops is the successor to the college of the apostles in teaching authority and pastoral rule; or, rather, in the episcopal order the apostolic body continues without a break. Together with its head, the Roman Pontiff, and never without this head, the episcopal order is the subject of supreme and full power over the universal Church. But this power can be exercised only with the consent of the Roman Pontiff.[3]

The whole of chapter three of the Constitution on the Church should be read to understand the teaching of the Second Vatican Council on the collegiality, as it is called, of the episcopate. The Council clearly affirms the existence of the college of bishops as part of the divine institution of the Church by Christ. It also states that this college when taken as including the Roman Pontiff has supreme and full power over the universal Church. But throughout it is repeatedly insisted that this must not be understood as derogating from the position of the Pope as defined in the First Vatican Council. The theoretical and practical problems of reconciling a meaningful and effective corporate government of the Church by the bishops with the primacy of the Pope as defined and strongly reaffirmed are not solved. There are grounds for thinking that little more has been done than with verbal dexterity to juxtapose two incompatible views of Church government. Evidence is still awaited that episcopal collegiality can be made effective without modifying the content and implications of the definition of papal primacy in a manner so far bitterly resisted. The set-up of the Synod of Bishops does more to ensure papal primacy than to make episcopal collaboration genuinely effective.

[3] Constitution on the Church, n. 22, in Abbott, *op. cit.*, p. 43.

However, my present point is the claim that the Church is hierarchically structured by divine institution.

The analysis of the episcopal office assigns to bishops the fulness of the ministerial priesthood. This means that there is in the Church a special or hierarchical priesthood not possessed by the laity. It belongs in its fulness to the bishops and is shared by priests of the second order as co-operators with them in their ministry. This hierarchical priesthood differs in essence from the common priesthood of the faithful. In the second chapter of the Constitution on the Church we read:

Though they differ from one another in essence and not only in degree, the common priesthood of the faithful and the ministerial or hierarchical priesthood are nonetheless interrelated. Each of them in its own special way is a participation in the one priesthood of Christ. The ministerial priest, by the sacred power he enjoys, molds and rules the priestly people.[4]

This hierarchical priesthood is seen as coming from the mission given to the apostles and their successors by Christ.

Since the essential features of the social structure distinctive of the Roman Catholic Church are thus taught as being of divine institution by Christ, the conclusion follows that the Roman Catholic Church alone is in the full sense the Church of Christ. The exclusive claim of the Church of Rome to be alone the one, true Church of Christ has been modified in recent theology and in the documents of the Second Vatican Council itself, so as to allow for the existence of other Christian bodies pertaining in some way as communities to the Church of Christ, being means of grace used by Christ and even in some instances deserving the name of Christian Churches. For that reason in the first chapter of the Constitution on the Church, it was stated that the Church of Christ "subsists" in the Catholic Church rather than "is." Nevertheless, an exclusive claim is still made:

This Church [the unique Church of Christ], constituted and organized in the world as a society, subsists in the Catholic Church, which is governed by the successor of Peter and by the bishops in union with that successor, although many elements of sanctification and of truth can be

[4] *Ibid.*, p. 27, n. 10.

found outside of her visible structure. These elements, however, as gifts properly belonging to the Church of Christ, possess an inner dynamism toward Catholic unity.[5]

The document of the Second Vatican Council that does most justice to the role of the other Churches in the mystery of salvation is the Decree on Ecumenism. Yet, even so, it reiterates the exclusive claim of the Church of Rome, as indeed it must do because of the teaching on the papal primacy. In the first chapter we read:

It follows that these separated Churches and Communities, though we believe they suffer from defects already mentioned, have by no means been deprived of significance and importance in the mystery of salvation. For the Spirit of Christ has not refrained from using them as means of salvation which derive their efficacy from the very fullness of grace and truth entrusted to the Catholic Church.

Nevertheless, our separated brethren, whether considered as individuals or as Communities and Churches, are not blessed with that unity which Jesus Christ wished to bestow on all those whom He has regenerated and vivified into one body and newness of life—that unity which the holy Scriptures and the revered tradition of the Church proclaim. For it is through Christ's Catholic Church alone, which is the all-embracing means of salvation, that the fullness of the means of salvation can be obtained. It was to the apostolic college alone, of which Peter is the head, that we believe our Lord entrusted all the blessings of the New Covenant, in order to establish on earth the one Body of Christ into which all those should be fully incorporated who already belong in any way to God's People.[6]

In brief, then, according to the Roman Catholic faith, Christ instituted a visible Church and gave it a definite structure. He established an hierarchical authority of ruling, teaching and sanctifying in the bishops as successors of the apostles. He instituted the papal primacy in Peter. Thus, the essential lines of the social structure of the Roman Catholic Church are unalterable because of divine origin, and the Church of Rome alone fulfils all the requirements for being the one, true Church of Christ. I will return later to the question of infallibility.

I am sorry if I have bored some readers by elaborately stating the

[5] *Ibid.*, p. 23, n. 8.
[6] *Ibid.*, p. 346, n. 3.

obvious. It was necessary at this point to make precise what is the social structure I am rejecting, and why in rejecting it I had to leave the Roman Catholic Church. The points I have mentioned are not offered as a full account even of official Roman teaching on the Church. To give that teaching fully, I should have to take up the biblical themes on the Church which are used and developed in the first two chapters of the Constitution on the Church and show the advance made on previous documents. Then it would be necessary to expound the rich teaching on the laity as given in the Constitution on the Church and in the Decree on the Apostolate of the Laity. Again, I have already mentioned the new vision of the Church's mission set forth in the Pastoral Constitution on the Church in the Modern World. My purpose, however, is not to criticize every element in the self-understanding of the Roman Catholic Church, nor do I wish to convey the impression that Roman teaching on the Church is in these post-conciliar days still merely an hierarchology. But my quarrel is with the structure of the Roman Catholic Church as a social entity. And this social structure derives its specific determination from being hierarchically constituted. Further, the hierarchical constitution does and, according to official teaching, is intended to affect the life and government, the attitudes and actions of the whole Church and every member of it. Thus, any role given to laity must be reconciled with a firm maintenance of the functions of hierarchical authority. So, while the growing prominence of other elements in the Church, notably the function of the laity, may to some extent counterbalance the present stress on hierarchical authority, that authority will remain what specifically determines the structure of the Roman Catholic Church as a distinctive social entity, unless that Church loses its essential identity as a social body and relinquishes what it now teaches in the name of Christian faith.

I have explained how the hierarchically determined social structure (and therefore the Roman Catholic Church as a social entity) lost its credibility for me because in its concrete existence and working it does not manifest sufficient signs of being, as the Church of Christ must be, an embodiment of Christian faith, hope and love. The evidence, I have argued, points to the conclusion that it is an obsolete structure no longer appropriate to the contemporary situation and therefore now a considerable obstacle to Christian life and mission. The question at present is whether that conclusion is ruled out of court and shown to be false by the biblical and historical data. Are the data sufficient to establish that, however marred the Roman Church may be by abuses and defects, it must be accepted as the one, true Church of Christ because it alone possesses the social structure laid down by Christ for his Church? Further, do the data show that any Christian reform, however radical, must stop short of changing the features of Church structure the Roman Church claims as coming from Christ himself?

The conclusion I came to was that the biblical and historical data did not make the Roman Catholic Church and its teaching sufficiently credible.

2. THE ORIGIN OF MY DOUBTS

After I had finished my studies at the Gregorian University, Rome, I went back to St Edmund's College, Ware, to teach. There for the first three years I taught Fundamental Theology or, to use the more popular name, Apologetics. This gave me a reasonable familiarity with the standard arguments and proof texts. At the end of that period I changed over to teaching Dogmatic Theology. However, in accord with recent thinking on how theology should be taught, I developed a full treatise on the Church as part of my course. This considerably deepened my understanding of the nature of the Church and gave me the opportunity of becoming acquainted with modern theological writing on the subject. At the same time, my course included a treatment of papacy, episcopacy and the general social structure of the Church, now from a doctrinal rather than an apologetical standpoint.

I regard the fifteen years that extend from my first taking up my teaching post in 1949 to my attendance at the Third Session of the Second Vatican Council in the autumn of 1964 as a period of assimilation. During this time my vision of the Church was immensely enriched. I was enthusiastic about the new writing on the Church, with the shift of emphasis it brought.

There were difficulties, but these could still be regarded as unresolved problems rather than as questions imperatively demanding an answer. I was largely unaware of the growing tension in my mind, a

135

tension chiefly due, I think, to the conflict between my vision of the Church and its concrete reality. In other words, I felt within myself the tension of the movement for renewal—the drive forward, which corresponded with my own creative urge, but the constant frustration, which had its counterpart in my own struggle to conform. But this unrest came into consciousness not as doubt but as impatient eagerness for renewal. Then the expectation aroused by the calling of the Council and the hopeful boldness of the writings that followed the announcement were enough to stifle any hesitation and postpone any calm questioning of the credibility of the Church. I remember the thrill with which I read, in German even before its translation, Hans Küng's book on *The Council and Reunion*.

As a matter of fact I did not during this period of growth bother much about theoretical difficulties concerning papal primacy. I assumed too easily that "hierarchology," as Fr Congar calls it, was now a past phase in the doctrine and theology of the Church. Questions about papal power receded into the background, and my view of the Church was dominated by such ideas as the Mystical Body, the People of God, the basic sacrament, the Eucharistic community. I recognised that in my course the section on the papacy was a somewhat heterogeneous element because of its excessively juridical content and unbiblical tone. The contrast with the rest of the course was similar to the contrast, which will immediately be felt by any reader, between the third chapter and the first two chapters of Second Vatican's Constitution on the Church. With the third chapter the document moves into a new world, remote from the New Testament and dominated by an excessive stress upon juridical functions. But I presumed in reflecting upon this uncomfortable clash within my theology of the Church that it would eventually be eliminated when the doctrine of the papacy was rethought in a more biblical fashion. I think that the difficulty of relating papal primacy, which though supreme in the Church is in essence a juridical function, with the Church understood as a sacramental reality did nag at my mind. All the same, while expounding the standard doctrine, I did not worry about the biblical and historical difficulties it raised.

Attendance at the Third Session of the Second Vatican Council, the session which saw the great debate on episcopal collegiality and the detailed hammering out of the text of the Constitution on the Church, brought me right up against the doctrine of the papal primacy as defined by the First Vatican Council. In following the discussions and studying the texts, it was impossible to slide over the implications of the papal primacy as defined and leave uncomfortable questions undisturbed at the back of the mind. The tenacity with which that definition was defended, the resultant weakening, almost neutralising of the declaration on episcopal collegiality, and the concrete working of the papal power, which culminated in the addition of the notorious *Nota praevia* or Prefatory Note of Explanation, hedging around collegiality with further restrictive statements: all this, as I can now see, deeply affected my mind, creating a yet unformulated awareness of how little I believed in papal primacy in any sense that would be regarded as reconcilable with the First Vatican Council. The anxiety of the progressives to declare their full allegiance to the teaching of the First Vatican Council and their earnest desire to keep papal primacy intact struck me as a naïve failure to face the real issue, combined with a sense, unadmitted even to themselves, of the tactics necessary to push through collegiality. I did not at the time confront my own deep thoughts. Especially when caught within a dogmatic system, the mind has a knack of shying away from the full implications of its own thinking. Professor Robert McAfee Brown has recorded a remark I made during the Third Session when he challenged me with the question: "You say the Holy Spirit presides over the councils of the church. Well, then, where was He at Vatican I? If it weren't for Vatican I, there would be no insuperable roadblocks to unity." My reply was: "If the Spirit hadn't been there, it would have been a lot worse."[1] I was trying my utmost to be honest and sincere. The answer truly reflected my then state of mind. With such half-answers it is possible for a long time to ward off a conclusion that would shatter the framework of one's life.

In the autumn after my return from the Council I moved to Heythrop College, Oxfordshire. There my teaching was at a higher level and more specialized. It did not include the theology of the Church. In January of 1966, however, I had to give the Maurice Lectures at King's College, London. They have been published under the title of *God's Grace in History*.[2] The preparation of these lectures kept me grappling with the problem of the Church in the

[1] "A Loss to Us All," *Commonweal*, April 7, 1967, p. 93.
[2] Fontana Books, Collins, London, 1966; Sheed and Ward, New York, 1967.

modern secular world. In the autumn of 1966, my course at Hey-throp was on biblical Christology. This made it necessary for me to enter more closely into the questions raised by New Testament criticism, in particular with the conclusions of the form critics. I found that my own approach to the New Testament documents became much more radical than before, without this upsetting my hold upon the substance of the Christian faith.

Against this background and in the context of the impending crisis about the Church provoked by the other causes I have previously described, I had to prepare a theological paper for a meeting between Anglicans and Roman Catholics, arranged for January 1967, at the Italian village of Gazzada. My reading for it did not tell me anything I did not know before, but it forced me to examine the state of my own convictions on the papacy and on the Roman Catholic Church as a social entity. I found that I no longer believed in the papal claims as defined in the First Vatican Council and repeated in Second Vatican and that my general understanding of the Christian Church put me outside the Roman Catholic body.

Clearly, the other reasons for my rejection of the Church had an influence upon my intellectual judgement of the biblical and historical basis for the papal claim. But it is in any event impossible to examine the data except from a particular standpoint. Those who accept the papal interpretation are influenced by a desire to remain within the Roman Catholic Church and by the other reasons they have for doing so. Again, I think that the line of argument I have previously developed against the credibility of the Roman Church was the chief motivating force in my own rejection. The consideration of the biblical and historical data took second place. Nevertheless, those data were powerless to check the conclusion I was forming on other grounds; and the interpretation of them as opposed to the papal claim did not on reflection seem to me to be sudden and arbitrary, but rather the consistent and inevitable outcome of the evolution of my thought on the Church over years of study.

Since this book is a personal statement, not a specialist study, I am not going to offer a detailed examination of the texts and arguments. I have in any case little desire to add to the already considerable literature on the subject. The various points have been endlessly argued, and it is more general considerations that in fact determine the solutions given. I made no new discoveries about the evidence. For the theological paper I have mentioned I simply gathered a representative selection of Anglican, Protestant and Roman Catholic writing on the Church from the Heythrop library. What I did discover was the change in my own assessment of data long since familiar. My purpose here is to try to describe that shift of judgement.

I must, however, confess that I was surprised by the no doubt unconscious arrogance of those Roman Catholics who contemptuously dismissed my statement that the papal claims were without sufficient biblical and historical support as a resuscitation of the old Protestant arguments. Are they not aware of the world of scholarship outside the Catholic Church, a world on which Catholic biblical scholars are largely dependent? Objections are not invalid because they are of long standing. And if Anglicans and Protestants in attacking the papacy have constantly modified their arguments, so too have Catholics in defending it. What is clear, however, is that anyone who claims that Christ himself instituted the papacy has a Herculean task before him in these days of modern biblical criticism. And to maintain that fundamentally the papacy is not the result of social and political forces but a divine institution is in the light of modern historical study to defend a difficult thesis. Roman Catholics should at least recognise the dimensions of their task. Difficulties cannot be automatically solved by bringing them under the umbrella of development. Development is not a panacea for all the pains and stresses of Catholic doctrine and theology, but a principle that requires careful and justified application.

3. THE GENERAL PROBLEM

What hit me with almost overwhelming force when I turned from a calm study of the complex biblical data on Christ to a consideration of Roman Catholic teaching on the Church was the sheer exorbitance of the papal claim. The antecedent improbability of proving the definition of First Vatican from Scripture is enormous. Apart from the difficulty of claiming the sanction of Christ himself for so definite an institutional structure, the kind of authority and power attributed to the Pope bears little relation to the outlook and general teaching of the New Testament. *Qui nimis probat, nihil probat.* He who proves too much, proves nothing. If the New Testament data cannot stand what the Pope actually claims, then the method of interpretation that results in such an extravagant conclusion becomes seriously suspect.

Not only in regard to the papal claim, but also with the general thesis on the hierarchical constitution of the Church, the same impression is given, namely, that the conclusion goes well beyond the evidence. The transition from the apostles, eyewitnesses of Christ and leaders of the first community, to a permanent hierarchy of bishops with apostolic authority not derived from the general community is a transition that the New Testament does not itself make nor compel one to make.

Here reference is made to tradition. The formation of an episcopal hierarchy was the manner in which the Church in fact structured itself in the first centuries, and in doing so it claimed to be preserving its continuity with the apostolic community. Granted; but what follows is that in its past historical situation that was the appropriate manner for the Church to structure itself, resist contemporary forces of disintegration and thus keep its identity with the apostolic community. In that sense it could claim to be obeying the intention of Christ and the apostles. It does not follow that, whatever the social, political and cultural developments that occur, the particular structure then chosen should be regarded as invariable and imposed upon every age and area of the Church by the institution of Christ. What the early Church did should be regarded as normative in the sense of providing a paradigm of how the Church should adapt itself to the needs of its situation and mission. More proof is required than is usually cited for the thesis that what the Church did in the past must now be regarded as unalterable.

No doubt the papacy and the historic episcopate have served the Church for centuries. But for all we know these centuries may be a short period compared with what is to come. Be that as it may, it is a fact that the Church has entered into a situation radically different from any that it has previously experienced. It has to confront a secular, post-Christian world and penetrate cultures very different from that in which its structure was formed and developed. One might argue the advantages of retaining the existing structure, but I do not see that one can block the suggestion of a radical restructuring by an appeal to New Testament or tradition. The data show what happened in the past; there is, as far as I can see, no sufficient proof that the structures then adopted are unchangeable.

Any appeal to development must allow the development claimed to be tested for its authenticity. And a development that is claimed as irreversible must retain permanent signs of being authentically Christian. If hierarchical structure and papal primacy are regarded as irreversible developments, then they must remain sufficiently credible as Christian institutions. In that way the argument from the biblical and historical data, which nowadays is usually supplemented in Roman Catholic authors by an appeal to development, merges into the argument I have previously discussed about the credibility of the Church as an existing reality. If the hierarchical and papal social structure is no longer credible in its concrete existence and working, it cannot be claimed as an authentic irreversible development. It may have been an authentic form of the Church in an earlier period, but it is not so now. The attempt to complete the biblical and early historical data by recourse to the concept of development fails. Only a decisive argument from the Bible and early tradition without appeal to development could suffice to offset a lack of credibility in the present Church. However, the absence of such a decisive argument is increasingly recognised.

4. THE EARLY CHURCH

To come now closer to the data.

Only in a carefully qualified sense can Christ himself be said to have instituted a visible Church.

Using various methods, namely source criticism, form criticism, redaction criticism and tradition history, modern biblical critics endeavour to distinguish and assess the historical value of the diverse material found in the Synoptic Gospels. They distinguish different layers in the Gospel material. The critics themselves work backwards from our present Gospels, applying successive criteria to disentangle the different strata in the Synoptic tradition. But if we take the strata in their historical order, they are: the original Jesus tradition, namely the words, works and final end of Jesus of Nazareth; the post-Easter development of that tradition, governed by the Easter faith, with the formation of various units of tradition, shaped to serve the practical needs of the community—the community tradition was first Palestinian, then Hellenistic; the collection together of similar units of material; the primary written sources, which are usually taken to be Mark and Q, and the primary unwritten sources, namely the special Matthaean material and the special Lucan material; finally, the later Gospels, which are Matthew and Luke. Needless to say, this is only a rough statement. Critics differ in applying the methods. Like all scholars, they have to work with conclusions of varying probability. There remain, too, more conservative schools of thought. The general fact, however, is that acceptance of modern biblical criticism prevents the simple attribution of all the sayings and deeds recorded in the Gospels to Jesus himself.

The various reconstructions offered of the original Jesus tradition do not allow one to attribute to Jesus the express institution and structuring of a permanent Christian Church. His preaching was centred on the Kingdom of God. He taught that in an anticipatory sense that Kingdom was already present in himself, but at the same time announced the imminent coming of the final Reign of God, bringing judgement and salvation. Jesus in his own teaching did not concern himself with an interval between his death and the final Kingdom. The understanding that there would be such an interval and the rethinking accordingly of the Christian message arose as the community of disciples adjusted itself to its post-Easter situation and assimilated the various experiences it underwent. The preaching of Jesus included an urgent call to discipleship, and he gathered disciples around him. But he did not construct a Church. The Church was the result of the impact of the resurrection upon the disciples, an impact which they described as the coming of the Spirit. The Spirit established them in faith and power as witnesses of Christ and drove them out into the world to preach Christ. In that sense the Church comes from Christ and is based upon Christ. But the understanding by the disciples of the person of Christ and the meaning of his work gradually developed, so that we can distinguish various stages in the formation of Christology. Likewise, the form and structure of the Christian community and the understanding of its mission only gradually evolved as the disciples met and reacted to the various problems and needs of their Christian mission.

Granted an achieved understanding of the divinity of Christ, theologians may wish to argue *a priori* concerning the knowledge Jesus must have had of the outcome of his work and the subsequent development of the Church. But they should respect the historical data on what Jesus did and said. The data do not support the thesis that Jesus laid down the structure of a visible social entity, the Church, destined to embody his work and teaching in a permanent community existence until the coming of the final Kingdom. That thesis does not correspond to the perspective that governs the teaching of Jesus himself.

When the community that arose out of the events of Easter

began its life and mission, it naturally grouped itself around those who had been the closest disciples of Jesus. These acted as the leaders of the community. They appear in the Gospel narrative as the Twelve. The number had meaning, because it recalls the twelve tribes of Israel and manifests the community of believers as the new Israel, the messianic community. It was important, therefore, for the place of the one who had failed in his mission, namely Judas Iscariot, to be filled by the selection of another companion of Christ, Matthias. That Jesus chose the Twelve as an inner group and kept them around him may be readily admitted, although some would dispute it. But the statements concerning their authority and mission reflect the growing understanding of its role by the early Christian community. The Twelve stand as its representatives, summing up the community in themselves. The prominence given to them also reflects the first organisation of the Christian community.

But they do not appear as a clearly defined hierarchy, concerned with the perpetuation of its hierarchical authority. There are several indications of this. When James, the brother of John, is killed, he is not replaced; he had fulfilled his role as one of the Twelve on whom the new Israel was founded. Nothing is known of the activity of most of the Twelve. They disappear from the historical scene, and the later stories about them are legendary. Again, in the New Testament the term "apostle" is a wider term than the Twelve and includes others who were eyewitnesses of the resurrection and for that reason claimed an apostolic mission. Further, a person, James, whom many scholars do not regard as one of the Twelve, makes his appearance as the head of the community in Jerusalem. Then there was Paul, who claimed a direct commission from the risen Christ. He acknowledged the necessity of joining himself to the original leaders and being in agreement with them, but he was not appointed by them.

In brief, the picture is of a community under various leaders, with different reasons for being regarded as leaders. We do not find a fixed hierarchy of twelve apostles, ensuring the deployment and perpetuation of their authority by strict succession to themselves. The development of the community, with its organisation, problems and needs, is reflected in the present Gospels, because that development considerably influenced the formation of the Gospel tradition.

Peter was pre-eminent among the leaders of the first community. There is no reason to doubt the historical truth of the position accorded to him in the first part of the Acts. Nor should we question that this corresponded to the pre-eminence he enjoyed among the disciples during the lifetime of Jesus. But none of the Petrine texts in the Gospels can be simply attributed to Jesus without allowing for the modifying influence of the developing tradition of the community upon their formation. This is so even in regard to the text with the greatest claim to authenticity, namely the famous Petrine passage in Matt. 16. The promise to Peter has been inserted here from another context, even though it has been skilfully woven into the narrative by the redactor. Verse 17 has literary affinities with Gal. 1: 15-16; that and the use of "church" in verse 18 have led some to argue to a Pauline influence in the formation of the text. Whatever the circumstances of its origin, it was put together in its present form within the community. The Aramaic substratum of part of the text is not a sufficient criterion for attribution to Jesus himself; that of itself would take it back only to the Aramaic-speaking Palestinian community. There was undoubtedly a stress upon the role of Peter in some early Christian circles. The other texts confirm this. Their basis is the role Peter in fact played in the first community and among the original disciples.

When, however, allowance is made for the heightening effect of the community tradition about Peter, the prerogatives granted to him are not essentially different from those assigned to the other apostles. The Church is "built upon the foundation of the apostles and prophets" (Eph. 2:20); and we must add to that statement the consideration that the description of Peter as Rock includes a reference to the content of the faith he professed. All the apostles are given the power of binding and loosing (Matt. 18:18). Peter is made key-bearer, but clearly in subordination to Christ, who has "the keys of Death and Hades" (Apoc. 1:18) and is "The holy one, the true one, who has the key of David, who opens and no one shall shut, who shuts and no one opens" (Apoc. 3:7). The meaning of the text is, therefore, that Christ who has the keys makes Peter his key-bearer; in other words, his steward, the servant in charge of the household, who carries the keys. But the other apostles, too, are "servants of Christ and stewards of the mysteries of God" (I Cor. 4:

1), all like "the faithful and wise steward" of the parable, "whom his master will set over his household" (Luke 12:41). As for the role assigned to Peter in John 21, the other apostles, too, are called to be "fishers of men" (Mark 1:17) and, if I Peter is by Peter, he himself urges the elders, "Tend the flock of God that is your charge" (I Pet. 5:2). And Paul in Acts is said to have exhorted the elders of Ephesus with the words: "Take heed to yourselves and to all the flock, in which the Holy Spirit has made you guardians, to feed the church of the Lord" (Acts 20:28). The function of feeding and tending the flock is not confined to Peter. While, then, the role of Peter as the pre-eminent apostle is thrown into relief, the import of the Petrine texts should not be exaggerated. They apply to Peter the general themes used of the disciples of Christ and the leaders of the first community.

Nowadays it is not necessary to go to Protestant authors to discover the gap between the biblical data and the papal primacy as defined. Fr John McKenzie writes:

The position of Peter in the apostolic group was one of pre-eminence; this is a commonplace in Catholic theology, and it has within recent years been set forth very clearly by the Protestant scholar, Oscar Cullmann. It is also beyond dispute that to call Peter the "Pope" of the apostolic college is to imply a position of which the New Testament knows nothing. Here again the Acts of the Apostles and the epistles of Paul are our best witnesses; in these Peter appears as a leader, but not as endowed with supreme jurisdiction. We cannot define the position of Peter exactly in any of the terms which we use; and the New Testament has left his position undefined in its own language. The thesis of the primacy is weakened if one attempts to find in Peter the jurisdiction which has been exercised by the Roman Pontiff for some 1700 years. This is a long time, and it takes one back very near to the apostolic Church; but Peter lacks that position in the New Testament which he ought to have if he or anyone else thought of him as Pope.[1]

Let me add two remarks to that quotation. First, I should in fairness say that I am not claiming Fr McKenzie's support for my own radical views on Church structure. Second, I have already pointed to

[1] John L. McKenzie, S.J., *The Power and the Wisdom: An Interpretation of the New Testament* (Geoffrey Chapman, London, 1965), pp. 179-180.

the weakness of the argument from development. Like many biblicists today, Fr McKenzie is able to handle the biblical data with
great freedom because he passes the buck of defending later Roman
Catholic doctrine to the dogmatic theologian. Increasingly the
theologian is left grappling with the inadequacy of the biblical data
as interpreted even by Roman Catholic scholars.

Even if one is prepared to allow much greater force to the Petrine
texts than I have done, there remains the problem that the New
Testament does not expressly speak of any succession to his office.
Even comparatively conservative Catholic writers admit this. Thus,
in an article which defends the traditional interpretation, Fr Refoulé
writes:

> Was Peter able to transmit his prerogatives to a successor? That ques-
> tion is for Cullmann, for example, the crucial question. Taken of them-
> selves the Gospel texts expressly neither affirm nor weaken the possibility
> of such a transmission. In fact exegetes and theologians deny it or affirm
> it in the name of a particular concept of the Church and of the grace of
> the New Covenant in comparison with the Old. Thus different theologi-
> cal syntheses confront each other, and that is the reason why the debate
> has remained so far somewhat fruitless.[2]

Admittedly, the author goes on to cull some indications that in his
opinion *suggest* an affirmative answer to the question of transmission. But it is plain from his own exposition that these are not
decisive. They are in any case counterbalanced by the absence of
any clear evidence for transmission in the first two centuries. The
point here, however, is that succession to Peter is not established by
the biblical data, but rests upon a particular understanding of the
Church. The whole of this book is an argument against the Roman
Catholic view in its application to Church structures.

---

[2] *Pierre pouvait-il transmettre à un successeur ses prérogatives? Cette question
est pour Cullmann, par exemple, la question cruciale. Les textes évangéliques
pris en eux-memes n'affirment ni n'infirment explicitement la possibilité d'une
pareille transmission. Exégètes et théologiens de fait la nient ou l'affirment au
nom d'une certaine conception de l'Église et de la grace de la Nouvelle Alliance
en comparaison avec l'Ancienne. Des synthèses théologiques différentes s'affrontent
alors et c'est la raison pour laquelle le débat est demeuré jusqu'ici si peu fructueux*
—"Primauté de Pierre dans les évangiles," F. Refoulé, O.P., *Revue des sciences
religieuses*, 38 (1964), p. 39.

I must now again pick up the theme of the gradual development and structuring of the first Christian community.

What should be stressed is the immense scope of that evolution. People are still inclined to think of the Church as existing ready-made on the day of Pentecost. In fact the Church had gradually to develop from being phenomenologically a Jewish sect, with attendance at the Temple for worship and observance of the Jewish law, to being a social entity distinct from Judaism with a consciousness of a universal mission. The creative power of the Spirit in building the Church, a power given as a permanent gift to Christians, is magnificently illustrated in the breaking down of the barrier between Jews and Gentiles and the joining of the two into one body. The scope of the early development and the great advance in Christian consciousness it implied are set forth in the article of Fr David Stanley, S.J., "Kingdom to Church."[3] There he shows how the Church emerged from an evolutionary process, and he describes the underlying development of doctrinal understanding. The conclusion should be noted that the Gospels of Luke and Matthew reflect the achieved result of a considerable development.

On the narrower question of the evolution of the ministry, the evidence of Paul is fundamental, because his Letters are earlier than the other New Testament documents in their present form. In the indisputably genuine Letters of Paul we find a variety of ministries, and the ministerial functions are included among the charismatic gifts. This does not mean that the Pauline churches were directed through some kind of free movement of the Spirit, acting through men subject to extraordinary inspirations. Paul had a wider view of charismatic gifts than that, and he insisted upon order being preserved by the subjection of extraordinary manifestations to the needs of the common life of the Christian community. But the general organisation was evidently fluid, with a diversity of functions, each member being considered as having his gift for the building up of the community. The classical text is I Cor. 12; there we find listed among those God appointed in the Church: apostles, prophets, teachers, workers of miracles, healers, helpers, administrators and

[3] Originally published in *Theological Studies* 16 (1955), pp. 1-29; reprinted in Patrick J. Burns, S.J. (ed.), *Mission and Witness: The Life of the Church* (Geoffrey Chapman, London, 1965), pp. 25-60.

speakers in tongues. The structure based upon elders (*presbuteroi*) and overseers (*episkopoi*), anachronistically attributed to Paul in Acts, has not yet made its appearance in the undoubtedly Pauline Letters. Finally, it must be added that Paul kept a personal authority over the churches he founded.

In the later documents of the New Testament, notably the Pastoral Letters and Acts, a development in the structure of authority can be observed. Individual communities were placed under elders and overseers. The distinction between the two is not clear and probably varied. Some notable men, co-workers of the apostles, continued to exercise a wider commission over a number of churches, appointing officers in them.

The general trend towards a firmer institutional structure is what biblical scholars call the "early Catholicism," discernible in the sub-apostolic writings of the New Testament. This represents the reaction of the Church to the problem of retaining its apostolic identity and continuity after the passing of the apostles and first leaders. Part of the solution it adopted was to establish an orderly succession to their ministry. This was the origin of the idea of an apostolic succession in the ministers of the Church. But in its New Testament form the idea does not demand that the ministers should be considered as possessing an authority different in essence from the community as such and that a uniform structure of authority should in principle be imposed upon the whole Church. The most that can be concluded is that Christian communities should have ministers in some way duly authorised, that having a special function these receive a charism from the Spirit for its exercise, and that their duty is to preserve unity a among the various Christian communities and continuity with their predecessors of acknowledged authority in the apostolic ministry. The manner in which the ministry is structured may vary widely according to time and place. Nor is there any simple guarantee of continuity. History shows that the system chosen has its breakdowns and defects, which have to be remedied according to the exigencies of each particular situation.

The structure still inchoate in the New Testament itself emerges at the end of the first century, or the beginning of the second, in the Letters of St Ignatius of Antioch in the form of a monarchical episcopate, namely one overseer (*episkopos*) as head of each local community, surrounded by elders (*presbuteroi*) and deacons. Precisely how the transition took place from the groups of overseers and elders to the monarchical episcopate is not known. Nor was this structure at the time of St Ignatius found throughout the whole Church. Nevertheless, it spread rapidly, and the Church was soon structured according to the pattern taken for granted ever since. I have already given reasons for not regarding it as unchangeable.

We should also notice the discontinuity that underlies the measure of continuity preserved by the retention of the threefold ministry, with the bishop as the single head of the community. Only in a limited sense is the episcopate as found in the early Church the same office as that of the feudal bishops of the Middle Ages or that of the heads of modern dioceses. Sociologically and doctrinally, the episcopate has undergone profound changes in the course of its history. The concept of the office, the scope of episcopal authority, the relation of the bishops to priests and people—all this has been subject to much development and many vicissitudes. The present *mystique* of the episcopate as set forth by the Second Vatican Council is attractive in many ways. The points to be decided, however, are: whether it bears any true relation to the concrete facts; whether the authority claimed should not be drastically modified; whether the monarchical episcopate is to be imposed on all Christian bodies striving for unity; and whether in any case it is an appropriate form of structure for the needs of Christian mission in the world today.

A further point should be made about the New Testament data. The New Testament does not apply the theme of priesthood to the ministers of the Christian community. It is well known that the word "priest" (although the English term comes from *presbuteros*, meaning elder, I use it here as the equivalent of the Greek *hiereus*, which is the word for priest in the commonly accepted sense) is not used in the New Testament of the Christian ministers. The word and its derivatives are applied in a Christian sense only to Christ or to the Christian community as embracing all its members. It was only at the turn of the second century that the priestly vocabulary was applied in a more restricted sense to Christian ministers and the Christian ministry understood as a priestly class with a special priesthood not possessed by other Christians. Then in the sixth century anointing with oil, long used for the initiation of all Christians, was introduced to serve as the special priestly consecration of bishops and priests. Before then, the imposition of hands sufficed to express the appointment to a particular office and function within the Christian community. Needless to say, the idea of a special priesthood, different in essence and higher in dignity than that of the ordinary faithful, has undergone a considerable doctrinal development.

In this matter there is an initial insight that is sound enough. The Epistle to the Hebrews teaches that the work of Christ can be understood as the offering of the great High Priest who both fulfilled and transcended all that was foreshadowed by the priestly cult of the Old Law. His work was unique and all-sufficient, excluding repetition and not requiring any supplement to reinforce its efficacy. But Christians are joined to Christ in his priestly experience, a union achieved in virtue of the power of Christ as High Priest to unite all men to himself. They do not simply draw benefits from Christ's sacrifice; in him they enter into the same sacrificial process, dying and rising with him, passing with him into communion with God. In that sense the whole Christian life is priestly and sacrificial, and the Christian community is a priestly people. The mission of the Church is a priestly work, and all the functions within the community are an exercise of its priesthood. Since the Christian ministry is a particular and important function within the community, it is a particular and important realisation of the priesthood belonging to the Church as united to Christ. In that sense it is a particular sharing in the priesthood of Christ.

But the subsequent development has distorted that original insight, with harmful consequences for the structure and life of the Church.

The Epistle of the Hebrews presents the unique work of Christ as Mediator by comparing and contrasting it with the Jewish priestly cult. The analogy clearly has its limits. Although what Christ did was a sacrifice insofar as it fulfilled all that the previous priestly cult was striving to achieve but only succeeding in foreshadowing, his unique work was not a ritual sacrifice after the manner of the Jewish or pagan sacrifices. Likewise, although the life and functions of Christians are priestly and sacrificial as sharing and embodying the work of Christ, Christians have no ritual sacrifice in the Jewish or pagan sense; they have no material temple or altar and, it should be added, no priestly class. Ritually the Eucharist is not a sacrifice; it does not require or allow a priestly mediation by a special class of men. That would be a return to a pre-Christian dispensation. Considered ritually, the Eucharist is the symbolic fraternal meal of the Christian community. As the act of a structured community, it will be presided over by authorised ministers; but this does not imply that these have a priesthood different in essence from the rest of the community or interpose a priestly mediation. Since the Eucharist expresses the work of Christ and the union of Christians with Christ, it is in that sense a visible sacrifice. The work of Christ and the life of Christians in union with him may, as I have said, be understood as sacrificial; in the work of Christ, in which all Christians share, is found the reality behind all sacrifices. The Eucharist is the supreme symbolic action of the Christian community; an action which is not an empty symbol, but in which the reality of Christ, in his work and in his union with Christians, becomes really present. It is, therefore, the Christian sacrifice in a pre-eminent sense. But the whole life of the Christian community is also in a measure sacrificial as visibly expressing Christ and participating in his reality and work. The Eucharist cannot be isolated from the general life of the Christian community and set apart as a new ritual sacrifice, requiring like the pre-Christian sacrifices a special priestly class and a special priestly mediation. It is simply the supreme expression of that reality present and embodied in the Christian community as united to Christ.

The making of the Christian ministers into a priestly class, set apart and possessing a priesthood different in kind from the rest of Christians, disrupted the Christian community. It led to the degradation of the laity, the obscuring of the nature of Christian life and mission, the distortion of the Christian liturgy into hieratic ritual and its eventual fossilisation. All these consequences the Church is now struggling to overcome. But the movement of reform is blocked by the unyielding insistence upon the false principle from which all these consequences have in fact flowed. The liturgy remains essentially the function of a special class of priests possessing a priesthood different in essence from the rest of the community. In the ultimate analysis the ordinary faithful need not be present and the Mass may be private, even though their attendance and active participation are urged. Likewise, the mission of the Church belongs in a special and inalienable way to the hierarchy on account of its essentially higher priesthood. The laity can act only in essential subordination to a priestly class. That constant warnings against derogating from the hierarchical priesthood should have been found necessary in the recent documents on renewal shows that the inner dynamism of the reforming movement clashes with the retention of such an hierarchical priesthood.

Some would consider that the consequences for Christianity have been even greater than those so far described. The formation of a priestly class meant the structuring of Christianity into yet another religion on the old style. It set up the Church as a religious system, functioning in much the same way as other religions, and lost the essential newness of the Christian reality. The work of Christ marked the death of all religious systems, including the Jewish. Man was no longer to seek his salvation in the paraphernalia, ritual and laws of religion. By its universality Christian faith could not be enclosed in a religion as a cultural institution. Christians had a new relationship to the world. Christ was the head of mankind and the lord of history; in him the world and history had their meaning. Christians, therefore, should not have been concerned with the creation of a religious world, set apart from the ordinary life and affairs of men, existing as a self-enclosed and self-perpetuating institution, removed from the mainstream of human history. They had a mission to go out into the world, disclosing to men the meaning of their ordinary lives and the direction of human history as revealed in Christ. To do this they were freed from the baggage of religion, empowered by their faith and the Spirit, and needing only a few simple symbolic actions, linked like the bread and wine to the fundamentals of ordinary human living. Instead, with the creation of a special priestly class possessed of hierarchical authority, Christians have built the most elaborate religious system yet seen on earth and, imprisoned in it, are now lamenting that the course of human history has left them behind as quaint survivors of a past culture.

Finally, the doctrine of a special consecration of Christian ministers, understood as endowing them with a permanent priestly character, has resulted in an excessive rigidity in the organisation of the ministry. At present it is hindering the wide diversification of the ministry, with the separation of the numerous functions once performed by each bishop or priest and now needing to be made distinct offices in this age of specialisation. It is the basis of the opposition to a part-time ministry and the combination of a Christian ministry with a secular calling. In principle it excludes the idea of a temporary call to the ministry, which would allow people to exercise a ministerial function for a time and then leave it aside when change in themselves and in the circumstances of their lives led them to fulfil their Christian mission in another manner. The doctrine that the Christian community was the subject of Christian mission and priesthood and that the ministry was a function, admittedly an important one, within that community, but not of essentially different Christian value or dignity than other functions, would lead to a much more flexible approach to the problems of Christian ministry today. And that doctrine, I suggest, would be more in accord with the original data than the one prevalent in the Roman Catholic Church. Once more a particular historical development, probably inevitable and not without value in a past situation, has hardened into an unchangeable doctrinal principle.

5. THE DEVELOPMENT OF
THE PAPACY

To turn again to the papacy.

There is no cogent evidence for the existence and exercise of a papal primacy of jurisdiction in the first two centuries. The evidence in fact indicates its absence. This has recently been admitted by a Roman Catholic writer, Fr McCue, who, however, makes the expected appeal to development, an appeal I have already discussed.[1] But other writers have said more or less the same. I repeat that a recognition of development must be accompanied by an acknowledgement that developments, especially institutional developments, are often relative to particular historical situations and are not without further proof to be taken as irreversible and unchangeable. For that reason, apart from the limitations of this book, I am in regard to my present purpose not much concerned with the stages according to which the papal primacy gradually emerged.

That it emerged only when a fair time had elapsed after the apostolic age and without a discernible line of continuity with that age seems reasonably clear. We may readily grant an early and understandable prominence of Rome as a church of apostolic foun-

[1] James F. McCue, "The Roman Primacy in the Second Century and the Problem of the Development of Dogma," *Theological Studies*, 25 (1964), pp. 161-196.

dation, with a claim to Peter and Paul as its founders. This provided a basis, although an insufficient one, for the later claims.

Rome was led to a sharper consciousness of its apostolic authority when it defended orthodoxy against the interference of the Emperors and resisted the growing caesaro-papism of the East. In the name of traditional authority it also opposed the imperially supported claim of the See of Constantinople. Rome staked out its own claim as the See of Peter and gave new emphasis to its previous pre-eminence.

Then social and political conditions in the West left the bishops of Rome with an important social and political role, which reinforced the ecclesiastical dominance already possessed as the one Western patriarchal see. A great development of papal authority took place, which eventually resulted in the construction of medieval Christendom. In the Middle Ages the papal claims were conceptualised more elaborately and defended with a dossier of arguments.

There is much that is praiseworthy in the development of the papacy. Only polemical distortion could lead one to say that it came from an unchristian imperialism. Rome had reason to defend orthodoxy with an appeal to apostolic authority in the doctrinal disputes of the Empire. It shouldered in a Christian manner the role that devolved upon it in relation to the peoples of the West. But what remains open to question is how far it was led to claim too much. Certainly, some of the claims of the medieval popes are generally recognised as excessive. Were it not for the unfortunate definition of the First Vatican Council, the papal supremacy of jurisdiction as there defined would, I suggest, be frankly regarded as likewise excessive by many Catholic writers today. The Christian West itself has never fully acquiesced in the papal primacy in that sense; there have always been opposing views and tendencies. The Christian East rejects it. And, even if we prescind from the lack of evidence in the first two centuries, I do not think that the later data adduced, when placed in historical context, come even near to proving that the papal primacy as defined is an irreversible development and a matter of Christian faith.

I have left until now the question of papal infalliblity, because it is a corollary of papal primacy and stands or falls with it. Since the Pope has full and supreme jurisdiction over the whole Church in matters of doctrine, there is attributed to him as a personal prerogative "the infallibility with which the divine Redeemer willed his Church to be endowed in defining doctrine concerning faith or morals."[2] A personal prerogative, not indeed in the sense of belonging to him as a private person, but personal to him in his office as shepherd and teacher of all Christians. The meaning of this is set forth more fully in the Constitution on the Church of the Second Vatican Council:

> Therefore his definitions, of themselves, and not from the consent of the Church, are justly styled irreformable, for they are pronounced with the assistance of the Holy Spirit, an assistance promised to him in blessed Peter. Therefore they need no approval of others, nor do they allow an appeal to any other judgment. For then the Roman Pontiff is not pronouncing judgment as a private person. Rather, as the supreme teacher of the universal Church, as one in whom the charism of the infallibility of the Church herself is individually present, he is expounding or defining a doctrine of Catholic Faith.[3]

The conditions required for this infallibility to be present are well known. In the words of the First Vatican Council the conditions are fulfilled when the Roman Pontiff "speaks ex cathedra, that is, when, acting in the office of shepherd and teacher of all Christians, he defines, by virtue of his supreme apostolic authority, doctrine concerning faith or morals to be held by the universal Church."[4] This papal infallibility is defined as "a divinely revealed dogma"[5]; so that "if anyone presumes to contradict this Our definition (God forbid that he do so): let him be anathema."[6]

There is the same objection to papal infallibility as to papal primacy, namely, that the doctrine has not any adequate support in the biblical and historical data. It has indeed even less claim to our adherence than papal primacy, seeing that it developed as an implication of that primacy.

---

[2] The First Vatican Council. English translation in *The Church Teaches: Documents of the Church in English Translation*, edited by John F. Clarkson, S.J., and others (B. Herder Book Co., St. Louis, 1955), n. 219. Latin text in Denzinger-Bannwart, n. 1839.

[3] Walter M. Abbott, S.J. (ed.), *The Documents of Vatican II*, p. 49, n. 25.

[4] *The Church Teaches*, n. 219; Denzinger-Bannwart, n. 1839.

[5] *Ibid.*

[6] *Ibid.*, n. 220; Denzinger-Bannwart, n. 1840.

A further objection, however, can also be made. Has it not distorted the understanding of the indefectibility of the Christian faith by attaching that indefectibility indissolubly to the *juridical* authority of particular declarations? Let me explain what I mean.

The Gospels teach that Christ promised to be with his disciples until the end of the world, and the New Testament shows that he fulfilled that promise by sending the Spirit as a permanent gift. From this follows the conviction of Christians that Christian faith and mission will never fail in this world. Until the end of time faith in Christ will persist and the mission coming from Christ will continue by the Spirit to be operative in human history. In that sense the Church of Christ, which is the community of believers and the bearer of the mission, is indefectible and will never be destroyed or overcome by the forces of evil and error.

But it does not follow that particular errors will not at times be rampant among Christians, obscuring the meaning and implications of the Christian faith. The biblical promise would seem to be fulfilled if sufficient faith remains for any errors eventually to be overcome. Nor does it follow that Church authorities may not make mistaken or only partly true statements, which later have to be corrected and modified by the interplay of other forces within the Church. And there is even less reason for asserting this when the statements are concerned with what is peripheral to the Christian message. Christian faith is not destroyed in the world because of a mistaken declaration, later corrected.

The authority won by some past Councils does not in fact rest upon their juridical authority alone. In some instances this juridical authority was defective, and there were some Councils of equal juridical status that never won acceptance. The list of Ecumenical Councils we now find in Roman Catholic writers is a post-medieval production. It would also be plain anachronism to apply the juridical conditions now laid down for Ecumenical Councils to the early Councils of the Church. No, the authority of the great Councils of the early Church cannot be separated from a process of acceptance, according to which they were acknowledged in the Church as expressing the genuine Christian faith. There is no merely juridical method of ensuring infallibility. And it must be remembered that much of the insistence that there was upon the juridical authority of some of the early Councils came from the desire of the Emperors to ensure a uniformity of doctrine within the Empire for political reasons.

A conviction that Christian faith will never fail in this world would lead one to hold that when Christians as a body have over a long period accepted a declaration as enshrining their genuine belief, then that declaration should be accepted as a true statement of faith. For that reason a person who dismissed, say, the authority of the Council of Nicaea would put himself outside the Christian tradition. But this criterion requires careful application. It is not easy to establish a definitive commitment of Christians where the matter is not central to the Christian faith and life, but only peripheral. Moreover, sometimes a particular declaration is insisted upon because in the historical context no other way was available for preserving Christian truth. Later a better formulation may be found or the circumstances such that the past declaration is no longer useful or necessary. Particular formulations always belong to particular historical situations; they should be interpreted and evaluated as such. Nor does belief in the indefectibility of Christian faith demand the exclusion of every element of error from particular formulations recognised as authoritative.

What seems clear to me is that the unfailing continuance of Christian faith in the world cannot be taken as proving the existence of a juridical method of guaranteeing statements as of infallible authority. This is precisely what the doctrine of papal infallibility tries to do. Once the Pope has made a definition it must be accepted as irreformably true of itself in virtue of infallible authority. No doubt it could not in principle, so it is said, contradict the faith of the Church. But such a definition stands of itself, in its own right, subject to no further test or process of acceptance for its authority to hold good. This is a claim far beyond anything warranted by the biblical and historical data. Nor does it correspond to the process through which the unfailing Christian faith has been preserved and developed with many ups and downs in the course of Christian history.

While the principle behind papal infallibility is erroneous and dangerous, papal infallibility as defined is of far less practical importance than the ordinary exercise of papal doctrinal authority. Here we observe the process called "creeping infallibility" by some authors. This means the tendency to treat noninfallible declarations of the Pope for all intents and purposes as though they were infallible. One is not allowed to descend from generalities and urge that a particular noninfallible papal declaration—unless it belongs to the remote past—is in fact erroneous.

But, however deplorable its results, the insistence upon the wider authority of the Pope is understandable, because papal infallibility as defined is practically useless in regard to any of the real problems facing the Church. It is in fact a theoretical construct, with little bearing upon the processes actually governing doctrinal commitment within the Church. The Pope today could not exercise his infallible authority in any doctrinal debate where a decision had to be verified from the biblical and traditional data. He does not dare to decide the question of birth control infallibly, despite its urgency and the reservation of the decision to himself. Even less so, I suggest could he intervene effectively with infallible authority in regard to the problems about the interpretation of the fundamentals of the Christian faith now increasingly confronting the Church as a result both of biblical criticism and of secularist philosophy. Those problems have to be worked out by open debate among Christian thinkers, and there is no way of excluding temporary errors and imperfect solutions. An infallible intervention by the Pope is conceivable only when there is no longer any need for its authority, because the problem belongs to the past and the results of the debate are secure.

I know without being told the usual explanation that infallibility implies only negative assistance. It does not mean inspiration or revelation, and therefore the Pope may not be able to give an answer to a pressing problem. Infallibility means only that if he does give a decision it will be true. All right. But there is little point in having a doctrine of papal infallibility unless it expresses a genuine element in the doctrinal processes by which the Christian faith is preserved and transmitted in the world. What I am contending is that not only is papal infallibility without adequate biblical and historical support, but it is also as defined a theoretical construct without practical value in the concrete order. That is why what may be called a practical infallibility has to be assigned to ordinary papal teaching in order to make papal authority actually operative.

Corresponding to this analysis is the fact that the two instances where the conditions of a papal *ex cathedra* definition have been fulfilled to the letter, so that their status is beyond dispute, are both Marian dogmas. The first, issued before the definition of infallibility by the First Vatican Council, is the definition of the Immaculate Conception by Pius IX in 1854; the second, issued after First Vatican, is the definition of the Assumption by Pius XII in 1950.

It is easy enough to make definitions in the field of Mariology. They affect only the exclusively religious sphere and, unlike moral statements, do not come up against the hard facts of human reality. Further, the two definitions are incapable of proof or disproof from the Bible and early tradition, because they are so remote from the data that they can only be defended as long-term developments.

They must be taken in fact as self-justifying.

I know that Roman Catholic theologians would protest against that judgement. I once argued against it myself. But I think that it is true. Theologians can trace the long, slow, disputed evolution of the two doctrines to the point where they gained general acceptance in the Church, but to show that they are a divinely revealed part of the Christian faith is another matter.

There are many aspects in the development of Marian doctrine which are questionable and which are in fact questioned by many Roman Catholic theologians today. I find it hard to suppose that the present retrenchment in the field of Mariology would stop short at these two doctrines had they not been defined. There are signs that the great growth of Marian doctrine should be regarded as a temporary phenomenon in the Church, due to causes that are now being combated, such as the neglect of the humanity of Christ and an excessively juridical concept of the Church, both calling for a human and feminine counterbalance. Moreover, the close association of Marian doctrine with papal infallibility is not surprising. The glorification of Mary has gone hand in hand with the exaltation of the Church. Mariology is in many respects the myth and cult of a triumphalistic Church. These are circumstances which make it difficult to accept two definitions that rest simply upon a complex development which only now we are beginning to see in perspective and assess critically. The genuine Christian faith of the Church on which the definitions are said to rest cannot be discerned by taking a vote or amassing petitions. A sifting of historical influences is required. And the only clear criterion for accepting the two dogmas as an unchangeable part of the Christian faith is the authority of the definitions themselves. These, then, have to be taken as self-justifying.

Moreover, I do not think that the principle of doctrinal development is rightly used as a basis for imposing upon the faith of all Christians matters that are peripheral to the Christian message and unsupported by any clear link with the faith of the apostolic Church. There is no need for certitude in such matters, and without a new revelation there are no grounds for certitude. Theories of the development of doctrine are intended to explain how the Christian faith remains the same when it becomes embodied in different cultural contexts and is repeatedly rethought and reformulated. This insertion of the Christian faith into the living dynamism of the human mind and the living processes of human culture leads to a constant development in the understanding of that faith and brings to light new aspects of its meaning. The process of development cannot be confined to logical deductions from the text of Scripture, because the struggle of Christians to meet new problems and answer new questions takes place not just by studying the past but with the permanent presence of the Christian reality amongst them and under the living movement of the Spirit. Nevertheless, all development is a process of understanding the original Christian faith and preserving it amidst change. Such a process does not lead to the discovery of new facts and events not recorded in the original revelation. Admittedly, both the Immaculate Conception and the Assumption are presented as transhistorical facts, not as historical events in the ordinary sense. But both are affirmed as facts, deeds that God accomplished in bringing about man's salvation. A developing understanding of the meaning of the original Christian revelation can never provide sufficient grounds of certitude for affirming the existence of facts not recorded in that revelation. A free intervention of God cannot be inferred; it must be revealed.

Further, both these doctrines, the Immaculate Conception and the Assumption, are tied to particular formulations of other doctrines, formulations that are now changing and likely to leave them behind as meaningless.

The Immaculate Conception depends upon an understanding of

original sin which sees it as the transmission by generation of an historically first sin. From the first moment of her conception Mary by a singular privilege was preserved from that sin, which otherwise she would have inherited through her human generation. However, despite official opposition, original sin is being increasingly understood, not as the transmission of a first sin, but as an attempt to express the sinfulness of the general human situation and condition into which each man is born. Christ, entering into that situation, dominated it as Redeemer. So do Christians in union with Christ, and we may say Mary did likewise. But it would not make sense to speak of an Immaculate Conception.

The Assumption, which means the anticipated resurrection of Mary, depends upon understanding the resurrection of the body as the glorification of our present bodies. This, however, is increasingly questioned.

Suppose we take the resurrection of the body as affirming the total redemption of man and as rejecting the idea that only a spiritual component in human nature is saved. We can then oppose the understanding of death as the separation of a soul from a body. What happens at death would be the passing of the total person into a new state of existence, bodily as well as spiritual, but a state of existence to which the corpse left behind is now irrelevant. Paul writes in I Corinthians:

But some one will ask, "How are the dead raised? With what kind of body do they come?" You foolish man! What you sow does not come to life unless it dies. And what you sow is not the body which is to be, but a bare kernel, perhaps of wheat or of some other grain. But God gives it a body as he has chosen, and to each kind of seed its own body. For not all flesh is alike. . . . So is it with the resurrection of the dead. What is sown is perishable, what is raised is imperishable. It is sown in dishonour, it is raised in glory. It is sown in weakness, it is raised in power. It is sown a physical body, it is raised a spiritual body (I Cor. 15:35-44).

(The contrast in the last sentence is not between a material and an immaterial body, but between a body of our old nature coming from Adam and a body penetrated with the Spirit and formed in the image of the heavenly Christ.) There is no evidence that Paul understood the resurrection of Christ himself as the reanimation of his corpse, and the general direction of his teaching would seem to favour a resurrection that was not the revivification of a corpse but the transition of the total man into a new state with a new kind of body. If we develop this idea, we can understand death, not as the beginning of a disembodied state, but as an immediate resurrection. Our resurrection takes place in stages. Already in this life we die and rise with Christ; our new existence begins. But we still await the fulness of redemption. At death we experience a dying and rising with Christ in a deeper fashion. Out of our present bodily existence comes by the power of Christ a new state of bodily existence. The corpse is left aside as the husk of the seed that was sown; it is no longer our body and can no longer serve as the expression of us as persons. Since, however, our redemption is not as individuals, but as forming one body of Christ with other men, after death we still have to await the final Kingdom, when the number of elect will be complete and the plan of God for mankind and the world brought to its conclusion. Our bodies are the way we are related to others. The fulness of the resurrection of the body will be given when we are all related to one another in the final Kingdom.

Now, if we argue along these lines, the conclusion is that we are all in a sense assumed, body and soul, into heaven. Or, to put it more accurately, the conceptual framework in which the question of Mary's Assumption arose would no longer be valid. She would enjoy the same resurrection at death as other Christians and would wait with them for the completion of her resurrection at the end of the world. Christ's own resurrection is already complete, insofar as he is source of the resurrection of all men. The final resurrection deploys what he already in principle possesses and therefore does not add to it. The same cannot be said of Mary. Consequently, it is difficult to see what meaning would be left to the dogma of Mary's Assumption.

The two definitions, therefore, are attempts to make irreformable dogmas of pious beliefs that are tied to relative and changeable formulations of other Christian doctrines.

It seems to me that the imposition of these two points—peripheral to the Christian message, remote from the biblical data, late developments in Christian history, dependent upon a particular and questionable formulation of other doctrines—as matters of obligatory Christian faith renders the papal system theologically indefensible. It confirms the more general arguments against papal infallibility.

6. THE QUESTION OF VISIBLE UNITY

Before leaving the question of the credibility of the Roman Catholic position in relation to the biblical and historical data, I have to consider one final point, namely, the claim to be in some exclusive sense the one, true Church of Christ.

This claim rests chiefly upon the papacy. It is because the Roman Church alone possesses the papacy, taken to be of divine institution, that it can consistently maintain that no other Church, whatever its wealth of Christian elements and values, has the complete structure as given to his Church by Christ. Every other Church is essentially defective, because it lacks the key element of the Petrine primacy. Certainly, the claim of the Roman Church *vis-à-vis* the Eastern Churches, which have retained an hierarchical structure and full sacramental system, would be difficult to sustain without grounding it upon the papacy.

Since I have opposed the claim of the papacy to be of divine institution, I have removed one of the main arguments for Roman exclusiveness. But there is another approach worthy of consideration.

The Church of Christ, so the argument goes, appears in the New Testament as one visible body, and throughout the New Testament great stress is laid upon the visible unity of the Church. When we turn to Christian history, we find a similar stress upon the existence and unity of the *Catholica*, the great Church. Schism is always understood, not as being within the Church and dividing it, but as being from the Church and constituting a breaking away from it. However weakened by these schisms from it, the *Catholica* remains. We find a persistent Christian conviction, going back to the New Testament and continuing through the vicissitudes of history, that the Church of Christ is one, visible body, united in fellowship and government, in faith and common life. If we interpret Christian history and the present Christian situation on the basis of this principle, then we will conclude that the Roman Catholic Church is the *Catholica*, the great Church. No other Church can convincingly make the same claim. All the other Churches have broken away from the Roman Catholic Church, which, though considerably weakened and damaged by the many schisms, remains essentially that one, visible body in unbroken continuity with the apostolic community and consequently in an exclusive sense the one, true Church of Christ.

I do not wish to deny the strength of this view. It formulates the deep conviction of ordinary Roman Catholics, who, whatever their ignorance of the details, interpret the New Testament and Christian history in that manner. They have a sense that their Church is visibly one and has always been one. Their conviction that their Church is the great Church, the Catholic Church, is confirmed by their experience; and they have some reason for seeing all other Churches as originating in a breaking away from their own Church.

But the argument has serious weaknesses. It rests upon a Roman Catholic understanding of visible unity and a Roman Catholic interpretation of Christian history.

First, it must be remembered that the Eastern Churches as a body make essentially the same claim. They, too, claim to be the one, true Church of Christ and alone in full continuity with the apostolic Church. On their side they regard the Roman Church as having broken away from the communion of the Christian Churches. Here, then, we have two opposing claimants, and it is difficult to decide in favour of the Roman Church without introducing the papal primacy, which in the form of a jurisdictional primacy as defined the Eastern Churches would firmly reject, with strong grounds in Scripture and tradition for doing so. True, the use of the phrase "Eastern Churches" indicates a different view of visible unity from that of the

Roman Church with its close governmental unity. But, despite their loose juridical structure, the Eastern Churches are deeply conscious of their unity of common faith and the communion that binds them together. Are we to say that the centralised structure of the Roman Church is alone in accord with the New Testament? It would be truer to say that the Church order of the East, with the underlying understanding of the nature of the Church, corresponds better to that of primitive Christianity. The world-wide spread of the Roman Catholic Church in contrast to the comparative confinement of the Eastern Churches cannot be dissociated from political factors. The Eastern Churches were hemmed in, while the Churches of the West were carried forward on the wave of Western expansion. The contrast, however, is now being lessened both by the presence of the Eastern Churches in the West and by the effects upon missionary expansion of the reaction to Western colonialism. Again, the Eastern case against the doctrinal and institutional developments in the Roman Catholic Church would have to be listened to in assessing the two claims.

Neither, however, would seem to fit the facts of Christian history. The Church of the early centuries did, it must be admitted, think of schism as being from the Church, a breaking away, and stressed the continuing visible unity of the great Church. But history has faced Christians with facts which were not then envisaged. From the fact to the possibility is always a valid inference. No argument from the New Testament or early tradition about what could or could not occur can prevail against the ascertained fact of what has occurred. When Christians are faced with disconcerting occurrences, they should not try to deny them on the basis of a previous understanding of the data, but return to the data to acquire a deeper understanding. Now, what has happened is schism within the one Church, not just the breaking away of Christians to constitute a false Church.

The schism between East and West can be reasonably understood only as taking place within the general unity of the Church, so that neither side was placed outside the Church of Christ. In the account given by historians today the division between East and West took place gradually over a long period by a process that was in part imperceptible but at the same time punctuated by a number of outstanding divisive incidents. However, communion was certainly severed to the extent that the Eastern Churches are not part of the visible unity of the Roman Catholic Church as a social entity. All the same, despite the schism, undoubtedly a large measure of visible unity remained. The unity between East and West which still persists amid division is not confined to the invisible order. A largely common profession of faith, the same Bible, the same sacraments and a large area of common tradition—all these constitute a considerable measure of visible unity. If we do not wish to exclude either East or West from the visible body of Christ's Church on earth, we must suppose that the visible unity essential to the very survival of that Church and therefore unfailing despite all human destructive and divisive forces should be conceived in a more flexible manner than in the Roman Catholic position. Visible unity has not been entirely destroyed, but it has been damaged and marred.

I will pass over the Great Schism of the West in the fourteenth century, simply noting that it illustrates how deep divisions can occur without one's being able to say that the visible unity of Christ's Church was preserved intact on one side, while the other side was outside the unity of the Church. But the upheaval of the Reformation was clearly much more serious.

Here the temptation for Roman Catholics is too readily to assume an interpretation based on Roman Catholic principles that are in fact open to question. Looked at without theological *parti pris*, what occurred was the break-up of the Western Church, not the mere breaking away of groups from the great Church. None of the resultant parties fully represented what had gone before. The Roman Catholic part was itself profoundly altered in the composition of its membership, in structural organisation and in doctrinal stance. Nor did the Reformers consider themselves as breaking away from the one Church, but as purifying and reforming it in doctrine, structure and life. Now, if one takes for granted that the papacy is of divine institution, that the previous hierarchical structure was unalterable, that doctrinal right was entirely on the Roman side and nothing but heresy and error distinctive of the Reformers, then it follows that the Roman Catholic Church represents the one Church of Christ, surviving the upheaval with its visible unity intact. But if one denies those points, which are in fact open to serious dispute, none of the bodies that emerged from the Reformation crisis represents the fulness of the Christian faith unmixed with error and is the essentially complete presence of the Church of Christ in the world. No; the visible unity of Christ's Church was profoundly damaged in the West; it did not remain gloriously intact in the Roman Catholic Church. It may be added that it is historically untrue to suppose that visible unity was apparent only in the Roman Catholic Church, while there was nothing but confused division among the Reformers. There was a great measure of unity in Churches of the Reformation, notably among the Calvinists, and the Counter-Reformation discipline covered over deep divisions among Roman Catholics, which persisted and emerged from time to time. What at any rate is clear is that the shattering effect of the Reformation upheaval upon the Church of the West cannot be healed by the return of the other Churches to the supposed fulness and intact unity of the Roman Catholic Church, but only by a change in all the Churches from their post-Reformation shape and stance. They have to learn from one another, each completing its own tradition in the light of other traditions and finding common structures in a way that does not cling to the past but meets the needs of the present situation.

The analysis I have given corresponds to the insights gained by those, including Roman Catholics, closely involved in the ecumenical movement.

Ecumenists have been led to a number of important convictions. They have discovered that all the Churches have much to learn from one another. All the traditions are at present one-sided; they all need correction and modification from the rest. The holding of any one tradition rigidly to the exclusion of the complementary insights of other traditions has led and still inevitably leads to error. Further, amid the divisions, ecumenists have found a surprising measure of unity already existing, a unity that has been obscured, not only by the doctrinal differences, but also by political, social and nontheological factors in general. The existing unity among Christians of different Churches is not simply the invisible unity of all in Christ; it is a unity rendered visible, although imperfectly, in a number of ways: in a professed faith more common than had been supposed, in a common reverence for the Bible, in a large measure of common tradition, in similar forms of Christian life and practice. Now that the polemical shouting has stopped, it is possible to reflect on the great extent to which Christians have remained one. There has always been a fair circulation of spiritual and theological writings among the Churches. More recently the biblical, liturgical and ecumenical movements in crossing denominational barriers have revealed how little these matter in comparison to the profound Christian convictions that unite people from the various Churches. This brings me to another discovery of the ecumenists. Their experience has shown them that the lines of the deeper divisions among Christians do not correspond to the boundaries of the denominations. People of one Church find themselves more united in faith and spiritual conviction with some members of other Churches than they do with many members of their own Church. The points on which they differ from members of another Church are less important in relation to the heart of their Christian faith and life than the points they have in common with them but which members of their own Church disagree with or ignore. Thus, the pattern of Christian groupings in relation to the Christian faith does not follow the denominational divisions. These divisions are often more the product and expression of political, national and social differences and barriers than of the Christian faith. All the less reason for taking any one of the existing boundaries as marking off the sphere of the fulness of the Christian faith and the expression of the intact visible unity of the Church of Christ.

At the same time, the increasing secularism of the West has made all Christians more conscious of the unity that they still have amongst themselves as Christian believers, despite their quarrels and divisions.

The conclusion I am leading to is that visible unity as a permanent, unfailing and indispensable feature of the Church of Christ cannot be conceived in the narrow sense of the unity of a visible social body, with a unified and undisputed structure of authority and a consequent full and unbroken communion among all the members. How far Christians have to work to achieve and preserve such a unity is another question. But my contention is that such social unity has not in fact been preserved in Christian history. Therefore, though it may be a task laid upon Christians, it has not been given them as a permanent and unfailing gift. There have been divisions within the one Church of Christ which have broken its unity as a single, visible social body. A measure of visible unity has always been preserved, but only amidst divisions of social structure.

That the unity of Christ's Church has remained unfailingly intact as the unity of a visible society is a cornerstone in the Roman Catholic position. Consequently, the exclusive claim. But this claim, as I have argued, does not do justice to the facts of Christian history and involves an exaltation of the Roman Catholic Church over against the other Churches that cannot be sustained in the light of the insights of the ecumenical movement.

However, in my opinion, the Roman Catholic Church has now virtually conceded the fundamental principle of the opposite conception of the permanent visible unity of the Church.

Following the previous contention of many Roman Catholic ecumenists, the Decree on Ecumenism of the Second Vatican Council admits that Christian bodies outside the visible boundaries of the Roman Catholic Church are to be regarded positively as Christian Churches or at least as ecclesial communities. The use of the two terms, namely "Churches" and "ecclesial communities" is intended to indicate that the appellation "Church" demands structural conditions not fulfilled in all the separated Christian bodies. However, no attempt is made to determine the exact application of the two terms to existing Christian communities, except that the Decree has no hesitation in using the word "Church" in speaking of the separated Churches of the East. But the important point for my present purpose is that the separated Christian communities are recognised as genuinely Christian social entities, even if they are still regarded as defective in various ways. Elements and endowments that build up the Church of Christ and give it life are found in their social structure; as communities they are means of salvation used by Christ; they are granted significance and importance in the mystery of salvation.

I have already quoted from the relevant first chapter of the Decree on Ecumenism. Here is another quotation, which overlaps the previous one:

Moreover some, even very many, of the most significant elements or endowments which together go to build up and give life to the Church herself can exist outside the visible boundaries of the Catholic Church: the written word of God; the life of grace; faith, hope, and charity, along with other interior gifts of the Holy Spirit and visible elements. All of these, which come from Christ and lead back to Him, belong by right to the one Church of Christ.

The brethren divided from us also carry out many of the sacred actions of the Christian religion. Undoubtedly, in ways that vary according to the condition of each Church or Community, these actions can truly engender a life of grace, and can be rightly described as capable of providing access to the community of salvation.

It follows that these separated Churches and Communities, though we believe they suffer from defects already mentioned, have by no means been deprived of significance and importance in the mystery of salvation. For the Spirit of Christ has not refrained from using them as means of salvation which derive their efficacy from the very fullness of grace and truth entrusted to the Catholic Church.[1]

Now, the cautious wording cannot disguise a fundamental change of attitude. Before, as I know well from my student days, the Roman Catholic position was interpreted to mean that only individual Christians existing outside the visible unity of the Roman Catholic Church could be considered as belonging to the one Church of Christ. Their sincere Christian faith related them to that Church, which in fact was visibly embodied in the Roman Church. But their Churches were false Churches and, as Churches or social entities, could not be regarded as belonging to the one Church of Christ or in any way forming part of it. In that way the claim of the Roman Catholic Church to be the one, true Church of Christ, unfailingly intact in its visible unity, was clearly maintained. Once, however, the separated Christian Churches are judged to be genuine, even if defective, Churches or ecclesial communities, they are held to belong as Churches to the one, true Church of Christ as visibly present in this world. The boundaries of the Roman Catholic Church can no longer be taken as marking the total, visible and social presence of the Church of Christ. That total, visible and social presence of the one Church of Christ includes the other Churches. This means that the visible unity of Christ's Church has in fact suffered division. In other words, there is an admission of schism within the Church, not just from the Church.

This essentially modifies the Roman Catholic claim. The contention cannot be that, in accord with the New Testament data, the Church of Christ as visibly present in the world has remained unfail-

[4] Walter M. Abbott, S.J. (ed.), *The Documents of Vatican II*, pp. 345-346, n. 3.

ingly one as a single social entity. It has not. Its total visible presence embraces several divided social entities. The claim must now be that one of those social entities, namely the Roman Catholic Church, has alone preserved the complete structural form of the Church, the fulness of the Christian faith and the complete range of the means of salvation. The Roman Church would thus be the central or Mother Church among the Churches that belong to the totality of the one body of Christ as visibly and socially present in the world. The Church of Rome would be claiming an intensive, but not as before also an extensive, completeness as the one, true Church of Christ.

But this claim cannot be based upon the New Testament data concerning the unity of the Church, because the New Testament does not envisage the situation of a divided Church. Once the previously rigid claim has been relinquished, the new claim has to be established on different grounds. The New Testament does not envisage what is now granted by the Roman Catholic Church, namely the existence of divided social entities belonging to the one Church of Christ. Hence it cannot appropriate the New Testament teaching on unity to myself without further argument. For this reason its claim to superiority over all other Churches requires proof. In fact it rests chiefly upon the thesis that the papacy is of divine institution. Take away that point, and it would be difficult to show more than that the Roman Catholic Church is at present the largest of the Christian Churches. Clearly, this makes it of outstanding importance, but it does not establish that it represents the complete structural form of the Church, the fulness of the Christian faith and the complete embodiment of all the gifts and means of salvation.

Christian history, therefore, compels us to develop our understanding of the unity of the Church.

All Christians believe in the unity of the Church. That unity is grounded upon the one Christ and the one Spirit. From the oneness of Christ and the Spirit arises the union of all Christians in Christ and the Spirit. This union of all Christians must be visibly embodied and manifested. Its visible embodiment constitutes the visible unity of the Church. The Church as visibly one is the visible presence in the world of the one Christ and the one Spirit.

Despite their divisions, Christians have in fact, as I have said, retained a measure of visible unity amongst themselves. Their union with one another has not been simply of the invisible order; it has been embodied and manifested in a variety of ways. The extent of this persistent unity has been brought home to Christians by the ecumenical movement.

Yet, the visible unity of the Church has been damaged and marred to an extent simply not envisaged by Christians of the early centuries. We must allow here for a development of understanding. Heresies and schisms certainly ravaged the early Church, but for centuries it was assumed that the visible unity of the great Church would always remain intact simply by a negative process of exclusion, however long it took to effect. Heretics and schismatics were presumed to be in bad faith and were treated accordingly. But history has taught Christians a greater sobriety in handling Christian truth, a greater caution in judging the efforts of their fellow Christians to understand and live the Christian faith in a changing world and a greater reluctance to break off Christian communion on account of differences of view and practice. It shocks us today to learn how easily Christians of an earlier age excommunicated one another, sometimes for trivial reasons or legitimate differences. Christians now, their consciences awakened by the ecumenical movement, can look around on the results of past intolerance and narrow-mindedness, on the effects of the refusal to listen, on the damage wreaked by the lack of concern for unity and love. They are divided from one another into different Churches, none of which can convincingly claim that its tradition in isolation represents the fulness of Christian faith and does not need to be complemented by other traditions, and none of which can claim to be the total visible presence of the Church of Christ. Christians can see that the unity which has persisted in the face of all the divisive forces and which is the lasting presence of unity as Christ's gift has been obscured for themselves and for the world not only by doctrinal differences but by political and social barriers they were sent to overcome.

All this has led Christians to the understanding that unity is not simply a static and permanent gift, but a task, a mission. Included in the mission of the Church and in a sense its chief expression is work for unity. Under the movement of the Spirit, Christians have to strive to keep, strengthen and manifest their union with one another in Christ. This understanding of unity as a task not just a permanent gift, as a goal not just an achieved fact, as a unity we seek not just a unity already possessed brings into relief an element in the New Testament formerly neglected by a triumphalistic outlook. For example, the constant exhortations of Paul to unity, the command reiterated in John to love one another and the prayer of Christ in John 17 as a prayer embracing the total mission of the Church until the final end. It corresponds, too, to the concept of the Church as a pilgrim people, still journeying towards the perfect unity that is its destiny but meanwhile buffeted by the divisive forces of human sinfulness.

But the unity of Christians is intended as an initial presence and manifestation of the unity offered to all mankind by Christ. The mission of Christians does not stop at the visible unity of the Church, but reaches out to bring all men into unity. Only, in fact, in bearing its mission to all men will the Church emerge as one, because the Church of Christ is shaped by its mission, formed through the movement of the Spirit from Christ to all men.

A strange feature of the ecumenical movement is that it is a movement that does not know precisely what it is working for. It is a movement for Christian unity, but its participants disagree about the kind of visible unity that should be the goal of their efforts.

It can be said that clarity ceases when it is a question of structures.

There should be a common faith. But this should allow for differences in understanding and expressing Christian truth. We live in an age when theological pluralism has at last been frankly recognised. But, apart from different theologies, a concept of faith as dynamic and inserted into the historical process should lead to the recognition that Christians will not all look at Christian truth from the same standpoint or all be at the same stage of development. There should be room for questioning and searching, for deep differences and discussion, for pioneers and laggards, without a rapid recourse to the authoritative exclusion of whatever clashes with official teaching. Heresy in fact has never been overcome by condemnation. When suppressed, it lies hidden to rise again later. Christians have to work to achieve a genuinely common conviction. The question, therefore, is what structures are best adapted in the contemporary situation to create, foster and spread a common Christian faith.

There should be fellowship among all Christians. This needs institutional expression. But what structures are most appropriate in relation to contemporary social consciousness and the mission of Christians to the modern world?

That Christian ministers should find recognition outside the community they serve is a simple consequence of an achieved communion among Christians. The same may be said of the forms and practices of the Christian life. But this does not mean that uniformity is desirable. If, as I have argued, the Christian ministry may be widely diversified, this may lead to differences between Christian communities, rendering interchangeability of ministers difficult in practice, despite general recognition of their status. And it is open to question whether even the sacramental practices used by Christians are as unchangeable as is often supposed.

The present ecumenical movement has lost its radical nature in the eyes of many Christians. This may be an unfair judgement, because it still includes many in its ranks who are working for radical reform. But insofar as the impression has been given, it is, I suggest, because the present structures of the Churches have been taken too much for granted and an immense effort expended on fitting them together. The work for Christian unity can be seen only in the perspective of the Church's mission to all mankind. The chief concern should not be with the existing structures of the Churches, but with the formation of new structures appropriate for the mission of the Church of Christ in its present situation. Since the present institutional structures are no longer suitable, many of the questions discussed in ecumenical conversations have ceased to be relevant. An increasing number of Christians are becoming impatient with the ins and outs of ecumenical dialogue, wondering whether it is worthwhile patching up and joining together structures that are no longer the effective expression of Christian faith, life and mission in the secular world in which they live.

Thus, consideration of the ecumenical movement brings us back to the question of the social structure of the Church of Christ as visibly present in the world.

I have moved rather far from the point with which I began, but I have no wish to be merely negative in my reflection upon the Roman Catholic Church. My rejection of that Church is closely linked to an attempt to grapple positively with the problem of a suitable structural form for Christian presence and mission.

Nevertheless, the negative element is there. I have now completed my account of the reasons why I no longer accept the Roman Catholic claim as credible in relation to the biblical and historical data. The Roman Catholic Church appeals to those data as establishing its credibility as the one, true Church, instituted by Christ with its particular social structure and alone in unbroken continuity with the first apostolic community. What I have offered is not a detailed refutation of its arguments, but a reasonably full explanation of the shift in my own thinking that made that Church lose its credibility for me. Many of the points I have discussed had been in my mind previously, but the circumstances I have described brought them together in a manner that prevented my counterbalancing the doubts I had on other grounds with an appeal to the biblical and historical data. On the contrary, those data led to a conclusion against the Roman Catholic Church.

Whether I looked at that Church from the standpoint of its existing structure and life, with a claim as the Church of Christ visibly to embody Christian faith, hope and love; or considered that Church in relation to the biblical and historical data as alone fulfilling what was there revealed concerning Christ's Church, I found an absence of sufficient signs of credibility and many counter-signs against its claims. For that reason I ceased to believe in the Roman Catholic Church and left it.

D.

Arguments against
My Conclusion

1. IS THERE A FLAW?

Was I right to go? Should I not have stayed in the Roman Church
to reform it from within?

Earlier in this book I promised to return to the consideration of
arguments that urge that my own attitude is excessively rigid and too
unqualified; that, granted the truth of many of my contentions, my
conclusion is still too hasty; that, when all had been said, I should
yet have remained within the Church to work with others to bring
about a clearer doctrinal understanding and a better practical state
of affairs. Some of the arguments to that effect demand serious
attention. They come from people who, reflecting honestly and earnestly upon the present doctrinal and practical situation, are prepared to go a very long way along the road I have followed. Indeed,
there is nothing startlingly original in the points I have made when
these are taken separately. What I have done is to draw together
ideas that are scattered abroad, that are of wide currency among
progressives in the Church, and say, "Look, this is what they add up
to." I have reflected upon them in the light of the traditional understanding of faith and credibility and drawn the conclusion that in
effect they remove the credibility of the Roman Catholic Church.
This corresponds to the role I have always fulfilled as a theologian: I
have taken what the pioneer thinkers have been saying, evaluated it

critically, accepted whatever I judged well-founded, and then weighed up and synthesised the result. All my writings exhibit the same mental procedure. But this time my evaluation and synthesis have led to a conclusion at which even the most radical thinkers jib: the rejection of the Roman Catholic Church. Have I blundered? Is there a flaw in the argumentation I have constructed from criticisms and ideas widely admitted? Why do not others draw the same ultimate conclusion?

I must now leave readers to test my case in detail for themselves. I have laid it before them as fully as I can. I merely ask those who dismiss it to state their reasons for doing so and not be content with consoling conjectures about my psychological reasons for leaving the Church. If it is a rationalisation, then the defects in the argumentation can be shown for what they are. Otherwise, I shall be entitled to infer that the rationalisation is on their side.

But I want to deal here with some general considerations urged by those who resist my final conclusion and decision. I will try honestly and fairly to weigh what they say.

2. FAITH AS PERSONAL COMMITMENT TO CHRIST

The first consideration is discernible in a number of comments upon my decision. I have not seen it worked out in detail.

What it comes to is this:

Faith is a personal commitment to Jesus Christ. The Church is made up of men; it is human. It serves as the vehicle and context of faith. But we do not believe in the Church as we believe in Jesus Christ. And we should not be surprised at the defects and failures of the Church. We have received our faith from the Church and we have to work out our Christian commitment within the Church. But no argument from the failure of the Church, let alone from the sins and stupidity of ecclesiastics, should affect our faith. After all, we have known all along that the Church was human.

The trouble with this argument is that it does not do justice to the nature of the Church. In saying this, I am not thinking only of the accounts given in the standard textbooks. The argument clashes even more violently with recent writing on the Church.

The Church is the Body of Christ, the visible presence of Christ in the world, the place of our encounter with Christ. Our faith is indeed a personal commitment to Christ. But we do not meet Christ face to face; we meet him only in and through the Church. Just as after the Incarnation commitment to God takes the form of commitment to

Jesus Christ, the embodiment of God's Word, so, too, after the Ascension commitment to Christ has to take the form of commitment to the Church, the permanent embodiment of his presence in the world. Faith in God is now realised as faith in Christ; faith in Christ becomes in the concrete faith in the Church. Not that Christ replaces God; he is the presence and embodiment of the Word who is God. Not that the Church replaces Christ; it is the presence and embodiment of Christ himself.

There is indeed a difference between the role of Christ, the incarnate Word, and the role of the Church, his Body. Jesus Christ is the Word in person, and therefore as a man is free from sin. We can commit ourselves unreservedly to him in his teaching and life. He is totally of God. The Church is a community of men who remain subject to sin and error. It is rightly said to be a human community. We should not be surprised to find it a Church of sinners and as a social body, not just in its individual members, marred by many defects and failings. Our relation with the Church has therefore to be discriminating. Not all that is of the Church is of Christ or of God.

But as the Church of Christ, the community of Christians, despite all sin and failure, essentially remains the visible presence of Christ. In other words, the Church of Christ is of its essence the visible embodiment of the truth and love of Christ, retaining sufficient signs of its credibility in that respect. Only thus can it mediate faith in Christ to men and continue to serve as the embodiment of Christ's presence in the world. If a social body ceases to represent the truth and love of Christ in its social structure and existence and no longer carries sufficient signs of credibility as the visible presence of Christ, then its claim to be the Church of Christ must be rejected on the ground of the Christian faith itself. Clearly that faith must have been mediated to us by a community that exists partly within that socially structured body but which cannot be identified with it as a social entity. Because the particular Church as a socially structured body is in fact an obstacle to Christian faith and a hindrance to the community that genuinely represents Christ, it must be rejected and opposed.

Further, Christian faith, though a personal commitment to Christ, has a content. We commit ourselves to Christ as revealed in word and event. To deprive faith of all content is not to distinguish faith in the true Christ from faith in false Christs. We have to commit ourselves to Christ as revealed, not to Christ as we or anyone else may arbitrarily conceive him to be. We can never indeed adequately conceptualise the content of faith. For that matter we can never fully conceptualise the content and implications of a human personal relationship. Even less can we express in concepts and words the relationship we have with God through faith in Christ. But the fundamental expression of the content of faith is given in the biblical record, and this has remained central in the historical tradition that has preserved and transmitted, developed and reformulated the Christian faith. In becoming Christians we are joining ourselves to an historical tradition of Christian belief, a tradition with the Bible as the record of its beginnings and the perennial centre of reference of its continuing life. Outside that tradition we have no assurance that we are committing ourselves to the genuine Christ and not to a Christ of our own imagining.

As Christians, therefore, we are bound to concern ourselves with the creeds and doctrinal declarations in which a particular Church claims to conceptualise the Christian faith. Even more so, when that Church imposes its teaching under pain of anathema, namely, exclusion from its communion and denunciation as a heretic in relation to faith in Christ. It is difficult, then, to see what justification there is for remaining a Roman Catholic if one does not accept the Roman Catholic profession of faith. Since faith is a social fact, the adherence to a believing community, it will not do to remain attached to a social body with a false profession of faith. At best there is no reason to belong to that Church rather than to some other; at worst one is conniving with a distortion of the Christian faith.

The arguments, then, I have given against Roman Catholic doctrine are very relevant to the question of membership of that Church. They cannot be side-stepped by an appeal to the truth that Christian faith is a personal commitment to Christ.

3. REMAIN WHERE YOU ARE

The second consideration I want to deal with was not directly aimed at myself, but its relevance as a criticism of my decision is so plain that I cannot pass it over without comment.

Dr Rosemary Ruether in a letter to the American newspaper, *The National Catholic Reporter*[1] was more perceptive than most in seeing that it was because I was a moderate rather than a radical theologian that I was led to break with the Church. My moderation far from making my decision more puzzling was what explained it. "He was under the impression that what he said he was supposed to believe had something to do with what he should believe. . . . We have 'reinterpreted' all those ideas out of existence, and so the reality of the church has lost its power to scandalize us. He tried harder."

The comment could not be fairer. When, however, I ask myself the reasons behind the implicit rejection of my decision as valid, I find them in an earlier article by the same author, written without reference to myself. I refer to "Post-Ecumenical Christianity," which appeared the *The Ecumenist*.[2]

In that article she recognises, as I do, the growth of a new Church

---

[1] January 18, 1967, p. 4.
[2] Volume 5, No. 1, November-December, 1966, pp. 3-7. This should be compared with her article, "Vahanian: The Worldly Church and the Churchly World," in *Continuum*, 1966, pp. 50-62, which fills in the background.

consciousness among Christians. "Post-ecumenism," she writes, "means, first of all, the development of a new church consciousness, a sense of standing in the whole Christian historical experience in all its diversity, and, while not losing the setting of one's immediate tradition, appropriating it by taking it up into a fuller identity."[3] Hence, "We have today a growing number of people who take for granted this fuller church consciousness as the matrix of their own Christian identity and who find themselves in concrete communities where it no longer makes sense to preserve traditional boundaries."[4] I could not agree more. And I am also at one with the author in holding that, while this development implies the relativising of traditions, there is still need for institutional structures, despite their ambiguity and limitations. Since, however, institutional structures are related to the centre of unity, namely the Word, only in a secondary way, Dr Ruether goes on to infer that people should stay where they are:

Thus we arrive at a relativizing of traditions and a final apprehension of the Church as a community that lives by faith and not by sight. This conclusion of the ecumenical quest seems to explain the fact that those (in the author's experience) who have broken through to the most mature ecumenical consciousness end by expressing this in the tradition from which they have come. In the words of one theologically acute friend (who began as a Presbyterian, was several years an Anglican, several years a Quaker and concluded as a Presbyterian), "Since non-salvation is to be found everywhere, I found I could handle non-salvation best where I began."[5]

Now, I agree with that to a great extent. A Christian aware of the present situation will recognise the relativity and incompleteness of the traditions of all the Churches. He will want to place himself in the Christian historical experience as a whole in all its diversity. No solution will be found in passing from one Church tradition to another. For that reason I myself have joined no other denomination. I do not think that the wholeness of Christian tradition has been preserved by any one denomination. It has survived amidst Christian

---

[3] "Post-Ecumenical Christianity," *op. cit.*, p. 4.
[4] *Ibid.*, pp. 4-5.
[5] *Ibid.*, p. 6.

divisions only through the plurality of Churches, with traditions that complement and correct one another. Had one Church succeeded in eliminating the others, the wholeness of the Christian tradition would have been lost. Further, I do not think that any Christian should attempt to erase his own background. His formation within a particular Christian tradition will have given him an outlook and insights enabling him to make a distinctive contribution to the common Christian task and the development of a better awareness of Christian faith and mission among all who believe in Christ. No good will come from a merely negative rejection of his own tradition; he should accept it and endeavour to correct and complete it. I myself have no intention of totally repudiating my past as a Roman Catholic believer and theologian. To do so would be both psychologically sterile and the destruction of my concrete Christian commitment. I will continue carefully and cautiously to discriminate those elements in the content of the Christian faith as I have received it which are truly grounded upon the Christian revelation as transmitted by the historical Christian tradition considered as a whole. In that sense I remain within the Roman Catholic tradition and am trying to correct and complete it. And I am not doing this in isolation, but with an endeavour to work in co-operation with all other Christians, including Roman Catholics.

But all this does not constitute or make possible formal membership of the Roman Catholic Church. That Church is a social body with a definite social structure and definite conditions for membership. It imposes as a condition for membership belief in its social structure as of divine institution. A person who openly denies its defined teaching, say that of the First Vatican Council, is in fact excommunicated and no longer a member in the eyes of the authorities who govern that Church. It may be possible for lay people to ignore the Church authorities and avoid the practical effects of their rejection of defined Roman Catholic doctrine. It was not possible for me; and I also consider it important for people honestly to make clear their own position. Further, I had no desire to continue to enjoy participation in the sacramental celebrations of the Roman Catholic Church by disguising my true convictions or my identity. I, therefore, had to adopt the position of someone who from the Roman Catholic tradition is working for a better understanding of

Christian presence in the world today, but who is compelled to do so outside formal membership of the Roman Catholic Church.

Moreover, as far as I can judge from Dr Ruether's remarks, I myself would grant more importance to structures than she does. They are essential to man as a social being. Consciousness itself is a social fact. One cannot be indifferent to existing Church structures; they are a serious obstacle to the development of Christian faith and mission. Further, if there is this new Christian consciousness, then it must find expression in new structures. This does not mean the creation of a new denomination, which is not the appropriate reaction to the present situation. Later in this book I will say something about what I think it does mean.

4. FUTURE DEVELOPMENT

A third way of opposing my decision is to appeal to a yet unknown but possible future development in our understanding of the *magisterium* and its teaching. I am basing my account of this argument upon what I have learnt from conversations and scattered comments. But it does represent, I think, the attitude of a number of competent theologians.

Biblicists and theologians have seen startling developments in their lifetime in the understanding and presentation of the Roman Catholic faith. They, therefore, feel justified in extrapolating to an equally momentous development in the future. After all, there is so much that is still unknown. No clear dividing line can as yet be drawn between infallible and noninfallible teaching; in the future much that is now regarded as unchangeable may in fact undergo change. Again, biblical criticism has transformed our understanding of biblical teaching. When similar methods are applied to the official documents of the *magisterium*, they may produce an equally radical transformation in the bearing of those documents upon our faith. Further, we are not as yet clear about the precise relationship between dogmatic formulations and divine revelation itself. Revelation keeps its transcendence over all attempts to express it. A better understanding of this transcendence may bring a greater stress upon the relative value of all dogmatic statements. In brief, while many problems remain intractable at present, it is best to hold them in

suspense. We should not allow ourselves to be overcome by difficulties and apparent contradictions, but continue to work patiently
with the confident hope that time will eventually lead to the solution
of what now troubles us. No good will come from giving up the
struggle and leaving the Church. A few decades ago, biblical scholars within the Church might well have been tempted to despair. Yet
now they have seen a truly astounding change of attitude within the
Church.

I sympathise with this argument. It kept me within the Church for
a long time. There was the hope that things would change both
doctrinally and practically. But a reasonable hope must be reasonably grounded. I am not so confident as before that things will
change. While there has been a remarkable change in the attitude
towards biblical criticism, the Church authorities are still very far
from accepting its full implications. Likewise, I do not think that the
reforming movement has as yet won full acceptance. There is a
measure of wishful thinking and an ignoring of recent official warnings in the confidence of those working earnestly for renewal, both
doctrinal and practical.

But, more important, development cannot be used to cover any
kind of future change. There are limits, unless we envisage an essential change in the present structure and teaching of the Roman
Catholic Church. Thus, although we do not know the precise dividing line between infallible and noninfallible teaching, we do know
that, unless the Church drops the doctrine of infallibility altogether,
the declarations of the First Vatican Council, and the Marian
Dogmas are infallible. Again, the analogy with biblical criticism is
not apt. More information may be needed about the historical context of some past doctrinal declarations, but the literary form of at
least the more recent is already clear. They are doctrinal affirma-
tions. Official documents do not in general present the same complexity of literary forms as the Bible. And we have enough historical
knowledge to determine the intended meaning of such recent dogmas
as those of the First Vatican Council. They cannot be circumvented,
but can only be denied. Further, unless the Church withdraws its
constantly reiterated teaching, no stress on the transcendence of
revelation over dogmatic formulations is going to result in the admission that these are not irrevocable and free from error. Finally, in

my opinion, if the present reforming movement is successful, it will dissolve the existing hierarchical structure itself.

So, if the Roman Catholic Church essentially changes, I will undoubtedly have to reconsider my relationship with it. But I do not see how I can support a present membership by the hope of a development, the implications of which I am not prepared to face.

5. CATHOLIC INSTITUTIONS AND THE HIERARCHY

I come now in the fourth place to the argument put forward by Fr Herbert McCabe in his notorious editorial in *New Blackfriars*.[1] This editorial gained its notoriety because the author's admission that the Church was "quite plainly corrupt" led to his being publicly insulted by Archbishop Cardinale, the Apostolic Delegate, in the *Catholic Herald*,[2] to his humiliation at the hands of authority and to his being deprived of his editorship of the journal. Apparently, those who turned upon him did not pause to consider that his main purpose in writing the editorial was to defend the Roman Catholic Church and its members against the conclusion I had drawn from the corruption within it. However, if those more concerned to defend the *status quo* with intolerant suppression than to enter into reasonable discussion felt themselves at liberty to ignore his argument, I myself at least should do him the courtesy of examining it. It has in fact some force.

[1] February 1967, pp. 226-229. This editorial, together with four other relevant pieces from *New Blackfriars* by other contributors, has been reprinted in the booklet *The Purification of the Church*, edited by Ian Hislop, O.P. (SCM Press Ltd., London, 1967).

[2] "And so one could go on and on to show that Fr McCabe is not in good faith; or to say the least is utterly immature and not enlightened in his judgment. In either case he is irresponsible and undeserving of credit" (*Catholic Herald*, February 10, 1967, p. 1). Outside the Church, where people are not the helpless victims of prelates, abuse of this kind is usually met with a libel action.

Fr McCabe denies my contention that many can remain Roman Catholics only because they live their Christian lives on the fringe of the institutional Church and largely ignore it. He bases his denial upon what he considers a better understanding of the meaning of the phrase "institutional Church." He writes:

Consider a few institutions: Spode House, the Newman Theology Groups, the Union of Catholic Students, the Young Christian Workers, University Chaplaincies, the Catholic press including even *New Black-friars*. None of these are exclusively for Catholics but no sociologist would hesitate to describe them as Roman Catholic institutions. It is within institutions such as these that a great many Catholics nourish their Christian lives. It is not true that merely because the dynamic of their lives is not derived from sermons or "religious education" that it therefore comes from outside the institutions of the Church. To think so would be to betray a clericalist view of what counts as a Catholic institution.[3]

He goes on to admit that it is the bishops who exist on the fringe of the institutions of the Church in that sense. They largely ignore those institutions. Further, no one in England expects to be guided and encouraged in his Christian life by pastoral letters. Things might be different in a more adequate Church, but at the present time in England the bishops provide merely an administrative context within which the really vital and immediately relevant institutions can exist. However, in saying this, he makes a remark that forms an essential link in his argument: "Nonetheless without the overall and relatively impersonal structure of the hierarchy these Roman Catholic institutions could not exist." Later in the editorial, the role of the hierarchy is emphasized more strongly:

It is because we believe that the hierarchical institutions of the Roman Catholic Church, with all their decadence, their corruption and their sheer silliness, do in fact link us to areas of Christian truth beyond our own particular experience and ultimately to truths beyond any experience that we remain, and see our Christian lives in terms of remaining, members of this Church.[4]

[3] *New Blackfriars*, editorial, op. cit., pp. 227-228.
[4] *Ibid.*, p. 229.

This argument seems to me to be the only reasonable way of defending continued adherence to a Church acknowledged as corrupt. If I deal with it with brevity here, it is because the points I have already made explain why I cannot accept it. A few further comments are, however, required.

I plead not guilty to the charge of having a clericalist view of what counts as a Catholic institution. The institutions listed by Fr McCabe and others similar to them I accept as Catholic institutions. They are set up and run by Catholics, even if others have some part in them. What interests me, however, is their relationship to the total social structure of the Church, a social structure in which the hierarchy are assigned an originating and governing role. Is that relationship essential to those institutions and fruitful or is it accidental and indeed largely a hindrance? I think that it is accidental and a hindrance. Although in present circumstances many such institutions do arise and exist within the framework of a particular Church, in this instance the Roman Catholic Church, an increasing number of Christian groups and institutions do not. According to some observers, for example, the denominational press has had its day. And I remain to be convinced that the continuance of the hierarchical structure is necessary for the formation and continued existence of the really vital and immediately relevant institutions. In my experience they would do far better without it.

Further, although Fr McCabe restricts his remarks to the English bishops, what he says would, I suggest, be applicable to the bishops of other countries. But the limited role he assigns them does not correspond to any doctrine or theology of the Church that I know. Take what he says and compare it with the part given to bishops in the Constitution on the Church of the Second Vatican Council. Clearly, if in the concrete the bishops are exercising only the minimal function he assigns them—and that I would accept as true—the official teaching on the episcopate represents a dream world. And dreams do not call for intellectual assent.

Finally, do the hierarchical institutions link us to areas of Christian truth beyond our own particular experience and ultimately to truths beyond any experience? I have previously argued at length that they do not. I wonder, however, that Fr McCabe did not advert to the intolerable paradox in his statement that they do. Are we to believe that decadent, corrupt and silly institutions are necessary to link us to transcendent truth and do in fact do so? Certainly, we need to be linked to areas of truth beyond what happens to be personally meaningful and personally liberating to ourselves. But this can be achieved by refusing to think in isolation and by not making an exclusively personal reference the sole criterion of truth. We have to join ourselves to the general community of Christians, which exists as an historical and present fact, and to the whole Christian tradition, which also exists as an historical and present fact. I have ceased to believe that an hierarchical authority has an essential part to play in preserving us from imprisonment in our own limited personal experience.

6. APPEAL FOR LOYALTY

The fifth and last place in this survey of general arguments against my conclusion and decision must be given to the appeal for loyalty to the Church.

Many of the comments I received, both publicly and privately, even from theologians, invoked the question of loyalty to the Church. The image most frequently used was that of the bark of Peter buffeted by storms. The crew should remain on board, not abandon the ship. I was failing in my duty, in the trust reposed in me, at a time when every hand was needed to battle with the tempest. My departure was a betrayal of the Church I should love despite its defects.

But can loyalty without belief be the ground for Christian community? To me such loyalty represents a corruption of Christian commitment and an obstacle to genuine Christian community.

What does such loyalty imply? It means that a person places the organisational unity of a particular denomination above the community of faith. This is a reversal of values. Christians should form communities on the basis of their faith. If they do not do so, but insist upon loyalties ungrounded upon faith, they are distorting the Christian witness to truth and hindering the expansion of Christian life and mission. The Church of Christ is the community of faith and should embody that faith. If a particular social structure does not do so, an appeal to loyalty to it is an appeal to betray the Christian faith. Thus, if my union in faith is closer to many Protestants than to a large section of the Roman Church, the former union should claim my prior attention.

Suppose just by way of hypothesis that I am correct in thinking that Christian presence in the world today is not embodied in the present ecclesiastical structures and does not correspond to their boundaries and divisions but is emerging according to a different pattern. Then to insist upon loyalty to the Roman Church, despite a lack of belief in its dogmas, is to obstruct the work of the Spirit.

I have no desire to provoke a hasty exodus from the Churches. My conviction is that people will be given different roles and different insights in this period of confusion. All the same, I am entitled to ask those who urge that people should remain in the Church whether they are doing so on grounds of faith or on grounds of loyalty. If on grounds of faith, they cannot shrug off difficulties against Roman teaching by tempering their belief with a shot of scepticism. Such scepticism is in fact rife within the Roman Church, and, in my opinion, it is destructive of the Church as a zone of truth and sincerity, especially when the doubts are covered over in public by silence. If they remain on grounds of loyalty alone, then my reply is that such loyalty simply prevents Christian witness to the truth and the clearer manifestation and better structuring of the genuine community of faith.

I do indeed sincerely love the Church as the community of Christians and the People of God. It is through such love that I retain my faith in Christ. For me personal commitment to Christ in faith and love means commitment to the Church his body, and to all its members. But for that reason I want to bear honest witness to the reality of that Church and relate my love to the real Church of Christ. Loyalty to a particular Christian denomination, without belief, would be for me a betrayal of my love for Christ's Church. And a protestation of loyalty covering over the emptiness of a lack of believing commitment sounds the hollow note of insincerity.

PART THREE

PROSPECT FOR
THE CHURCH

1. THE GENERAL PROBLEM

The long, second part of this book has been written in confrontation with the Church of Rome. This corresponds to the evolution of my own thought. I was a member of that Church, and so, in reflecting upon the situation of the Christian Church today, I had to struggle with the claims and teaching of the Church to which I belonged. My thinking inevitably became a debate about the truth of the Roman Catholic Church. Since this book is a personal statement, it had to fall into the same pattern. And because my reflections led me to disengage myself from the Roman Church, the book had to take the form of an explanation of my reasons for doing so.

However, although my account is thus cast into a negative mould, I have tried all along to give the positive vision that lies behind my rejection. Readers by now should have a fair insight into my positive understanding of Christian faith, hope and love, of the Christian Church as embodying these, of its visible unity and permanent mission. Hence this last part of the book can be comparatively short. Its purpose is to complete the picture of the Church of Christ in the world today. To put it in another way, my aim here is to tie up the loose ends I have left.

But a misunderstanding must be avoided. I did not in leaving the Roman Church nor do I now claim to have all the answers. Clearly, without abandoning the Christian faith altogether, I could not have left the Roman Church if I had not had some alternative and positive perception of the continuing existence of the Church of Christ in the world of today. And, as a matter of fact, I had for some time been grappling with the problem of Christian presence in the modern secular world, as is shown by my book, *God's Grace in History*, to which I have already referred.

But it is one thing to have sufficient light to leave the Roman Church, while remaining a Christian, and for continuing the search in another direction; it is another to present a completely rounded picture of the social structure of the Christian Church in its present situation. Apart from my own inadequacy for the task, that social structure is only now emerging from the break-up of the existing Churches. The initiative here lies with the Spirit. It is as yet too soon clearly to discern what the Spirit is doing. All that can be done is to recognise the direction in which the Spirit is leading and follow that path.

Sensitive Christians in all the Churches are trying to discern how to embody their Christian faith and life in structures that make sense in the modern world. There is not one of the Churches whose more perceptive members are not tortured by the obsolete irrelevance of its churchy institutions and practices. The Church of Christ is the permanent, visible presence of Christ in the world. In every period through the activity of Christians this presence has to find an appropriate embodiment. What should be that embodiment today? What is the institutional structure best fitted for the mission of the Church in the present situation? There are no easy answers.

I want to indicate the general direction of my own thinking, starting from the conclusions I have reached in my debate with the Roman Catholic Church. I must ask for the indulgence of historians and sociologists, impatient as these are with wide generalisations. Generalisations may indeed deceive as oversimplifications, but they can also serve as useful working hypotheses. It is for their latter function that I make them here. I see this last part of the present book as a sketch of themes for future books. My departure from the Roman Church is not the end of my work as a theologian, but rather a new beginning.

To open, then, with a general statement of the problem. Underlying all recent questioning about the social structure of the Christian Church is the long-delayed acknowledgement of the disappearance

of Christendom. Christians at last are now accepting the emergence
of the secular West as irreversible and the consequent need to understand and structure the new relation between the Church and the
world. Many deep questions are involved. They can be summed up
in this way: What is the relation between the purpose or mission of
the Church and the movement of secular history? How should the
Christian community be structured as distinct from the inclusive
society, whether considered as the nation or as the general community of mankind?

In my book, *God's Grace in History*, I gave reasons for welcoming secularisation when understood as a cultural process distinct
from secularism. Christians should cease to lament Christendom and
instead regard it as a transitory and now past stage in the history of
Christianity. The welding of the Church and society into the single
sacred, politico-ecclesiastical order of Christendom is historically
explicable and had advantages at the time. But it also had considerable disadvantages and should not be taken as the normative form of
Christian presence in the world. Secularisation, with its social, political and general cultural consequences, represents an advance of
human consciousness. It has brought a differentiation of the secular
and the sacred, with a healthy and fruitful acknowledgement of the
autonomy of the secular. Admittedly, owing to the intermingling of
secularism with the process, it has in fact done this in an ambiguous
way. But the positive value of secularisation should be recognised,
unless Christians are going vainly to attempt to force men back into
an earlier stage of social development.

In saying this, my general concept of secularisation is the effective
assertion of the proper autonomy of the secular. In other words, as a
cultural process, secularisation is the widening of the area of the
secular over against the sacred. By the secular I understand the
sphere of immediate reality. It is what lies open and present before
man; it is all that is in principle knowable by human intelligence,
subject to human investigation; it is the area of reality within which
man exercises a practical mastery. The sacred remains outside man's
understanding and control. Secularisation means that various areas
of man's experience, previously regarded as sacred and under the
tutelage of religion, are acknowledged as in principle subject to
man's intelligent mastery and, consequently, to his practical control.

Thus, nature, the State and society have all been desacralised. They have been released in their proper autonomy, freed from the tutelage of religion and made the object of intelligent investigation, with the consequent possibility of their being directed and controlled, modified and adapted by man's practical and organising intelligence.

Is this process of secularisation a pushing back of the sacred, with its eventual elimination? I do not think so. I see it as a process of differentiation. True, much that man formerly regarded as sacred has now become secular. But when man saw almost everything as sacred, he was confusing the sacred and the secular. To put it more accurately, he still had an undeveloped and undifferentiated consciousness. To overcome all confusion of sacred and secular, to differentiate clearly between them, enhances the sacred as well as the secular; it purifies man's concept of the sacred.

The sacred still remains. It is the area of mystery. But not mystery in the corrupted sense of an awkward puzzle, nor in the diminished sense of what yet awaits successful investigation. It is mystery in the sense of a presence in man's experience of a darkness he acknowledges as light but cannot see, of an intelligibility too bright for his gaze, of a transcendence that evokes his adoration. Mystery or the sacred is the presence of God. It is an undefined presence, which imposes itself upon man's experience but escapes his understanding.

Christians, however, believe more than that. They believe that God, the transcendent, has revealed himself within human history. This revelation has not removed the mystery; God remains the transcendent, distinct from all creatures and beyond man's grasp. But it has established a new relation between God and man. There has been a self-gift of God, resulting in a new presence of God to men through Christ and the Spirit. This gift has its repercussions upon human life and history. By a union with God through Christ a higher integration of human living is achieved leading to a new community amongst men, with a life and personal relationships based upon those higher values made known by Christ. And faith in Christ implies the conviction that only through Christ men, whether they know it or not, receive the liberation and fulfilment for which all men long, but which they cannot achieve of themselves. It comes to them as a gift from the transcendent God, who has revealed himself and acted in Christ. Faith presupposes an open and active receptivity to God's gift; a willingness not to remain enclosed in a human self-sufficiency. And it takes concrete and explicit form as a personal commitment to Jesus Christ. And this faith carries with it a conviction that through union with Christ and submission to his Spirit human history is being directed towards a final end, in which the purpose of God in creating will be achieved. All history will find its fulfilment in the final Kingdom, where the work of Christ will be complete.

It follows that there is an area in man's experience which is always sacred and can never become secular. And the sacred is not just a transcendent remaining at the background of man's consciousness. Owing to the self-gift of God and the repercussions of his intimate presence through Christ, there is an element in human life and human history which escapes man's understanding and practical mastery. And it is precisely that element which determines human liberation and fulfilment and the end of human history. The mystery of God as present to man demands faith. And without faith there is no salvation.

But Christians now recognise that, besides the visible form of Christ's presence in the community of Christian believers there is a universal, latent presence of Christ. This means that, although not all have the opportunity of an explicit faith in Christ, faith as an open and active receptivity for God's gift is a possibility for all. People will conceptualise that faith differently, even confusedly and inaccurately. But this need not prevent the basic relationship with God by faith, with its saving effects.

Recognition of the Universal, latent presence of Christ and the universality of God's gift through Christ leads to the conclusion that the differentiation of sacred and secular does not mean their separation in the concrete order in which man lives. There are secular realities and secular activities, which have their place and autonomy. God's gift, while taking these up into a higher integration of human living and thus enhancing them, does not destroy them in their proper consistency and autonomy. To refuse to acknowledge their secularity is a failure to recognise the transcendence of God's gift. The lack of autonomy granted to the secular in Christendom degraded the sacred as well as stifled the secular. But when we consider the total lives of men in the concrete, there is no self-contained secular order. History in the concrete is never a merely secular history unaffected by God's gift through Christ. And to speak of the secular world as such is to name an abstraction. When by the world distinct from the Church is meant the totality of the lives and activities of men outside the Church, then it is not exclusively secular. It is the effect of God's gift, the product of the universal presence of Christ among men. Not unambiguously so, because of the corruption due to sin. Nevertheless, Christ is the Lord of history. And the historical process is a working out of God's plan through Christ and a progress towards the Kingdom. God's plan embraces the whole of human life and history, not just the part directly related to the visible Church.

We have, therefore, to work with a concept of the visible Church which does not see it as an enclosed sacred and religious sphere surrounded by a secular world. The visible Church is not the exclusive area of the sacred nor the community of the exclusively saved. Nor does it mark the limits of Christ's presence in the world. There is no profane world in which to set such a Church. The Church is the visibility of what is universal, the disclosure of the meaning of all human life, the revelation of the direction of the whole of human history, the expression and embodiment of a Christ who is present universally. When understood as a distinction between sacred and secular, the distinction between the Church and the world is a false distinction. This has important repercussions upon our understanding of the structures appropriate to the visible Church. They should not be the structures of an enclosed religious system set in opposition to a profane world. The meaning of Christ as universal Redeemer implies the destruction of all such religious systems.

So far, I have outlined briefly what I have expounded at greater length, though still with brevity, in *God's Grace in History*. But it is now necessary to enquire more closely into the reasons why secularisation has been accompanied by secularism, which means the exclusion of the sacred altogether.

Here my purpose is not to give a total explanation, but to draw attention to the part played by a failure of the Church, the recognition of which should guide both a renewal and a restructuring. There is no need to deny the element of wilful apostasy in the rise of secularism. But Christians would do well not to adopt that simple explanation before they have eliminated the obstacles to faith erected by the Church. Again, it would be a mistake to exaggerate the import of the dechristianisation of the West. The faith lost by the average man was an imperfect faith, what might be called a cultural faith. Open dechristianisation is more the uncovering of the defects in Christian evangelisation and the breaking down of the political and social façade that hid those defects than the destruction of a genuinely personal faith among the general populace. All the same, the increasing hold of secularism upon our present culture cannot be denied. Likewise, we should ask the reasons for the obstinate rejection of the Church on the part of so many, who often show a greater perception of Christian values than church-going Christians themselves.

Secularism, I have said, is the exclusion of the sacred. It commonly takes the form of agnostic humanism. But secularism is less a philosophy than the presupposition behind a number of contemporary philosophies. Existing on the level of presuppositions, it finds expression in a variety of cultural forms. It is the assertion of the complete autonomy, as far as man is concerned, of the secular, the natural, the temporal, the relative, and the rejection or ignoring of all ultimacy. It leaves aside the search for or affirmation of an ultimate meaning or ultimate ground and cause of reality, of an ultimate order or coherence in the flux of phenomena, of an ultimate end or purpose of history. Since it excludes the transcendent, it is referred to as radical immanentism, which some see as typifying modern culture. Although its negation is now much wider, historically it emerged as the rejection of the Church and the God of the Christian Church.

The latter rejection raises a fundamental problem beyond the scope of this present book: modern atheism and agnosticism and their historical roots in Christianity itself. These are in part the effect of the inadequate concept of God fostered by Christendom.

I do not have in mind the metaphysical systems of the Scholastics. Admittedly, the limitations of these insofar as they were expressions of a particular culture should not be overlooked. But the Scholastic concept of God was not crude. And the debate about the status and scope of metaphysics, the possibility of a natural theology and the nature of religious language raises questions which, Christendom apart, would necessarily at some time have engaged the reflection even of believers and demanded elucidation. But the direction of philosophical debate usually reflects wider cultural preoccupations and changes in the economic, social and political orders. Without minimising its importance, we must therefore look outside the realm of philosophy itself for an explanation of the strength of the reaction against the Christian God and what has been called the death of God in modern culture.

At least part of the explanation is that the Christian God, whatever the distinctions of the theologians, was built into the cultural, social, politico-ecclesiastical system of Christendom as its ultimate ground and sanction. God was the supporter of the *status quo*. He was represented on earth by popes, emperors and kings as sacred rulers. The hierarchical order on earth reflected the hierarchical order of angels and saints in heaven, and God was at the summit. The whole was a static, sacral order, established and sustained by God. Needless to say, this was more of an ideal construct than a true account of the concrete reality even of medieval Christendom. But it was a world view that closely associated God, entangled him one might say, in a particular cultural complex. When various causes brought the cultural upheaval we call secularisation and social and political changes destroyed Christendom, the Christian God went with it. He had become too much the God of Christendom to survive its disappearance.

Further, Christendom never succeeded in purifying itself from paganism. That is evident enough in the insistence upon a static and enclosed sacral order, more a pagan concept than a biblical or Christian one. The biblical God is not a supporter of the *status quo*, but a God who breaks it up. He is the God who acts, and acts to shatter all the established orders which men erect for themselves. The Spirit was given for an ongoing mission, given as a liberating and creative force, constantly calling men forward, leading them to make and accept radical changes for the renewal and transformation of the face of the earth. He was not given as a gift at man's disposal, a permanent sanction for settled and unchangeable systems of law, a force to be tamed and safely distributed through what are called the usual official channels. And Christianity is an eschatological faith, a faith that looks to the future and to an end outside history. Insofar as it cannot be enclosed in any cultural complex, not even a Christian one, it is not a religion in the usual sense. Any religious system it forms in union with a particular culture is transitory. It cannot settle down in any order, even of its own creation, as if it were the final Kingdom. Involved in the movement of the whole of human history, it looks forward beyond history to the end and fulfilment of all history in the Kingdom of God. And all history, including its own, it regards as under God's judgement. Rather than being a settled nation, with a fixed hierarchical structure, the Church is a pilgrim, nomadic people, constantly uprooted, constantly on the move, needing constantly to improvise to meet new and unexpected situations. Christendom was a passing phase, and the God that Christians used to complete its sacral structure was not the true God of Christ. Christians have now the mission to show men that.

There were other pagan elements. Apart from the tendency of the Church to treat God as if he were at its disposal, with his truth in the possession of the Church authorities and his saving gifts in their hands for distribution as they saw fit, men still clung to their idols, though in Christian dress. The popular concept of God was often a projection of psychic needs. God provided a security men could not find elsewhere. He fulfilled their needs and was looked to for the solution of all their problems. Such a God could not survive the advent of secularisation, when men recognised the autonomy of the secular and looked to their own efforts to fulfil their needs and solve their problems. The transcendence of God's gift, leaving intact the secular in its consistency and autonomy and itself working within, enhancing not replacing the dynamism of man's own intelligence; the universality of that gift, not restricted to the operation of a religious system: these two points had been obscured, and so secular man in leaving his idols thought that he was leaving the Christian God. Within modern secularism is a protest, fundamentally Christian, against false gods.

So, the disappearance of Christendom has left Christians with a problem of God. Not just a problem for philosophical theology, but a cultural problem. Christians have to purify their concept of God from those elements which tie it to the culture and world view of Christendom. This is an immense task. The biblical language has been used so long according to a particular understanding that it has lost much of its force. And in any case a fresh understanding will require a fresh conceptualisation and language. But even such a purification will not of itself solve the problem of relating modern culture to the Christian faith. Modern man has developed his culture largely under the aegis of secularism or radical immanentism. He will not be easily converted. To convert the post-Christian is not the same as to convert the pagan. And the Christian Church will have to die in its present state before it rises again. Unfortunately, the Churches as institutions are clinging desperately to the outlook, structures and trappings they have inherited from Christendom. They prefer a decrepit survival to the hope of a resurrection through death.

I have said that I am not directly concerned in this book with the problem of God. I have introduced some remarks on it because it is related to the question of the Church. My concern is in fact with the Church itself.

We have to ask why the Church has failed so badly to bring the Christian faith to bear upon modern culture. That it has failed is indicated by the tension that exists in Christians themselves, who sense the incompatibility between their lives as modern men and the lives they are trying to lead as Christians. Admittedly, that tension could not have been completely avoided. Secularisation and the break-up of Christendom would in any case have left Christians with a difficult problem of God and the necessity of making other less major adjustments in their understanding of the Christian faith. But there is another element in the present experience of Christians: the sense that their membership of the Church is an added problem. The present structural forms of its life impede rather than help the confrontation with the modern world. The urgency with which the renewal of the Church is being welcomed and pursued shows that. The more perceptive already recognise that renewal of the Church will not of itself solve all the problems now facing Christians. But the sense of being blocked by the Church, hampered within its rigid framework, prevents a confident tackling of the deeper problems.

The indications are that the Church is persisting in a refusal to accept various elements in modern consciousness that it could accept without succumbing to secularism. It is opposing secularism not simply on grounds of the Christian faith, but by insisting upon past cultural elements built into its present structure. Since what it is insisting upon is obsolete and can no longer serve as the vehicle of Christian faith and mission, the Church is opposing modern secularism on the basis of an equally unchristian ideology. But secularism has at least the advantage of corresponding with man's contemporary consciousness. That is why an increasing number of sincere Christians in the conflict between the Church and the modern world find themselves drawn to the side of the world. In some respects its outlook harmonises better with the implications of their Christian conviction as held by themselves as modern men.

I have argued previously for a positive appreciation of secularisation. Continuing in the same vein, I want to point to various elements in the modern world and modern consciousness which the Church should but does not yet consistently accept. These elements clash with the present social structure of the Church and render it obsolete. They can be accepted only by restructuring the Church. Consideration of them, therefore, will guide us in determining how Christian presence should be structurally embodied in its present situation. And that is the chief question I am raising here.

Earlier in this book I described how after the French Revolution the political policy of the papacy had disastrous effects upon the mission of the Church and set the Roman Catholic Church in an undiscriminating and sterile opposition to the modern world. That considerably aggravated what would in any event have been a difficult transition. Institutions with a long history have a great tenacity. To have expected that the Church would smoothly undergo the break-up and restructuring demanded by the cessation of Christendom would have been extraordinarily naïve. But people who are now confidently awaiting those postponed radical changes to take place without a disintegrating upheaval are in fact indulging in such naïvety. I should like to know what basis they have in history, whether sacred or secular, for such confidence. Great institutions are usually either broken up and reshaped by revolutionary force or they survive as curious, empty shells on the shore of time. They are seldom radically altered by an evolutionary process of orderly change. The real question, it seems to me, is whether the Christian revolution now gathering force will succeed in breaking up and reshaping the present structures or, resisted to the end, sweep past them to leave them as quaint, meaningless relics. The hope of a steady renewal under official auspices simply ignores the magnitude of the change required.

It is its magnitude that makes this change one that affects all the present Churches, not simply the Roman Church. While the Roman Church is the archetype of the Christian institutions inherited from Christendom, every Church that is clinging to a rigid Church order from the past is refusing to accept the conditions necessary for Christian mission in the modern world. Hierarchical or rigid Church structures are no longer appropriate. They clash with the legitimate self-understanding of modern man.

What, then, are the elements in the modern mentality which the Churches are refusing consistently to accept? By a consistent acceptance, I mean one that includes a readiness to embody those elements in appropriate new structures at the cost of radical structural change. There is much talk in the Churches about the modern world. Our age is characterised by an escape into theology. Beautiful theological constructs without reference to concrete reality are taken as a substitute for reform. More of that later. Enough at the moment to state that I am concerned with an acceptance of modern consciousness sufficiently firm and coherent to bring about a change in the structure of the Church as a social entity.

I will first examine the shift that has taken place in man's self-understanding. Then I will draw out the implications of this for the manner in which men now order their social existence. Next, I will deal with the question of the approach to truth demanded by man's present historical consciousness. Finally, on the basis of these previous observations and with the help of recent theological insights, I will discuss the relation between the Christian Church and the wider or inclusive society.

A preliminary remark: in speaking of the change in consciousness that underlies the modern mentality, I shall not attempt to trace its historical roots or phases of development. I am content that the reader should judge whether what I am going to say makes sense to him as describing his own outlook and whether he feels the opposition I discern between that outlook and the Church as it is. Historians may trace the ideas I will outline back a very long way and may debate the exact moment when they decisively emerged. For my present purpose it is enough to note that the modern world is different from earlier periods, that a change of outlook has taken place and that the Church clashes with the contemporary consciousness. I do not think that many will dispute these general contentions.

2. THE CHANGE IN MAN'S SELF-UNDERSTANDING

I have said that there has been a change in man's self-understanding. This change can be designated as a shift from a concept of a fixed human nature to that of a person in the process of becoming himself in freedom.

The question here is not whether, philosophically speaking, the concept of human nature is a valid one. It is whether man understands what he is as man, his human nature, as a static reality, already complete, with its limits already definitively formulated. According to this understanding of man, human nature is always the same and any change is only an incidental modification introduced to meet merely incidental differences in the circumstances in which men are placed.

This view of man corresponded to the general understanding of reality as an hierarchically ordered cosmos. The world was static, not in the sense of motionless, but insofar as it remained in essentially the same state, with the same realities permanently ordered in the same graded relationships. Society was brought under the same pattern, with a similar hierarchy of orders, culminating in a sacred or divinely sanctioned ruler.

We have now become accustomed to an evolutionary view of the world and the idea of a mobile society. Just as important, perhaps more fundamental, is the shift in the understanding of man himself.

Men have now an historical consciousness. This means more than an awareness of history. It means that men are aware of themselves as historical beings, becoming what they are only in an historical unfolding. Men do not exist as ready-made persons; they become themselves only through a process of development. And the virtualities of human nature come to light only through the historical process. Historical consciousness is an awareness of becoming as the mode of being proper to men, whether individually or socially. There is a history of each person, but this individual history can be understood only within the context of history in the more usual, social sense. Each person becomes himself only in relation to others and in a wider historical setting. His becoming is socially and historically conditioned. Through and through, whether on the individual or social level, historicity marks the being of man.

But the inadequacy of the concept of a fixed human nature is not simply that it ignored man's historicity, but that, in considering man primarily in terms of substance, it prescinded from what was most distinctive of man, namely, that man was a conscious subject, intelligent and free.[1]

As a person, a man is an intelligently conscious subject. Not that we should fall into a false spiritualism. Man's intelligence is an embodied intelligence, and as a person man exists and develops only in relation with other persons, a relation achieved bodily, notably in language. Nevertheless, what distinguishes man as a person is his being as an intelligent subject, namely, as a self with that kind of consciousness specific to intelligent and free activity.

When we consider man, not just as a substance, but as a subject or conscious self, we find that he exists only in a continuous process of becoming. Man's intelligence begins as a mere potentiality. When it has emerged into full activity, it remains an open, restless dynamism, so that man is constantly growing, though indeed with much struggle and effort, in understanding and knowledge. Further, only through a slow maturation does a man achieve a genuinely

---

[1] Cf. Bernard J. F. Lonergan, S.J., "*Existenz* and *Aggiornamento*," in *Focus: A Theological Journal* (Regis College, Willowdale, Ontario), Vol. 2, 1965, pp. 5-14.

personal freedom, and even in maturity there is always need to widen the range and strengthen the effectiveness of self-possession and personal decision. In other words, man only slowly becomes truly himself and emerges as a person, not just a thing.

A man has to take charge of his own becoming. From the beginning of his life, a person is developing, physically, intellectually, and with growing freedom; but a critical point is reached when the man recognises that he must direct that process, determine what he wants to become, decide the kind of person he is going to be, so that he begins to make himself. Clearly he can do this only within limits. He is restricted by his background and situation, by his talents and capabilities, by his physical makeup and emotional temperament and by the lasting effect of some of the decisions he has already taken. But the essential condition for being truly himself is to make his becoming his own in the sense of deliberately guiding it. And experience shows that it is unwise to be too definite about the factors limiting development. Men have sometimes achieved the seemingly impossible when they have taken a radical decision about themselves and guided their personal development in a chosen direction, prudently assessing but then resolutely overcoming the obstacles that block the way. But the chief point here is not the obvious fact of limitations and difficulties in the development of every person, but the truth that to be fully a person, a man must make his becoming truly his own, take in hand his own growth as a free and intelligent subject or self and begin deliberately to make himself as a person.

In brief, the shift from the concept of a fixed human nature is the discovery of the person as a freely self-constituting or self-creative conscious subject.

In making himself man also makes his world. The world of each person as an intelligent subject is the extent of intelligently appreciated meaning; in short, all that lies within the horizon of his vision as an intelligent and knowing subject. And within that world a man exercises his freedom. Each man, however, makes his world in collaboration with other men and acting within a social context.

But the human world is not simply a world of discovered meaning, of meaning already there but unveiled by man's intelligence. The properly human world is the world of freely created meaning. Men create meaning and thus establish a distinctively human world.

When an individual assumes responsibility for his own development and through personal decisions orders his life in a particular fashion, he is creating meaning. His style or manner of life has meaning, but in being meaningful belongs to the world of freely created meaning. Likewise, men in collaboration freely establish meaningful relationships and institutions. A law-court, a university, a parliament: these and similar human institutions are instances of freely created meaning.

Community at the distinctively human level belongs to the world of meaning freely created by man. Granted the physical and emotional basis of human togetherness and social life at its more primitive levels, human community as such comes into existence as the product of men's intelligent activity, penetrating their social life with meaning, establishing complex and meaningful social relationships and embodying these in freely created social structures and institutions. Human community is the world of freely constituted meaning insofar as that world is socially created and socially embodied.

Men, therefore, as persons, that is as free and intelligently conscious subjects, have their being only in a continuous becoming. This becoming, however, takes place only in and through a relation with others. It is a common becoming, both social and historical. Moreover, to be fully a person, each individual must take responsibility for his own becoming and make it truly his own. And men together must assume responsibility for their common becoming. In doing so, both individually and collectively they create the world of freely constituted meaning. To that world belongs community in the distinctively human sense.

The fundamental condition for man's personal and social development when understood in this way is freedom. Men need it to become themselves. Without freedom they cannot do so. A few remarks on freedom are therefore required. Typical of the modern consciousness is the stress upon freedom.

We may distinguish essential freedom and effective freedom.[2] Essential freedom is the dynamic structure found in man enabling him to make free decisions; in that sense all men as men are endowed with freedom. Effective freedom is the actual operational

---

[2] Cf. Bernard J. F. Lonergan, S.J., *Insight: A Study of Human Understanding* (rev. ed., Longmans, Green and Co., London, 1958), pp. 619-620.

range of that dynamic structure. This varies. Effective freedom is subject to many limitations, both external and internal. What a man can freely do may be severely restricted by economic necessity. Likewise, a man's freedom may be greatly curtailed by psychological determinisms.

In general, effective freedom has to be won. A liberation is always needed. The liberation that leads to effective freedom is both interior and exterior.

Interiorly, liberation coincides with the development of the person as I have already described it. Each person must take possession of himself and become a freely self-constituting subject. This is not easy. It demands a knowledge of self, the overcoming of fear and insecurity, an objectivity that counteracts intellectual and emotional distortions, a disciplined willingness to act in accord with one's considered judgement rather than on the impulse of the moment: in short, an ability to judge objectively, to decide firmly even in a radical manner, and to execute the decisions made. The critical point in interior liberation is the assumption of responsibility for one's own becoming. But interior liberation is an endless process; we have constantly to strive to widen the range of our effective freedom.

However, just as individual development takes place only within a social context and as part of a common becoming, so, too, interior freedom requires exterior freedom for its achievement. Exterior freedom consists in those conditions that enable people to be and become themselves, that allow them to express their ideas outwardly and execute their decisions, that release them from oppressive threats and methods of persuasion which induce fantasy fears and play upon their emotional insecurity, and finally that guide them with truth and do not deceive them by half-truths or falsehood.

The growth of interior freedom is dependent upon exterior freedom. Man is a social being. It is false to make light of exterior unfreedom on the grounds that interior freedom is what counts. A man cannot reach interior freedom without some degree of exterior freedom. Whenever we find men who gain sufficient interior freedom to struggle against external oppression, there is something in their background and situation which has enabled them to win their interior liberation. A child does not first learn to think and then afterwards to talk. It first learns to talk or think aloud, and then afterwards to think without voicing its thought. Similarly, men do not first gain interior freedom and then strive to establish conditions of exterior freedom. Through exterior freedom they learn to become interiorly free. This indeed means that exterior freedom must not be conceived in a purely negative manner. It must include conditions that positively help people towards liberation. Among these conditions is authority, but authority understood as a creative and formative truthful guidance at the service of freedom both individual and social and adapted to the actual needs of men.

People who objected to my leaving the Church on the ground that, interiorly free, I should have worked for a greater freedom within the Church miss the point. I acted on the conviction that I could gain my interior freedom only by breaking out of the unfree system of the Roman Catholic Church. Others may be differently placed. But as a general principle it is true that exterior unfreedom causes interior unfreedom in all but exceptional cases. I was exceptional in gaining sufficient interior freedom to leave, but I could not have remained without relinquishing the little freedom I had attained and retreating into interior unfreedom.

I have spoken of freedom in terms of making free decisions. This is in fact the manner in which man's freedom operates. But such freedom is subordinate to freedom in the deeper sense of personal and social expansion. The dynamism of man is towards truth and love. Men are striving for greater truth and greater love and for the embodiment of these in personal life and human community. The choice of one possible course of action will exclude or restrict the choice of other possibilities. This limitation upon freedom of choice or decision is not a restriction upon freedom in the deeper sense of a personal and social expansion towards truth and love. Thus, the decision to commit oneself for life to a partner in marriage is a restriction upon one's choice of other partners, but it opens the way for the kind of personal expansion attainable only through such a life-long exclusive relationship. The promiscuous person is less free. Not only is he excluding the choice of a deep personal commitment to a partner in marriage, but in doing so he is blocking the personal expansion that brings. Likewise, the restrictions upon individual choice which are involved in social existence do not hamper freedom in the deeper sense if they are grounded upon the needs of a common becoming and a social expansion towards truth and love. Nevertheless, without the freedom of men, individually and collectively, to decide the direction of their lives and to assume responsibility for their becoming, there is no properly human development. Freedom of choice may not be ultimate, but it is the operational structure of human freedom.

The account I have given of freedom concludes my outline of the change in man's self-understanding. It enables us to see the general objection of modern men to the Church. The modern rebellion against the Church is the determination of men to be themselves. They want freedom to become themselves, and with some reason they are convinced that the Church would refuse this freedom if it could. Almost every step along the way of the development of modern man and his world has been opposed by the Church. But men have succeeded at last in throwing off the crippling shackles of an obsolete Church. And they will no longer tolerate the ecclesiastical refusal to allow human beings to grow and be themselves. Churchmen may thunder about modern licence. Ordinary people know well enough that what they are trying to do is simply to find themselves and attain the development appropriate to them as adult human beings. They do indeed make mistakes as they seek to direct their own becoming, but such mistakes are preferable to being kept in an infantile state by ecclesiastical interference and to finding the path to personal and social expansion blocked by the dictates of ecclesiastical authority. The Church gives the impression of wanting to hold men in a state of heteronomy, denying them their autonomy because this would disturb the *status quo* and call into question much that has previously been regarded as unchangeable. In its present social structure the Church is unable to allow a consistent acceptance of the change in man's self-understanding. So, instead of encouraging and guiding men's development as self-creative persons and the advance of human community through freely constituted meaning, it constantly tries to restrict men by insisting upon its own authority and by reference to a statically conceived natural law. Men, however, have had enough. They want to grow and be themselves. If the Church will not allow this: well, so much the worse for the Church.

3. FROM HIERARCHICAL ORDERS TO FREE ORGANISATIONS

If we ask why the Church is at variance with the freedom demanded by modern men for their personal and social development and adopts an attitude that prizes heteronomy above autonomy, we must turn to the second point I have listed for consideration: the implications of the self-understanding of modern men for the manner in which they order their social existence. After all, there is no intrinsic incompatibility between the concept of man as a freely self-constituting person and the Christian message. Christianity announces the liberation of man. That Christians look to Christ and the Spirit for the achievement of that liberation can hardly be interpreted as a denial of human freedom itself. It should be seen rather as its enhancement and as the disclosure of the source of the effectual realisation of the personal and social development for which men are striving. No, the clash is not with the teaching of Christ but with the obsolete structure of the Church.

Corresponding to the shift from the concept of a fixed human nature to that of a freely self-constituting person, there is the social change from fixed hierarchical orders in a closed situation to freely created organisations in an open situation.[1]

[1] Cf. Dietrich von Oppen, "Man in the Open Situation," in *Journal for Theology and Church*, Vol. 2: *Translating Theology into the Modern Age* (Harper & Row, New York, 1965), pp. 130-158.

Fixed orders in hierarchy were typical of society when men worked with the concept of a fixed human nature. Notice in passing that it is significant that the word "hierarchy" is used outside the strictly ecclesiastical sphere when it is a question of rigid graded orders. The usage indicates the link between the insistence upon static social classes and functions and an archaic, sacral view of society and the world. Fixed, hierarchically arranged orders, permanently dividing men according to class and function, were regarded as given and preformed in the same way as human nature was understood as a static reality, given and complete, with its limits already definitively formulated. They preceded the exercise of men's freedom. They were not the result of personal choice or the expression of meaning freely created; they were part of an established system, usually presented as divinely sanctioned.

Each man belonged to an order, determining his place in society and in the hierarchically arranged cosmos. His order embraced a man totally in the sense of forming the total, limiting framework of his life. He had his place, whether high or low, in the general structure of society and the world, and was expected to keep it. A man was good when he submitted willingly and without objection to his predetermined place in the divinely sanctioned state of things. His protection against oppressors was that the higher as well as the lower orders, rulers as well as subjects, had their rights limited and their duties allotted to them in the general hierarchical scheme. But while men might strive for their rights against unjust oppressors, they were not entitled to work in freedom to build a new and different structure of society. The hierarchical structure was given; it was not considered as the changeable product of the common activity of freely self-constituting persons.

Hence, men lived in a closed situation. The structures in which they were placed were resistant to change. There was not a general mobility nor a wide range for the exercise of their freedom, whether individually or socially.

Although that last statement is true, I am in general describing a theory of society and the world, not giving an account of the concrete reality of past societies. Just as the concept of a fixed human nature never adequately expressed the concrete reality of man, so also the hierarchical view of society was never fully in accord with the actual reality of society. The so-called divinely sanctioned structure was in fact the result of human decision and compromise, and society was always more mobile than the theory allowed. Nevertheless, the shift in man's self-understanding, with the consequent rejection of fixed hierarchical orders, has liberated society from the cramping effects of the attempted imposition of an unalterable structure and has opened the way to rapid social change. A development of consciousness inevitably had great repercussions upon the manner in which men ordered their social existence. The new consciousness is in fact the death warrant of all fixed hierarchical orders. It has already seen the death of Christendom and is now steadily bringing about the disintegration of the Church in its present form.

Modern society is built upon a structural principle different from the acceptance of fixed orders in hierarchy.

The typical feature of modern society is the freely created organisation. What has now been established is a technological-organisation state of life for man.

Organisations as distinct from fixed orders are the product of man's freely creative intelligence. They are not given and preformed, but made by men and explicitly acknowledged as such. This gives them definite characteristics, which must be examined.

Every organisation is limited in its scope and validity. It is concerned only with a particular, limited aspect of man's life and does not, or should not, claim to embrace him totally. Again, it is relative in value and essentially changeable; it should not claim any permanent validity.

To consider first the limited scope of every organisation.

Organisations are the product of man's intelligence. They therefore reflect the way that intelligence works.

In trying to understand complex data, man isolates particular features, aspects, objects or relations and, having grasped these in distinct concepts, proceeds to systematise his conceptual knowledge. Further, his aim is to relate the particular features or objects to one another, while prescinding as far as possible from himself as the observer or subject. He has to allow for the personal equation, but he does so in order to eliminate the subjective factor from the objectified result. In other words, abstraction in the sense of the distinguishing and isolating of particular aspects and objectification or the prescinding from the subject are typical of the working of man's intelligence.

Man's practical, organising intelligence works in a similar fashion. Particular features, relations or aims are distinguished, isolated and dealt with separately. Hence any one organisation is concerned with a limited feature of man's social existence and has a restricted purpose. This is the reason for the very great number of organisations in modern society and the increasing organisational complexity of the modern world. Again, the tendency is to objectify problems and relationships. In relation to a particular organisation for a particular purpose, the person is not considered in his total reality, but as an objectified instance of a particular problem or relationship. Thus, a person becomes a case for legal advice, for a surgical operation, for taxation, for housing, for a driving test, and so on. Organisations are based upon objectified relationships. Taken separately, they prescind from the total reality of the persons they relate. This is what makes organisations seem impersonal.

Modern technological-organisational society has long been subjected to negative criticism, a criticism that seizes in particular upon its impersonality. But a merely negative criticism is worse than useless. There is no point in indulging in a nostalgia for a past rural society, especially if that is idealised in retrospect. The organised, urban society of today reflects an advance in man's social consciousness. As concretely realised it has many defects. But the approach should be positive to appreciate the principles that underlie it, to learn how to live within it and to work to ameliorate it. Despite its defects, it has widened the opportunities for personal and social expansion. It is the social counterpart of the change in man's self-understanding.

What can at once be remarked is that the change to freely created organisations is a liberation of men from fixed and preformed hierarchical orders. Men are now able by their intelligence and free decision to organise their social existence as they see fit. Since men must do this together, individuals have to work with others to achieve their social aims. They have to make their contribution to social thought and criticism and engage in political and social activity to give effect to their ideas. All the same, behind the present development of organised society is the acknowledgement that social structures are not given and unchangeable; they are the product of man's organising intelligence and the exercise of his freedom. The freer men are from the bonds of fixed, preformed orders, the more they can become themselves.

The limited scope of every organisation, with the impersonal character this gives it, should also be seen as the liberation of the individual from imposed and preformed relationships. An individual's personal life is now more his own, and his deeper and more personal relationships a matter of free choice. It may sound attractive that the doctor should be the family friend, but it can also be an intrusion. Many prefer to get medical attention without extending the relationship with the doctor to friendship, unless they deliberately choose to do so. Likewise, one may expatiate romantically about the friendliness of the village shop, but it is a restriction upon one's liberty and privacy to be unable to buy goods without entering into a discussion with the shopkeeper about the details of one's personal life.

We live in fact in a world of differentiated relationships. Necessary relationships are objectified, limited to their particular purpose and kept within those limits. And even in regard to such necessary, limited relationships, those who live in cities will usually have a measure of choice. However, more important, by the limiting and objectifying of necessary relationships, people as persons are freed from imposed personal relationships. They are able to commit and involve themselves as persons according to their own free choice. A village community may seem to be a richer and more human form of society than the city with the anonymity with which it surrounds its inhabitants. It is, I suggest, less human, because it encloses men in a set of predetermined relationships. To have one's life thus enclosed and preshaped for one may provide a ready-made emotional security. Not everyone is prepared to meet the demands of freedom. But the absence of free choice, with the consequent inability to shape one's own life, often leads to personal relationships that remain comparatively superficial. Further, when the imposed relationships work out unhappily, the enclosed, preformed community can be sheer hell for a particular individual. The anonymity of the city and the general possibility of limiting the numerous, necessary relationships of social existence to their particular purpose leave men free to shape their own lives and commit themselves as persons by a truly free decision.

The deliberate limiting of many relationships within modern, organised society gives them an impersonal character, because they do not embrace the total reality of the persons involved. But this impersonality need not become in any way antipersonal. The conscious recognition that the particular relationship is limited should mean an awareness and respect for the undisclosed reality of the other person. It is where the limitation of the relationship is forgotten that the person is violated by its impersonality and treated as a mere object. A surgeon or lawyer or administrator who limits his relationship to his clients to what professionally concerns him is respecting, not denying, their integrity as persons. Only if he forgets that his relationship with them is limited and does not embrace their total reality as persons will he be guilty of treating them as mere objects for his professional skill. The bureaucrat is not wrong in limiting his attention to what concerns his administrative function. Where he often errs is in failing to recognise that he is dealing with only a very limited aspect of the reality and lives of the people who come under his administration. He reduces their reality to his administrative concern, instead of remaining conscious that it extends well beyond it.

As Harvey Cox has pointed out, we need a middle form of relationship between the I-Thou relationship of deep personal commitment and the I-It relationship that reduces persons to the status of things or mere objects. He suggests that we call it an I-You relationship, which is a limited relationship, but one where 'there remains an awareness and respect for the reality of the other person.[2]

What, then, emerges, from the consideration of the limited scope of every organisation is the essential need to recognise and constantly remember that limitation. Where the limitation is not recognised, the organisation becomes destructive of persons, because it reduces their reality within its own narrow limits. Where it is recognised, the differentiation of social existence into numerous limited relationships frees men to shape their own lives. The multiplication of organisations prevents men from being enclosed in a single all-

[2] Harvey Cox, *The Secular City: Secularization and Urbanization in Theological Perspective* (The Macmillan Company, New York, 1965), pp. 48-49.

embracing fixed order; none of the organisations can lay claim to the total reality of a person or presume to control his whole life. And each person remains free in regard to his deeper commitments and more personal relationships.

This brings me to the second characteristic I mentioned of organisations, namely that they are relative in value and essentially changeable.

The structural principle behind organisations is the creative intelligence of man. Organised society, therefore, must be placed in the context of the developing intelligence of man; it participates in the open dynamism of human intelligence. Modern society is essentially changeable because it is the expression of man's becoming. Behind that becoming lies man's restless, questioning intellect and his striving for greater freedom. As men engage in the process of making themselves and their world, they meet new problems and find new solutions to old problems. Socially man's becoming is expressed by the creation of new organisations and the leaving aside of old organisations, by the increasing differentiation of organisations as social needs and aims are more clearly defined and distinguished. Truth, I have said, becomes prejudice when it is taken out of the context of man's questioning mind. Likewise, if organisations are removed from the creativity of man's developing intelligence and made absolute and unchangeable, they cease to express and embody man's becoming and harden into irrational restrictions upon his intelligence and freedom. Organisations must remain open to change. They must be regarded as relative in value and without permanent validity. Otherwise, they are divorced from their structural principle: the creative intelligence of man. Instead of being the expression of the reality of man in his intelligent and free becoming, they block his development and imprison his humanity. It is when they refuse to change that organisations become inhuman and destructive of persons.

Thus, modern men live in a world that is immensely complex, but always changing. They experience the world as a succession of perpetually new situations. For that reason, they are or should be iconoclastic towards all organisations. Organisations should be open-ended. They should never become fixed in what they are, but remain constantly ready for change. There should always be the opportunity for improvisation, leading to new forms of expressing the reality of man and his becoming.

In a world that is in principle open to constant change, what is man's relationship to the past? Well, man in his becoming depends upon the past. A continuity with the past should be acknowledged in human development, both individual and social. For a person to repress and refuse to accept his own past is psychologically harmful and hampers his very development. To ignore the social past and think that every generation begins afresh is to destroy the possibility of historical development, in which each generation builds upon the work of previous generations. It is also to take away the meaning of education, the purpose of which is to bring each person to the point already reached in human development.

However, there is room for a distinction in viewing the past. There is the past that remains past in the sense that it is no longer relevant or meaningful for us. And there is the past that becomes present insofar as it is constitutive of our present being and thus meaningful for us. Now, we appropriate the past and make it living and meaningful only inasmuch as we look to the future; in other words, only inasmuch as we place it in the context of man's becoming. The past is falsified when it is made absolute, because this destroys its very authenticity as a past embodiment of man's reality. It is when we recognise it, not as an unhistorical absolute, but a past expression of man's historical being, that we can render it relevant and meaningful.

To return to my main theme.

The bearing of the remarks about the change from fixed hierarchical orders to freely created organisations is that men, both individually and socially, now live in an open situation.

By this I mean that their lives are not enclosed and shaped for them by the imposition of preformed relationships and restriction within fixed, unchangeable social structures.

The organisational complexity of modern society creates a variety of choice for the individual. Organisations in principle are freely joined and from them men can freely withdraw. Many factors, notably economic necessity, still unjustly restrict men's effective freedom in this respect. Again, social necessity justly limits the individual's freedom of choice. But the principle of the greatest possible freedom should be recognised. Even the modern, organised nation, granted many present restrictions, is freely joined by naturalisation or freely left by emigration. Within the nation, men have a fair range of choice in deciding their social function and planning their general social existence.

Further, the limited character of organisations leaves men free to form their own deeper personal relationships and thus shape their own personal and social life. Whereas in an hierarchical society a man was good if he submitted willingly to the order in which he was placed and which totally embraced his life, where a man today forgets the limited function of any organisation and submits himself and others totally to it, he disfigures his and their reality as persons. The extreme instance of this is the totalitarian State. Lesser instances are the organisation man, who identifies himself with the organisation for which he works, and the bureaucrat, who reduces people to numbers in a file. Only if the limited function and relative value of organisations are recognised, will modern organised society be preserved from inhumanity. Organisations cannot embrace the total reality of men as persons. They are but partial expressions of the rich and changing human reality.

Moreover, as I have said, organised society is a changing society, reflecting the open dynamism of man's creative intelligence. Not only individually, but also socially, men are now in an open situation, where all social structures are subject to constant change.

The open situation in which men are now placed has created the modern problem of loneliness. Not all are mature enough to embrace the freedom to shape their own personal and social life and exist stripped of preformed relationships. In the anonymity created by the city they remain lonely, cut off from social intercourse. Then there are social groups at an unfair disadvantage in modern society, deprived of reasonable social opportunities and unable to share fully in social life. The problems caused by modern society call for love towards those damaged and an active concern to eliminate the defects. But the problems cannot be met by attempting to return to an earlier state of society, but by trying to better the present, imperfect achievement.

However, this leads us to seek a deeper basis for modern society. Technological-organisational society will become truly human only when it is the expression of a common world of meaning and of a universal fellowship among men.

Freely created organisations have meaning. They are the work of men in freely creating and embodying meaning in the world around them and thus forming and developing the properly human world. In that sense organisations are never neutral. They are like language. They embody and communicate meaning, and through them meaning is created and unfolded. A programme, therefore, of modernising society, understood as its more efficient reorganisation, while ignoring meaning and treating organisations as neutral, is strictly nonsensical. It merely implies that one is the victim of unacknowledged ideology. A reorganisation of society cannot be separated from its renewal, which demands the conscious fostering and development of a common world of meaning, thought out and critically examined. Organisations should be subordinate to that common world of meaning, each expressing some feature, aspect or relationship belonging to it. Men must work freely together to create the world of human meaning; organisations are the language they use.

But it would be a mistake to suppose that a common world of meaning requires embodiment in a single, overarching organisation. That is untrue. Any attempt to bring the common world of meaning within the boundaries of an all-embracing super-organisation would be a disastrous failure to recognise the open, changing reality of man and the ceaseless activity of his intelligence and freedom. It would be to create a vast prison for mankind. No, the understanding that men are self-constituting persons, involved in an individual and social becoming, leads to the conclusion that their common world of meaning can be expressed and embodied only in a great variety of changing and changeable organisations. Each organisation, even if world-wide, will be limited in function. Men will be imprisoned in none, but will remain in an open situation. The present age is not an age of poverty of meaning, but of richness of meaning. Even were a common world of meaning achieved, which it is not as yet, many organisations would be needed to express its complex richness and open dynamism. And to attempt at present to establish a total organisation would be to frustrate the process that could lead to such an achievement.

To say that underlying the development of modern society with its freely created organisations should be the creation and development of a common world of meaning is to demand the acknowledgement of a universal human community or fellowship. As I have already said, community at the distinctively human level is precisely a common world of meaning, insofar as that world is socially created and socially embodied in institutions and relationships.

But again it would be wrong to suppose that the universal human community requires a single, overarching organisation. Men will express their universal fellowship in a variety of ways and through a variety of organisations. A single all-embracing organisation is neither essential nor practicable; indeed, it would be positively harmful. What is essential is that the whole of human social life should be subordinate to the conviction of the unity of mankind and should serve the promotion of universal fellowship. The fundamental principle of human community is not organisational unity, but the conviction of the unity of mankind and the gradual working for the achievement of a common world of meaning. Men will work for this through free intellectual discussion and practical collaboration in the building of society. A variety of organisations, limited in function and subject to change, corresponds better to the human condition than the establishment of a single, total organisation.

As individuals men will express their acknowledgement of the human community through three different forms of relationship.

There is first the I-You or limited relationship embodied in particular organisations. While this kind of relationship prescinds from the total reality of the persons involved, it is not antipersonal, but demands from each an awareness and respect of the other person. The doctor or lawyer or administrator, while keeping within the limits of his professional concern, is or should be exercising a just and loving service in relation to the other person. If the objectified relationship expressed in an organisation is a just one, there is no need to step outside its limits in order to manifest love and justice towards the other persons concerned. It is fallacious to suppose that love of the neighbour demands the impossible feat of establishing an intimate friendship with everyone. Man expresses human community through objectified relationships, provided they are just.

The second kind of relationship is also limited, but it is unorganised. It is the service of a fellow man in need, wherever he is met.

Man in an open situation should be prepared to help others outside any framework and whenever particular circumstances make this demand upon his love. No one can withdraw from such unexpected demands with the excuse that he is giving his service through established organisations. These are always inadequate. But the relationship thus embraced is limited to the needs of the particular case. As Von Oppen remarks in the article I have cited, the Good Samaritan did not take the wounded traveller into his house to live with him for the rest of his life, but bandaged him, took him to an inn, left money there for his care, promised to stop on his return, and then went about his business. The situation determined the nature of the relationship required; and it did not demand a life-long friendship. Thus, we should meet any demands a particular situation makes upon our love. What is required is usually limited; it is imperatively demanded, for all that.

In the third place there is the I-Thou relationship of deep personal commitment and intimate friendship. Here men today have the greatest freedom. Modern society, with its general mobility and the limited character of its organisations, leaves men freer than ever before to shape their own individual and social life on the deeply personal level. This in fact makes possible a deeper because freer personal commitment, as it has, for example, created the partnership marriage in place of the arranged union. I-Thou relationships cannot of their nature be organised. They will be found in intimate personal friendships freely entered into and also give rise to small, interpersonal groups. Such groups will be fluid in form and subject to the vicissitudes of all friendships as persons change and develop or just move away. Attempts to organise them and give them stability usually kill them. Notice that because the principle behind them is free commitment and association does not mean that they are motivated by selfishness. They require the same kind of unselfish outgoing towards other persons as all friendship.

After this somewhat lengthy account of the social change from fixed hierarchical orders in a closed situation to freely created organisations in an open situation, it is now possible to look in contrast at the hierarchical social structure of the Church.

At once it is apparent that it belongs to a different, archaic world; it is an obsolete survival of a past stage of history. The same applies to all rigidly maintained Church structures, even when they are non-hierarchical.

The imposition of an essentially unchanging social structure, hierarchical in form, clashes with modern man's social consciousness. It withdraws the social structure of the Church from the creativity and freedom, which constitute the structural principle according to which man now organises his social existence. So, Christians are prevented in this changing world from freely creating on the basis of their faith the organisational structures they require for the embodiment of their Christian life and mission. There is constant resistance to change and rejection of experiment and improvisation. There is an insistence upon fixed laws and traditional procedures, inadequate as these are in a period of rapid change. In brief, to maintain the hierarchical structure, the Church is attempting to keep men in a closed situation, instead of recognising that they are now in an open situation. What insistence upon an unchanging social structure means in effect is a denial of the social implications of the concept of man as a self-creative person. That is why modern men see the Church as oppressive.

But the problem is even greater than the continuance of a fixed hierarchical order from the past. The past is always falsified in making it an unhistorical absolute. A fixed hierarchical order in a modern context has not the same nature and effects as it had in the past. Out of its proper historical context it has become distorted.

The social structure of the Church has not been unaffected by modern organisational society. It has taken into itself the organisational complexity of the modern world and formed itself into a vast administrative structure, endeavouring to control, arrange and systematise the activity of Christians. Thus, the closest model for a modern bishop is a business executive. But in combining organisational complexity with the claims of a fixed hierarchical order it has left aside the features of organisational society that prevent its becoming inhuman and destructive of human personality. The protection of man's personality and freedom in the face of modern highly organised society is the firm maintenance of his open situation, with insistence upon the limited scope of every organisation, the essential changeability of all organisations, their multiplicity and variety and the absence of any single, overarching organisation embracing his total reality as a person. By its maintenance of a fixed social structure and its stress upon its hierarchical authority, the Church refuses the application of these principles to itself. Hence throughout its structure it shows the worse, inhuman, bureaucratic features of modern organisational society without allowing and fostering its advantages. By attaching its claims as a divinely sanctioned and unchangeable hierarchical order to what has now taken on the characteristics of a vast administrative organisation with modern techniques, the Church is crushing the humanity of Christians and frustrating their personal and social expansion as Christians.

4. THE HISTORICAL APPROACH TO TRUTH AND FAITH

However, before going on to examine positively how the visible Church should be organised in the context of modern society, I must first deal with the question of the approach to truth demanded by man's present historical consciousness.

The modern historical approach to truth can best be seen in contrast to its opposite extreme. This is extrinsicism. The extrinsicist view of truth holds that objective truth, precisely because it is objective, exists already out there, outside history in some unchanging realm. In other words, it exists apart from its possession by any subject, stands complete and fixed outside living minds. For that reason it is not involved in the historical process and can be formulated in immutable concepts and propositions. There are developments only in the sense that the same truth, while remaining unchanged, may find different applications in the changing, historical world, with perhaps as a consequence an incidental touching up of previous formulations. Linked with extrinsicism is conceptualism. The conceptualist holds that concepts are primary and static. Concepts are taken in themselves apart from the understanding of living minds. They are considered as stable and unchanging, so that they can be ordered and systematised without reference to the developing intelligence of men.

233

Now, it would be wrong to say that all the thinkers of the past before the coming of modern historical consciousness were extrinsicists and conceptualists in their approach to truth. That is untrue, for example, of Thomas Aquinas. But the modern sense of historicity has further drawn out the implications of what some previous thinkers had already recognised, namely, that truth exists only in living minds, that, although it is objective, it is always related to the knowing subject, so that all human truth is involved in the developing process of human intelligence. Genuine concepts are the product of human understanding and remain at the service of a dynamic intelligence, sharing in the imperfections, progress and frequent tentativeness of all human thinking.

The existence of human truth only in human subjects means that truth as attained by man is conditioned by the historical process. There is an historicity of truth reflecting the historicity of man. What is truth for man must be related to his becoming. He has his being only in an historical unfolding and attains truth in the same manner.

I have earlier in this book outlined the main principles of an historical approach to truth. Let me recall the points made, with some further precisions concerning their application to Christian faith.

Man's relation to truth is that of unceasing pursuit in the context of open questioning. Truth is no longer held as truth, but as prejudice, if it is removed from the open dynamism of human intelligence, which seeks truth by questioning.

All the same, in pursuing truth man does reach limited certainties. A man may be said to be certain when in regard to a particular point there are no further present relevant questions. The answer that thus meets the questions at issue may be therefore affirmed with firmness or certitude. The certainty affirmed is, however, limited for two connected reasons. First, men always grasp and know truth from a particular standpoint. They can never entirely prescind from or escape the limited perspectives imposed upon them as subjects involved in an historical process. For man there is no God's-eye view of reality, namely a view that would be entirely unaffected by the limitations of every human standpoint. Human knowledge is always a knowledge conditioned by the existing limitations of personal and social development. Second, because every man is involved in both a personal and social becoming, standpoints and perspectives are constantly changing. Hence, although there may have been no further relevant questions disturbing an answer given from a particular standpoint, new and unexpected questions may arise when the standpoint changes. A problem once reasonably judged as solved may then have to be reconsidered from a different point of view or in the light of fresh related developments in knowledge. For these two reasons, all man's certainties are limited and perfectible; existing in the context of the developing human mind, they must always remain open to revision and correction. So, human truth cannot be definitively formulated in unalterable propositions and immutable concepts.

Nevertheless, this does not mean that human knowledge lacks all objectivity, that it is entirely relative to the individual subject or historical epoch and without objective reference. What both indicates and secures the limited though essential objectivity of human knowing is that man by ceaseless questioning constantly transcends each particular standpoint. He moves from one standpoint to the next, from one historical perspective to another, and, in doing so, reviews and perfects his certainties, corrects subjective distortions and overcomes the limitations of his previous point of view. This dynamic thrust of man's intelligence, with the constant revision and correction of his certainties it imposes, is inexplicable without a reality independent of the subject, to which man is striving to relate himself in his knowing. And, although man can never disengage himself from every limited standpoint and gain a total view of reality, a view freed from the conditioning of any perspective, he is able by his endless questioning to approximate his knowledge ever more closely to objective reality and avoid imprisonment in any particular subjective standpoint or historical perspective. In other words, as a knowing subject man is like a person who cannot obtain a complete, aerial view of a region, but has to move from hill to hill gradually to build up his mental picture of the lie of the land, except that with knowledge in general the hills to be climbed are without number.

Those remarks are not intended as an answer to all the difficult problems surrounding the objectivity of human knowledge. Their purpose is simply to indicate that a recognition of the historicity of human knowing does not necessitate a denial of its objectivity and the acceptance of a pure subjectivism or relativism.

A further point, however, should be made. When we adopt an historical approach to truth, we see that particular truths usually have error intermingled with them and particular errors usually contain some truth. Because all particular truths are limited and are affirmed from a particular standpoint, they are usually bound up with elements that later prove erroneous and have to be left aside. Likewise, an error often has an element in it that points in the right direction, raises a useful question or lays its finger upon an inadequacy in accepted views. It can thus serve a valuable function in man's intellectual development. It is related to truth, though in an oblique fashion. It is worth noticing that only at a later stage of development can the truth be separated from the erroneous elements with which it is intermingled or the error that contains some truth be completely discarded because that truth has been grasped directly. At the time, truth and error or error and truth are inextricably entangled. A development is needed to distinguish between them. We should recognise the limitations of human knowing and both the inevitability and frequent usefulness of error in the historical process of man's learning.

Now, faith can exist only in the dynamic context of man's intelligence and freedom. Faith, as I have already explained, cannot be rationally demonstrated; it is not a conclusion that can be proved by reason nor the holding of a doctrine that can be incontrovertibly verified. But it is the response to a perceived duty, the answer to a call of God which manifests itself with sufficient clarity to make our free response a reasonable action for an intelligent being. Led by God's Spirit, we leap beyond the world where the human mind proceeds by proof and verification. But neither our intelligence nor our freedom are violated; they are indeed enhanced.

Christian faith is a personal commitment to God through Christ. It is not just an intellectual assent to a body of doctrine, but a total self-giving to God as present in the man Jesus. It has therefore the absoluteness of an irrevocable self-surrender to another person. At the same time, the personal commitment of Christian faith would be meaningless without a doctrinal content. The presence of God is mediated to us through his Word, and if his definitive Word is a person, Jesus Christ, the presence of Christ is mediated to us today through the preaching of the Gospel. Without a doctrine of Jesus Christ, of his message and his work, commitment to Christ would be indistinguishable from personal fantasy or historical and philosophical invention. The Spirit within us acts in conjunction with the historical tradition of Christian belief coming to us from without.

Indissolubly linked to a doctrinal content, the personal commitment of Christian faith inevitably undergoes conceptualisation and formulation. And the absoluteness of that commitment is reflected in the continuity of the historical tradition of Christian belief. The Christian believer is committed to an acknowledgement of that continuity. Irrevocably committed to Jesus Christ as mediated in his Gospel (as preserved and transmitted in history), he does not envisage any development that will render Christian commitment and its essential doctrinal content obsolete or untrue.

All the same, the doctrinal content of Christian faith was given and could have been given only within the historical process. The message was originally presented in the setting of a particular culture and therefore formulated from a particular standpoint. And all subsequent conceptualisations and formulations are likewise made within particular cultural contexts and from particular standpoints. The absoluteness of Christian belief consists in a continuity that subordinates all the limited, perfectible formulations to the preservation of Christian commitment in a succession of different cultures and to the drive towards a better understanding of Christ and his work and in the fact that no development leads to the dissolution of that commitment. It does not and cannot consist in the achievement of unalterable concepts and immutable propositions existing outside history or in gaining a total, God's-eye view of Christ, unconditioned by any particular standpoint or historical perspective.

It is impossible, therefore, to isolate an absolute, unchanging core of Christian belief. To try to do so is an illusory project, because it is in effect an attempt to remove Christian belief from history. Some of the efforts to extract the Christian *kerygma* from the rest of New Testament teaching seem to me to fall into this error. Granted that a central message can be distinguished from secondary elements, the formulation of that message is always culturally conditioned and from a particular standpoint. Each age will ask new questions about its meaning and seek to formulate it afresh. There is no pure essence of Christian belief, abstracted from historically conditioned teaching. We live our Christian commitment and grasp its content only within the serial reality of history.

To say that Christian truth exists in the context of the questioning dynamism of man's intelligence is only to express the same point in a different way. Since every formulation of Christian belief is limited, it is open to further questions, leading to its bettering or correction. The Christian believer will be confident that no questions will lead to the destruction of Christian faith, but that confidence should be expressed by the bold and honest confrontation of all relevant questions, not by their suppression. To suppress relevant questions would mean that Christian doctrine is no longer held as truth, but as mere prejudice. The believer will not expect to prove his faith, but he will recognise that genuine questioning will lead to its better understanding.

Recognition of the historicity of Christian truth as held by men also implies the acknowledgement that Christian believers do not and cannot avoid all error in grasping and formulating it. Particular formulations are usually intermingled with elements that are later seen to be erroneous and left aside. The imperfections of man's view from limited standpoints and the unavoidable interference of physical, emotional, social and cultural factors upon his intellectual development and activity even as a Christian would make the exclusion of all error miraculous. And it would be an unnecessary miracle. The Spirit can sufficiently secure the indefectibility of Christian faith by constantly counteracting and overcoming error, without the need to exclude it. As long as there remains a sufficient hold upon Christian truth among Christians to form the basis for a renewal and eventual opposition to any error, the continuity of Christian tradition is safeguarded.

Christian history would suggest that such is in fact the manner in which Christian truth has been preserved. Particular errors have often been widespread, sometimes universal, among Christians, but there has always remained a sufficient basis of Christian truth from which they were in time counteracted and overcome. And when we look at particular formulations of Christian teaching, we find elements in them that later had to be rejected. At the same time, many errors have had an important function in pointing to truth and urging the inadequacy of a one-sided formulation.

What is true of Christian tradition generally is true of the Bible. The Bible is a unique and indispensable witness to God's revelation, which culminated in Christ. It is not, however, free from the limitations of its cultural context, or rather contexts, nor is it entirely without error. The limitations and errors do not destroy the unity and continuity of its teaching nor the fact that it embodies the absolute truth of God's Word. At the same time, it is a human and historical document, subject as such to inevitable imperfections and limitations. While it will remain the perennial centre of the Christian tradition and never be rendered obsolete, both in itself and in its interpretation it must be regarded as existing within the historical process. It cannot be isolated from history as an unhistorical absolute.

After this brief examination of the historical approach to Christian truth, we can now ask what social structure of the Christian community is implied by it.

It seems to me that the structure should be such as to keep Christian truth within the context of history and in interaction with human historical development, both individual and social. Once it is removed from the historical process, it ceases to be truth for man and becomes antiquated legend or obstinate prejudice. On the same count, it must be kept within the open, questioning dynamism of human intelligence. Questions must not be suppressed, the value of particular formulations not exaggerated, and errors met by carefully examining their implications, not by supposing that they can be immediately condemned from a total possession of the truth.

These conditions, I am convinced, will be realised only by regarding Christian truth as belonging to the Christian community as a whole, as in fact being the common world of meaning that constitutes it as a community. Only by being firmly placed in the hands of the Christian community as a whole will Christian truth be fully engaged in the process of man's becoming, fully linked to his individual and social development. And Christian truth as a common world of meaning will be preserved and transmitted by open communication. Open communication will secure that relevant questions are not suppressed, but are taken up by others and met by common effort. Through it the inadequacy of particular formulations will be revealed and counteracted by fresh thought to meet new situations and problems. Open communication can provide the remedy for errors. Particular Christian groups may fall into serious error, blinded by national or racial prejudice or influenced by specious arguments. Other groups or individuals can resist these errors and work to overcome them. When an error spreads generally among Christians, open communication allows for the dissident voice that eventually makes itself heard.

Christians will believe that the processes of open communication are effective in unfailingly preserving the presence of Christian truth in the world because of the support and guidance of the Spirit. Nevertheless, the Spirit acts through humanly relevant structures. As we see it in the modern world, open communication is achieved by personal relationships and social intercourse, by writings and meetings, by numerous organisations directed to particular purposes, by teaching but now understood as a procedure involving dialogue and discussion, and by the use of other modern means of communication. There is no reason why the Spirit should not be seen as acting through such means.

Such processes of open communication establish the scientific community as a common world of meaning, transcending national, racial and even cultural barriers, without the need for an overarching organisation or for an external authority issuing scientific edicts. And if this is repudiated as a possible analogy for the Christian community on the grounds that the scientific community embraces only an élite—a point which is questionable when one considers the full extent of its pervasive influence—similar analogies may be drawn, not only from schools of thought and literary traditions, but also from tenaciously persistent folk cultures and traditions. There are no rational grounds for asserting that a common world of meaning cannot be preserved, transmitted and developed outside the framework of an overarching organisation ruled by a teaching authority empowered definitively to decide questions that arise. The Christian world of meaning is indeed founded upon the authority of God's Word. But it does not follow that the Spirit in evoking faith in that Word must act through a system of hierarchical authority. The authority of God's Word may be seen as embodied in the Christian community as a whole with its common tradition and biblical record and then preserved and transmitted through open communication.

The Christian tradition is a present and historical fact. Despite the many divisions among Christians, it exists recognisably as a common world of meaning to which all Christians, with the possible exception of some fringe groups, belong. The individual should not and does not need to create a Christian belief for himself. He joins himself to the historical Christian tradition and enters into that world of meaning. He does so through some meeting with other Christians. These introduce him to the Christian faith through their own understanding of it, and usually at present they owe allegiance to a particular Christian denomination. The new Christian will therefore at the moment generally become a member of one of the Churches that now divide the Christian community. But his understanding of his faith should not remain static. He can develop his Christian belief by gaining a deeper and wider knowledge of the Christian tradition as a whole through his own reflection, through contact with other Christians, through reading within the vast range of Christian writing, through benefitting in general from the processes of communication amongst Christians. This will lead him considerably to modify his original understanding of Christian belief, but to do so within the general context of the Christian tradition.

The point I am making is that the refusal of an overarching organisation for the Christian tradition and of an hierarchical teaching authority does not mean that each individual is left free to create his Christian belief *ab initio*. The Christian tradition or historical Christian faith exists as a matter of fact. It is not embraced by any single social structure, and all the present institutions are under question. But it certainly exists as a common world of meaning to which a person can join himself by a commitment to Christ, a commitment mediated through it. His Christian commitment will then share in his own becoming, guiding and animating it. And the Christian will participate in the common, historical becoming of the Christian community by communicating with other Christians, by working with them and by joining one or more of the various organisations embodying and serving the Christian faith and mission.

An overarching organisation and an hierarchical teaching authority are not merely unnecessary for the preservation and transmission of the Christian tradition, but they also embody an archaic approach to truth, out of keeping with modern historical consciousness.

An hierarchical teaching authority rests upon a view of truth as static, just as hierarchical orders in general presuppose a view of society as static. The deposit of faith is regarded as an unchanging, timeless body of truth, capable of being definitively formulated in authoritative statements imposed as irrevocable. Christian tradition in what concerns its essential preservation and transmission is taken out of the hands of the community as a whole and given to a special class empowered to decide any controverted question. Any role assigned to the community must, despite the increasing stress upon such a role, be kept essentially subordinate to the hierarchy and is controlled by it. This removes the Christian tradition from the context of open questioning by the community of believers, with the striving such questioning implies towards a genuine consensus, strengthening, enriching and developing a common world of meaning. In the hierarchical system, questions are treated as either difficulties or aberrations to be countered by reference to a static body of truth held in trust by authoritative teachers. And an hierarchical teaching authority establishes a paternalistic order in the Church in relation to truth—an order appropriate only when education is a limited privilege. The general body of the faithful are grouped together as the taught and placed under a special teaching class. Teaching itself is conceived in an old-fashioned manner as an authoritative didactic rather than heuristic procedure, dialogue and debate being admitted only by way of concession, so that, for example, the Pope can remove a point from discussion if he wishes. But, as I have already remarked, belief in the authority of God's Word and in the working of the Spirit does not necessitate the acceptance of obsolete procedures.

The hierarchical teaching authority has become increasingly irrelevant in the life of the Church, and the hierarchical system has already to a great extent broken down. The general movement of thought is forging ahead in the Roman Catholic Church, and papal statements, when not hostile to it, are largely inadequate and restrictive formulations of ideas already widespread. Little notice is taken of their inadequacy and restrictions, and theologians continue on their way, simply garnishing their books with suitable selected quotations. The same may be said of the documents of the Second Vatican Council, which unlike those of previous Councils, including Trent, did not add, but only cut back the understanding already achieved. The hope cherished by many is that the authoritative acceptance of ideas will promote their spread within the Church, but such authoritative sanction is beginning to matter less and less. And it is becoming ever more evident that the hierarchy simply do not command sufficient authority to decide any really controversial matter. It is unlikely that they would dare to do so. If they did, the probable result would be disastrous for the Roman Church. Hence a series of unheeded warnings is taking the place of authoritative teaching. What is now happening to papal and conciliar authority occurred some time ago in regard to the teaching of individual bishops. It is long since that teaching was taken seriously because episcopal.

Some may argue that the existence of hierarchical authority is a safeguard against popular error and majority prejudice. It prevents the Church from being dominated by a contemporary, local *milieu*, with its blindness and limitations, and allows it to insist upon temporarily unpopular ideas. Pastors are more detached and independent than their flocks.

The facts, however, show that this is not so. With all its claim to authority, the hierarchy concerned with its own prestige and with the preservation of the institution does not dare to take an unpopular line, especially in any matter with social and political repercussions. To keep its authority it does not resist majority prejudice. Carl Amery has shown this conclusively with reference to the Church in Germany, and his book has a wider bearing.[1] Open communication, with the freedom it allows for dissidence, is the only true safeguard against popular corruption.

---

[1] *Capitulation: An Analysis of Contemporary Catholicism*, trans. by Edward Quinn (Sheed and Ward, London, 1967).

5. THE CHRISTIAN CHURCH AND THE WIDER SOCIETY

This brings me now to the final point in this discussion of the prospect for the Church: the relation between the Christian Church and the wider or inclusive society. Here I have to pick up again and apply what I have already said about the social change from fixed hierarchical orders in a closed situation to freely created organisations in an open situation. But first I need to present what I consider a sound understanding of the nature of the visible Church.

The visible Church is no longer regarded as the community of the exclusively saved. The problem of the salvation of the unevangelised came into theological prominence with the geographical discoveries of the fifteenth century, which made theologians aware of the millions of men cut off from the preaching of the Gospel. From that time onwards it was impossible to treat the unevangelised man of good will, living in ignorance of the Christian message, as an exceptional case to be solved by appeal to extraordinary interventions. After much complicated theological discussion, agreement has eventually been reached that the gifts of salvation are universally available outside the visible boundaries of the Church. All men, whatever their historical and cultural situation, can reach a faith and love, a sharing in the life proclaimed by Christ, sufficient to participate in redemption even here on earth. Since, according to Christian belief, there is no salvation apart from Christ, the universal availability of salvation implies a universal, though latent and unrecognised, presence of Christ in his saving activity. In brief, the saving gifts of Christ are not confined to the visible or empirical Church, but are present and operative throughout mankind. And the visible Church does not mark the limits of Christ's presence in the world; he is present universally within the historical process as a whole.

The recognition of the universal presence of Christ and his saving gifts demands a change in our understanding of the relation between the visible Church and the world. What it implies is the rejection of the concept of a secular, profane world from which the Church is set apart as the exclusive area of the sacred. Some writers have expressed this by saying that Christianity has abolished the distinction between the secular and the sacred. I think that this statement is too sweeping and creates confusion. Christianity retains and has indeed clarified the distinction between the secular and sacred dimensions of reality and of man's existence. It is important to recognise both the autonomy of the secular and the transcendence of the sacred. But to distinguish secular and sacred within the complex totality of human existence, affected as this is by God's transcendent gift, is not to separate them. And the universality of the sacred, namely, of God's saving gift through Christ, means that there is in the concrete no secular world, no merely natural or secular order standing over against the visible Church. The visible Church is not an enclosed sacred area within a profane world. There is no profane world in which to place it. The sacred gifts proclaimed by the Church are present throughout mankind and within human history as a whole. And if the world is understood in the Johannine sense as the realm of those who reject Christ's salvation, that world exists within the visible Church as well as outside it.

How, then, shall we conceive the visible Church and its purpose? The visible Church is the disclosure of what is present universally in human life and history. It stands as the permanent embodiment of the explicit revelation of God's purpose for all mankind. Its purpose is to manifest the meaning of human life and history as a whole and make known the source and manner of the salvation God offers to all men. It is thus the manifest as distinct from the latent presence of Christ. Through the Church Christ remains visibly in the world and provides a visible sign of salvation and anticipatory expression of the Kingdom. And as the visible presence of Christ and his saving gifts, the Church is intended to be an effectual sign, serving the mission of Christ to men as a pioneer force under the movement of the Spirit. The visible Church is Christ's vanguard in the advance of mankind through history to the final Kingdom.

We can deepen this concept of the Church by comparing Christian existence with ordinary human life as found in the concrete—notice, not with a merely natural human life, which is only an abstraction.

Christian faith is not the introduction of an entirely new world of thought nor the exclusive attainment of a special kind of commitment nor the possession of an esoteric body of knowledge. It is the explicitation of a commitment and convictions found in the form of an implicit faith among all sincere men, who follow their consciences and thus remain open to the hidden promptings of the Spirit. Christian beliefs and values are perceived and cherished by men who have not come to an explicit faith in Christ and remain outside the visible Church.

The Christian life is the strengthening, promotion and celebration of all good and genuine human life. It is not the creation of a special kind of existence nor the erection of a separate form of religious life nor the following of an exclusively Christian way of life.

Christian fellowship is the discovery and building up of universal human fellowship. It is not the establishment of an exclusive Christian fellowship.

The purpose of Christian liturgy is not to achieve a deeper and exclusive community experience among a special group. It is the disclosure in symbol of the meaning and basis of the human community itself.

In brief, the consequences of denying the existence of a secular world over against the visible Church is that the Christian community or visible Church is the manifest emergence of that common world of meaning which is constitutive of the human community itself. It is the coming into explicit consciousness of that world of meaning which men are endeavouring, though only with a slowly growing awareness, to make incarnate in a universal community of mankind.

All genuine community at the human level is, as I have previously explained, constituted by a common world of meaning, freely created by the active intelligence of men and embodied in social relationships and social structures. This is also true of the Christian community as a human community. It is constituted by the Christian world of meaning, which is grounded upon the free commitment of faith, deepened and extended by the developing understanding of that faith, and embodied in social relationships and structures.

We have been accustomed for so long to identify the visible unity of the Church with a clearly defined social structure and with organisational unity that it is difficult to accept the more flexible concept of the visible Church required by the new understanding of the relation between the Church and the world. But the fundamental principle of the visible unity of the Church is not organisational unity but the unity of a common world of meaning as socially embodied and expressed. Since, however, the Christian world of meaning, constitutive of the visible Church, coincides with the common human world of meaning, constitutive of the human community itself and present already universally, though struggling for expression and implicit in great measure, it is impossible for the visible Church to have clear boundaries. The centre is located, but the boundaries are blurred. The centre is Christ, visibly present through those who are explicitly committed to him by faith. But it is difficult to say where even an explicit faith in Christ begins or ends among the varieties of its formulation. And who can say where Christian meaning in general, as found in particular values, beliefs and actions, ceases to be socially expressed in a world where Christ is universally present? Every human community is constituted by meaning as socially created and socially embodied. Community begins and ends where the common meaning constitutive of community begins and ends. The Christian community or visible Church is the social expression of that common world of meaning which, through the universal presence of Christ's salvation, is constitutive of the emergent universal community of men. The boundaries of that social expression will inevitably merge indistinguishably into the general human community. And this corresponds to the experience of Christians, who find that the lines of their visible and social unity as Christians with other men do not correspond to the organisational boundaries of their Church.

Granted however the lack of clear boundaries, Christians with an explicit commitment to Christ will create, develop and embody their Christian world of meaning in social relationships and social structures. The social relationships they will create and embody in structures will correspond to the three kinds of relationships I have already analysed in discussing the human community. Insofar as these relationships are grounded upon an explicit Christian faith, they become constitutive of the visible Church.

We may first take the I-Thou relationship of deep personal commitment and intimate friendship. Sharing a common faith that affects the depths of personal and social existence, Christians in meeting one another will form personal friendships and small interpersonal groups. These small groups for intimate, face-to-face association and co-operation cannot be organised in any strict sense. They arise according to opportunity and circumstance and depend upon personal initiative and the many unanalysable factors that lead to friendships. Their grounding upon the Christian faith is not achieved in any formal manner, but secured by the genuinely personal, living and active faith of the persons involved. In the environment of such groups, each one's faith is strengthened and developed and each one in his turn contributes to the Christian becoming of the others. What such groups do varies. They are in general hidden centres of Christian mission in regard to both the formation of the participants and the bearing of a Christian witness to others. These groups are not selfish and enclosed, but like all genuine friendships provide a secure basis for an outgoing love towards other men. Increasingly such groups are ecumenical and find denominational differences irrelevant to their deep Christian commitment. And some people who are not Christians are brought within them and meet the Christian faith in this way. If they do not themselves become Christians, they learn to respect the Christian faith and find a unity with Christian believers. These interpersonal groups are the deepest form of Christian presence in the world and constitute the origin and animating core of the wider Christian movements and organisations. Christian renewal has generally sprung from such groups.

However, to meet its wider social functions and be commensurate with man's social existence, Christian faith needs a more general social expression. It requires embodiment in organisations, with the objectified or limited relationships these carry with them. But in keeping with present social consciousness, the organisation of the Christian community will reflect what I have said about the organisation of society in general. The organisations will be freely created by Christians themselves; their structural principle is the freely creative intelligence of the believer, an intelligence enhanced, not destroyed, by faith. They will be many and various, each organization limited in function and purpose. All the organisations will be relative in value and open to change. There will be room for improvisation, and organisations that no longer serve a useful purpose will be allowed to die. New organisations will be created or old ones adapted as the need arises. Further, the Christian will be left in the open situation characteristic of the present stage of man's development, because no organisation will embrace or claim to embrace his total Christian existence.

Some of the organisations will be distinctively Christian. They will be created by Christians for a distinctively Christian purpose. Thus, they will gather Christians together in wider groups, though in differing ways, to express their faith and engage in public worship. Or, they will organise Christian evangelisation more systematically and on a wider front than can be achieved by small interpersonal groups. Or, they will promote Christian education and by various means foster an open communication amongst all Christians, and in that way serve to keep Christian individuals and groups in touch with the Christian tradition as a whole.

In other organisations, whether created by Christians or not, Christians will work with others in a general service of mankind and for the practical recognition by everyone of the unity of all men. Such organisations form part of the embodiment of the Christian world of meaning. I repeat that it is wrong to try to establish clear boundaries. Indeed, some Christians will fulfil their Christian mission within purely secular organizations. Insofar as they ground themselves upon the Christian faith and, while respecting the proper autonomy of the secular, see what they do as being within the general context of the Christian world of meaning, their work forms part of the visible presence of Christ and his Church in the world. The visible Church reaches out to the total human reality and merges into the universal human community.

The third relationship in which the Christian world of meaning is embodied is that created outside all established and organised relationships by chance encounter with a fellow man in need. This relationship is determined and limited by the demands of the particular situation, but there is an imperative need for the recognition and fulfilment of such *ad hoc* demands if the open situation in which men are now placed and the complexity of modern organised society are not to lead to the destruction of many individuals. The teaching of the Gospel is an unambiguous summons to meet such demands with generosity and alacrity, so that Christians are left without excuse for any neglect. In many ways such unorganised love, meeting the needs of others, however inconveniently and unexpectedly they may be thrust upon us, is the most characteristically Christian expression of commitment to our fellow men.

These, then, are the three forms of relationships in which the Christian world of meaning finds social embodiment and is thus made constitutive of the visible Church. There is, I maintain, no necessity to bring them under a single, overarching organisation and within a unified social structure. The unity, preservation and transmission of the Christian world of meaning will be secured by open communication among Christians within a diversity of social structures and relationships.

The desire for an overarching organisation embracing the totality of Christian tradition, life and mission springs, it seems to me, from a threefold misunderstanding.

First, it is in effect nostalgia for a static, hierarchical view of reality and society, now, however, irretrievably past. Such a view does not correspond to modern social consciousness. But there is always the *laudator temporis acti*, and I need not tell the reader that there are those who lament the advent of modern society and yearn for the stable, relatively unchanging orders of the past. Needless to say, the past is usually conceived idealistically. But apart from that, the past cannot be recreated. Within a modern context, an hierarchical order is distorted into a vast organisation without the safeguards provided by a truly modern approach, which insists upon the relative limited value and changeability of all organisations. There is no overarching organisation for secular life today. Even the State and nation embrace only part of our lives, which culturally and socially are increasingly international. I do not see the need for a total Christian organisation. To attempt to form one would create immense dangers. God forbid that the present Churches should unite to form one, vast unified organisation.

Second, the desire shows a failure to recognise that the only all-embracing framework for the saving mission of Christ and the work of Christians is mankind and human history, not the visible Church. The visible Church cannot be demarcated by clear boundaries from the human community itself. Christians should not attempt to confine it within the limits of a single, exclusively Christian organisation.

Third, the desire rests upon a misconception of the relation between the visible Church and the world. The visible Church is not an exclusive area of the sacred, marked off from a profane world. The visible Church is the human community itself as rendered manifest in its nature, destiny and dependence upon Christ's salvation. Christians bear a mission to foster an explicit consciousness among men of the common world of meaning already embodied in Christian social relationships and structures. But there is no call to embody that common world of meaning in a single organisation or institutional structure set over against the world. The total embodiment Christians are working for is not the visible Church, but the universal community of mankind, which coincides with the final Kingdom.

In brief, the Christian community is a present and historical fact. There is no need or possibility for an individual to create his own Christian Church. It is already there in the world. At present, it is divided into different social entities, which have drifted or broken away from one another and are only now overcoming their mutual antagonism. These divisions obscure the common world of meaning, which persists, despite the divisions. Christians must engage in a renewal, which will draw them closer together in fellowship and open communication, make possible common Christian activity across the denominational frontiers and render the unity of Christian faith and mission more apparent to themselves and the world. But such renewal requires expression in a reorganisation, which will not patch up existing institutions nor seek after a single organisational unity, but which will restructure the Christian community in accord with modern social consciousness.

It should be clear from the account I have given of the social structure appropriate to the Christian Church in the modern world that the relation between the Church and the wider or inclusive society will be fluid and incapable of being juridically formalised. Christian groups and organisations, grounded upon the free, personal commitment of faith, will be many and various, scattered among the other voluntary groups and organisations found in modern, pluralist society and not always clearly distinguishable from these. For that reason the Church will have a pervasive influence throughout society.

Perhaps it would be helpful to contrast this fluid structure with the two earlier ways in which the relationship of the Church to the inclusive society has been structured, namely, the societal Church and the sect.

In using the phrase "societal Church" I have two features in mind.

First, the Church itself is formed into a society, existing as a complete, juridically organised and unified social entity. Its structure, though given a spiritual meaning and competence, reflects the political organisation of a State. Like a State it is a power structure, with a central legislative and executive authority and administrative officials, though all is given a spiritual interpretation and directed to a spiritual purpose.

Second, this Church is integrated as a society or unified social entity into the public social order of the wider society. The integration has been achieved in different ways. In the Middle Ages Church and State were merged into a single politico-ecclesiastical unity, though with a constant tension and struggle between papal and imperial or regal authority. Later there were the established Churches: the Church of the nation was given an exclusive or privileged status and thus, with varying degrees of freedom, made part of the public order of the State. More recently the association between Church and State has generally become much looser. But even without establishment the State will often give the Church juridical recognition, perhaps to the extent of paying Church ministers or arranging Church taxes. And where there is no juridical recognition by the State, a Church existing publicly as a society inevitably becomes a *de facto* public institution, forming part of the public social order, with a place alongside other public institutions. The voice of the Church is identified with the statements of Church officials. Church officials will negotiate with State officials when they consider that Christian or ecclesiastical interests are at stake. And if policy demands that account be taken of the Christian reaction or point of view, State officials will approach Church officials, either publicly or privately.

A societal Church is ill-adapted to the needs of Christian mission in the secular world of today. In all its forms it is really an obsolete survival of the past order of Christendom.

Established Churches violate the principle of the secularity of the State, which, as I have argued in *God's Grace in History*,[1] Christians should now fully recognise. When establishment of the Church still possesses effective meaning, it restricts, threatens or even directly violates religious freedom. When largely meaningless, it cheapens and confuses the genuine mission of Christians to society.

But even where the association with the State is loose and informal, a societal Church cripples the witness of Christians to the Gospel. It almost inevitably makes Church officials anxious about the public standing of the Church, concerned with institutional position and privilege, frequently to the extent of compromising the uncomfortable truths of the Gospel when these have social and political repercussions. I have already discussed this effect earlier in the book. And since the voice of the Church is identified with the silence or *castrato* notes of Church officials, the more vigorous witness of ordinary Christians is treated as dissonance and ignored by other Church members and by the world at large. Further, the existence of the Church as a public institution alongside other public institutions is now having the paradoxical effect of restricting the influence of the Church to the private sphere. Because the Church exists alongside the other institutions of society, it remains outside of them, cut off from all the decision-making processes that determine social, economic and political life. It organises itself around the residential community, which in modern society is increasingly a private sphere, kept separate from public and business life. Although the Church is constantly urging Christians to bear witness to Christ in the environment of their secular vocation, this remains secondary in relation to Church life. As an organised body the Church is primarily and indeed almost exclusively present in the private sphere. Its presence in

[1] Fontana Books, Collins, London, 1966, pp. 26-30.

the public sphere, apart from providing a ceremonial adjunct, is limited to a defense of Church interests and protests against legislation it considers immoral. It is not present as a vital force within the ordinary working of social institutions.

For all these reasons I consider the more fluid structure of the Church I have described a more effective vehicle for Christian mission. Only when the Church ceases to be a separate public institution will Christians through their informal groups and limited, adaptable, multiple organisations carry their witness to Christian truth and love throughout every area of social and political life.

The sect is another earlier form of the relation of the Church to the wider society.

A sect is characterised by its opposition to the dominant order of society. Since the established order it opposes is usually both ecclesiastical and political, its opposition takes the form of a spiritual protest with political and social repercussions. Historically, sects have been based on a refusal to conform to an established religion or Church. Hence they have clashed with both ecclesiastical and political authority. Sects, therefore, are made distinctive social entities largely by what I believe sociologists call collective negativity. In other words, they are essentially opposition groups, or the negative counterpart of a dominant order. For that reason they are usually enclosed, tightly knit groups, showing the features we designate as sectarianism. Their narrowness has often been aggravated by their advocacy of a world-denying spiritualism.

The flexible structure I have proposed for the Church would not make the Church a sect, because it is an open structure, marked by a positive acceptance of the world and co-operation with society. Despite the rejection of a societal Church, the proposal refuses the narrow, enclosed organisation of a sect and urges an openness to all Christians and to society generally. And I am not advocating an exclusive Church of the spiritually pure.

Nevertheless, the opposition of sects to the established order does contain a measure of truth, which should not be overlooked. If Christians are true to their mission, they will constantly find themselves in opposition to the *status quo*, to the established order of society, to what is fashionable and commonly accepted. Complacent acceptance of any dominant order is a betrayal of the Gospel. All

social institutions—and this includes all Christian organisations—
are ambiguous. They are marked by the sinfulness of men, by their
imperfect grasp of truth and by their failure to love earnestly and
consistently. Every social order, every social organisation, every social policy and practice should be constantly subject to criticism and
correction in the light of the Gospel. Despite their openness and
positive intent, Christians will often have to become dissidents. It is
important, however, that they should learn that their own policies,
practices and organisations also come under the judgement of the
Gospel.

6. THE SACRAMENTS

After this outline of the social structure of the Church and the nature of Christian presence in the world today, I cannot avoid a question which I am sure many readers have been waiting to ask: How do the sacraments fit into this scheme?

A sad consequence of a person's leaving his Church is that he is cut off from those forms of sacramental celebration, especially the Eucharistic liturgy, through which he has expressed and deepened his union with Christ. I have not escaped suffering in that respect. After celebrating Mass for years as a priest, I have not been able to cease to do so without a painful wrench and a sense of spiritual denudation. Precisely because the sacraments affect one's whole personality, sensuously and emotionally as well as spiritually and intellectually, the pain of their loss cannot be quenched by theological reasons, however well grounded these might be. From personal experience I can therefore understand the attitude of those who, despite all doubts and difficulties, stay within the Roman Catholic Church because they cannot relinquish the sacraments, especially the Mass. I know some who admit that their only reason for remaining is that. I would not disturb them. What is important is that people should cling to Christ according to their present understanding. And I have no desire to impose my own suffering upon those who have not the understanding to endure it. Nevertheless, I must explain why I could not myself adopt their attitude.

Strangely enough, it was my very study of the sacraments that enabled me to make the break. All my reflection led to the conclusion that the seven sacraments, including the Eucharist, could not themselves be regarded as fundamental. The fundamental sacrament is the visible Church itself. Christ is the Great Sacrament as the presence and embodiment of the saving union between God and men; in other words, as the effectual sign of God's self-giving and man's response. The visible Church is the fundamental sacrament insofar as it is the permanent, manifest presence of Christ in the world, the visible expression and embodiment of his union with men, the effectual sign of his saving gifts. As a sacrament, the Church does not replace Christ nor confine his presence in the world, but it gives continuing visibility to his mission and, in doing so, embodies the reality and action of that mission in a manifest form. The seven rites are called sacraments because they are seven outstanding actions which the Church performs as the fundamental sacrament. In a pre-eminent fashion, they apply and make actual in a particular situation and for a particular community or person what the Church as the fundamental sacrament is permanently and does continually.

Because of the permanent presence of Christ in the Church and his union with it as his Body, the seven sacraments are actions of Christ. Through them he acts upon us to deepen our union with him and bestow his saving gifts upon us. But they are actions of Christ insofar as they are in their structure actions of the Church. They are a deployment of the presence of Christ in the Church.

The seven sacraments are actions of the Church. All of them are professions of faith, hope and love on the part of the Christian community. Made up of words and actions, the sacraments are symbols in which the community proclaims its faith, unfolds its hope and declares its love—a love that includes repentance. Looking at the sacraments we can see what is the mind of the Church in regard to Christ and gauge the manner of its commitment to him.

In the setting of this Christian faith and commitment, six of the sacraments are actions of the community in relation to particular members. The Eucharist as the chief sacrament is the general gathering together of Christians for a common celebration of the total mystery of Christ.

And within this community context each sacrament is an expression of the personal response of the individual Christian to Christ.

Now, since the seven sacraments are actions of the Church, their structure is determined by the structure of the Church. It is wrong procedure to begin with the existing structure of the sacraments and use that as a basis for defining the structure of the Church. The general structure of the Church as a community must first be determined and then it will be possible to see how that community will express its Christian faith and commitment in its chief and distinctive actions, namely, the sacraments.

That this is the correct approach is confirmed historically. The structure of the sacraments has always reflected the contemporary structure of the Church. This is particularly so with the Eucharist. The transformation of the Eucharist from a fraternal sacred meal to an hieratic sacrifice, from a community celebration to a priestly action on behalf of the faithful, with a return now to a combination of hierarchical action with community participation, simply reflects the changing structure of the Church itself. The vicissitudes in the structure of Penance likewise follow general changes in the Church, such as the differing relation between episcopal and priestly ministry, the emergence of monks and later of friars, the growing importance of jurisdiction in the concept of the Church. The practice of baptism reflects the self-understanding of the Church, so that at one time whole peoples could be baptised with their king and baptism in a Christian country be as much a social and cultural as a religious action, while today both indiscriminate and infant baptism, are causing great difficulty because membership of the Church is seen as grounded upon the free, personal commitment of faith. I have already pointed out that changes in the concept of Holy Order and in the manner of ordination went hand in hand with a changing understanding of the Church. Here indeed the change in the sacrament and the change in the general structure of the Church coincide. The changing relation of the Church to marriage corresponds to changes in the understanding of its hierarchical power.

Thus, the sacraments can be understood and structured only on the basis of a prior understanding of the nature and structure of the Church.

And what is also becoming clear biblically and theologically is that Christ can be said to have instituted the sacraments only in the sense that the Church, of which they are the distinctive actions, owes its origin to him. What has already been said about the institution of the Church by Christ would lead us to expect that the sacraments, including the Eucharist, although given a basis in the words and actions of Christ himself, owe their origin and development as formal rites to the first community and reflect its culture context. And that in fact is a reasonable interpretation of the data.

It follows from all this that a radical transformation of the general structure of the Church must lead to a radical transformation in the structure of the sacraments.

Thus, a denial of the appropriateness of an hierarchical order for the Church is a refusal of an hierarchical structure for the sacraments. Certainly, there will be a differentiation of function, but not one made static and unchanging by permanent consecration.

Likewise, the multiplicity and variety of Christian organizations will imply an absence of any attempt to impose liturgical uniformity. Indeed, there will be no all-embracing authority to effect this.

Moreover, although respect for the Christian tradition as a whole will lead to a continuity in themes and practices, the general acceptance of change and relativity will result in the alteration and adaptation of the sacramental rites to contemporary Christian needs. During every creative period of liturgical history, the liturgy was profoundly affected by the contemporary outlook and culture. Greater change and adaptation than ever before are now needed. And I see no compelling reason to regard either the number seven or any particular sacramental rite as absolute and unchanging.

Further, the new understanding of the relation of the visible Church to the world will have great repercussions upon the sacramental practice of Christians. First, it brings under question any exclusive regulation for participation. While the sacraments as distinctively Christian actions are grounded upon an explicit faith in Christ, I do not see the need to exclude anyone who, understanding what is being done, finds himself able to take part with honesty and sincerity. Participation in the sacraments should not be more clearly defined than the boundaries of the visible Church, which, as we have seen, are blurred. Second, and more important, it demands a rejection of the present structuring of the sacraments as elaborate religious ritual. This reflects an understanding of the Church as a self-contained religious system set apart from a profane world. The sacraments have to be reformed into very simple symbolic actions, closely linked to man's ordinary life in the world and serving to disclose the depth of meaning in all human existence.

What does all this involve in concrete detail? Frankly, I do not know. For my decision it was enough to see two points: first, that the problem of the sacraments was dependent upon the question of the general structure of the Church and could not be allowed to block a clear conviction about that; second, that experience confirmed—I will return to this point in a moment—that a radical alteration of sacramental practice was imperatively required. These two points were sufficient to assure me that, whatever the wrench to me personally, I was not denying anything essential to the Christian faith in cutting myself off from the closely ordered sacramental system of the Roman Catholic Church. Furthermore, I knew that the problem of the sacraments today could not be solved by theoretical discussion alone, let alone by the reflection of a single individual. On the grounds of my general understanding of the Church, I was prepared, therefore, to take part in those sacramental celebrations of Christians which were open to me and where I was welcome, and then to engage in discussion and experimentation with Christians generally to clarify the problem of the sacraments and work towards a solution. Apart from my general view of the Roman Catholic Church, there seemed little hope of making much progress with the restrictions, both doctrinal and practical, that Church at present imposes. I had reached a point in my own study of the sacraments where I could no longer accept these restrictions and had to seek a freer environment.

Although I have some ideas about what should be done, I am living, therefore, without a practical solution to the problem how the sacraments should be structured and celebrated in the present situation of the Church. I do not find the sacramental celebrations of other Churches more satisfactory than those of the Roman Catholic Church; indeed, though this may be due to my background, sometimes less so. Not that I am at all troubled by the Roman refusal to recognise their validity—a refusal I consider both untrue and based upon obsolete principles. But the general problem still looms large:

the Christian liturgy at present is simply out of keeping with the consciousness and needs of Christians in the modern world, nor does it correspond to the more recent understanding of the relation of the Church to the world.

But in this respect the situation I am now in is not essentially different from that I experienced as a Roman Catholic. While years of personal participation surrounded the liturgy with associations that were spiritually meaningful to myself, I increasingly recognised how much the meaning I gave it was adventitious to the liturgy as it existed in fact and was actually celebrated. And much of what I wrote about the liturgy was a beautiful construct, which did not correspond to the liturgy as it is in the concrete. It was notional, describing a sheerly spiritual faith, unsupported by the present liturgical facts. But precisely because liturgy is in the order of symbol and visible expression, liturgical theology should be reflection upon actual liturgical experience. If the Mass is not visibly and experientially a community action, it is a contradiction to maintain that sacramentally it is. Faith may be needed to accept the reality expressed in the liturgy and to commit oneself to it, but the intended meaning of the expression and the structure of the sacrament are of their nature open to verification. What in fact people are doing is deriving the meaning of the liturgy from books or talks, not from the liturgy itself, and then trying to impose that meaning upon a ritual that only in part supports it and frequently contradicts it. And even the meaning they learn notionally does not adequately correspond to their present consciousness and needs. No wonder that many, especially young people, are overwhelmed by the unreality of the liturgy, while others find it a constant source of frustration and tension. As for myself, the pain of losing the spiritual associations of childhood, youth and manhood has been offset by the cessation of the previous, continuous pain of being constantly involved in external forms that could no longer express and were often in conflict with my Christian faith and experience.

The liturgical renewal in the Roman Church has reached an impasse. The liturgy has been put into the mother tongue and generally stripped of accretions. Many of the desires of the reformers are being translated into rubrical regulations. But the changes have only served to reveal the underlying problem in all its starkness. Any further progress will depend upon much more radical thinking about the Church itself.

Meanwhile it is necessary to recall that the reality the liturgy embodies and conveys is greater than itself and is not confined to the liturgy.

It is because it is a human action that the liturgy is not an empty symbol. The liturgy is not just a visible pointer, like a sign-post, indicating a reality distant from itself. It is a symbol in the sense that language is symbolic, embodying as one with itself the truth it expresses; or in the sense that a gesture or action of love is symbolic, containing and conveying the love it intends to express. With man bodily action and spiritual reality become one. The liturgy is the outward actions in which Christians, not merely express, but also embody and deepen the reality of their faith, hope and love. And the liturgy embodies the presence and action of Christ, because faith, hope and love constitute a union with Christ and are dependent in their reality and expression upon his initiative and sustaining action. It is in deepening our union with Christ by genuinely expressing it that the sacraments give grace. They are effectual after the manner of an action of love that in truly expressing the love deepens it. They are not automatic dispensers of amounts of grace.

The reality of our union with Christ is wider than the sacraments. Although the sacraments should be pre-eminent symbols of it, the means of expressing it are many and various. At a time when the sacramental rites are in a state of inadequacy and lack genuineness, it is necessary to give priority to the reality they were intended to serve and seek to express it in ways that are genuine and can truly embody it. Only if Christians do this and thus improvise will they find the answer to the problem of a Christian liturgy adapted to the present situation. To give priority to the present external forms is to lose the reality for a past expression and to falsify the Christian life for people today.

This also gives another reason for not subordinating the Church to the sacraments, instead of the sacraments to the Church. If a Church in its general structure is not an embodiment of faith, hope and love, its sacraments are to that extent falsified. How can one in the Eucharist celebrate the reality of a community of faith, hope and love, if that reality is not found in the general life of the Church?

Hence the frustration of Roman Catholics in proclaiming and celebrating in the Eucharist a community of truth and love which does not correspond to the Church as they experience it. This makes the liturgy false and unreal. The Church must first change if the celebration of its reality in the liturgy is to ring true.

7. CREATIVE DISAFFILIATION

What I have said about the unreality of much liturgical theology draws attention to the pressing need to base theological reflection upon the concrete reality of the Church and to translate theological ideas into practical effect. I should like to stress this point because it is the reason why I have given such importance to the questions I have raised about the social structure of the Church.

The present time, it seems to me, is characterised by an escape into theology. This is the modern form of the retreat into the spiritual which has prevented earlier movements of reform from achieving an effectual and decisive renewal of the Church. We are dazzled by what is fundamentally an uncommitted theology, deluged with a spate of theoretical ideas that are not thought through consistently to their ecclesiastical, social and political consequences. Conceptually the theology is wonderful, but it represents an unreal world. It is not based upon the actual life or situation of Christians, nor is it allowed to have practical effect or social expression in the life of the Church. Unbelievers are wrong in demanding rational proof of Christian truth, but they are right if they ask for some connection between the conceptual constructs of theologians and the perceived reality of the Church, between the beautiful analyses of the Christian faith and the attitude, actions and experience of Christian believers. But the easier course for the theologian is to brush aside the corruption of the concrete Church and escape into theology. Nowadays, as long as he can remain within the realm of pure theology, the more erudite the better, it is increasingly less likely that he will be disturbed. He has to be cautious, but the Church authorities are coming to know that there is little they can now do to control theological thinking. But touch a practical point, which need not affect the Christian faith itself but simply official policy or the established order, and there is uproar. No wonder theologians are reluctant to translate their theoretical ideas into their meaning for Church structures and Christian living in the world today. I do not blame the theologians. After all, they are intellectuals, and their beautiful theological world is intellectually so satisfying. It is a pity to spoil it by contact with the messiness of concrete reality.

If someone remarks that theology is based upon the Word of God I cannot but agree. But the Word of God as contained in the New Testament is not a theoretical construct erected in the refined atmosphere of a scholar's study. It is the translation of the Christian experience of the first community, a formulation achieved with the help of concepts from the Old Testament, but developed as the primitive Church struggled with the real problems of Christian living and mission. And if that biblical record is to be made intelligible to men today and formulated afresh, it will be by the Church struggling with the problems of Christian living and mission today under the permanent presence of Christ and his Spirit.

Institutions and social structures have meaning. The Christian faith as it exists in concrete fact is not to be found primarily in what theologians write about it, but in the meaning embodied in the structures and institutions of the Church and in the relationships, attitudes and actions these give rise to. If the social structures of the Church no longer embody a valid meaning, the Church is presenting and living a corrupted and distorted faith. Theologians may write learnedly about the concept of God, but the God of the Church is the God represented and implied in its institutional structure and social life. That is why I cannot remain indifferent, as most theologians have, to the recent Roman document on indulgences, which implies a primitive concept of the deity and his relationship to man.

And Christians urgently need an adequate and appropriate social expression for their faith. I am thinking of the innumerable unattached Christians there are at present. People who in their essential outlook are Christians, who perhaps have professed the Christian faith in the past, but who simply cannot contemplate or have not been able to endure life within the present Churches. Having had no alternative manner of being Christians put before them, they have drifted away from the Christian faith. The faith of many of these people could be brought to maturity if they could be shown how to live and socially structure the Christian faith without imprisoning themselves within the obsolete structures of the existing denominations. I am thinking, too, of the Roman Catholics I know who are desperately lonely within the existing structure of their Church. No one who has not talked to such people, some of them priests and religious, can fathom the depths of loneliness and despair that can overwhelm a person within that vast Church. They often have a sense that no one has the same difficulties and problems as themselves or feels the same needs; the official line is so pervasive, the pressure that any lack of conformity is due to personal perversity is so insistent. What they are being deprived of is a socially structured environment that will correspond to their actual consciousness and needs as Christians in the modern world and a sufficient personal formation to embrace it, despite the strictures of the Roman Church, with a personal, radical decision. It is these people I am trying to help.

To continue to play the present institutional game within and across the present denominational structures is to hinder the coming into full visibility of a radically different and better form of Christian presence in the world. And it will be to watch an increasing number of people ceasing to profess the Christian faith because they identify it with the present Churches. They do not recognize that it is often the Christian faith they have that leads them to reject institutional structures inimical to the self-understanding and freedom of man and to Christian truth and love.

What I suggest for all Christians is, to borrow a phrase from Harvey Cox,[1] an attitude of creative disaffiliation.

Disaffiliation is required, because one must recognise that the existing social structures of the Churches are inadequate and obso-

---

[1] *The Secular City: Secularization and Urbanization in Theological Perspective* (The Macmillan Company, New York, 1965), p. 230.

lete. Insofar as they can be made useful, they must be regarded as limited in function, relative in value and essentially changeable. The Christian should embrace his open situation and refuse to be enclosed in any total organisation. Obedience to the Gospel and to the Christian community as a whole will frequently today demand opposition to the claims, prescriptions and official attitudes of the existing Church institutions. This is not an invitation to individual licence. The individual Christian will endeavour to ground his thinking upon the Christian tradition as a whole and will enter into communication with other Christians. But complete conformity to the official line of his Church is irresponsibility as a Christian.

But the disaffiliation should be creative. It will include an acknowledgement that the visible Church or the manifest Christian presence in the world today is still largely constituted by Christians with a denominational allegiance. While the Christian community as a whole is struggling to find a new social embodiment, it is still linked to past structures, and sincere Christians are trying to work within the framework of these structures. It will be some time before they completely free themselves from them, and, furthermore, some of the structures are capable of adaptation. There is need, therefore, to work positively with Christians of all denominations, to respect their point of view and generously to appreciate whatever is of value in the structures to which they cling. History has to run its course, and a purely negative attitude is always disastrous.

What creative disaffiliation will involve for the individual will depend upon his personal understanding and situation. For an increasing number it will mean a renunciation of their denominational membership. For others it need not do so. They will find sufficient freedom and scope for honest and sincere Christian living and mission within formal membership of their Church. The renewal and reorganisation of the Christian Church will be achieved by people working from either direction, from without as well as from within the present Church structures.

EPILOGUE

I come now to my final word.

I have tried to give fair measure to my friends and critics. Throughout the book my aim has been to give as honest an explanation as I could of the reasons, both negative and positive, which led me to leave the Roman Catholic Church. I have hidden nothing of which I have been conscious. And, surely, any unconscious motivation is best left alone, not conjectured by amateurs working at a distance from me.

Nor have I tried to work up my case *post factum*. I am writing these last lines in the middle of June 1967, not yet six months since I publicly announced my decision. I have done practically no reading directly for this book. For one reason, I have not had the time; for another, I wished to write it before substantially developing my thought. I wanted to record for myself and for others the state of mind in which I made my break with the Roman Church. All that I have done is to consult a few books and articles which have helped me to document or formulate my own thinking. Many of the themes of this book will be familiar to those to whom I have lectured in recent years. They have led me to a conclusion that will surprise my former listeners as it caused an upheaval in my own mind. Certainly, both the demands of writing and the many discussions I have had with people about my decision have helped me to dot the i's and cross the t's in formulating my thought. No one can wrestle day after day for months with a book he is writing without clarifying his thinking on the subject he is writing about. But as far as the human conditions allows, this book represents the actual grounds on which I left my former Church.

I have not, therefore, tried to don the mantle of a radical theologian. It would ill become me. I am well aware that parts of this book will seem curiously conservative to those who are asking very radical questions about the central doctrines of the Christian faith. I have not attempted to be other than my usual self as a theologian. I can see well enough that the fundamental intellectual problems for Christians today are the problem of our knowledge of God in relation to modern philosophy and the question of the uniqueness of Christ in the confrontation with the other world religions. But for the reasons I have explained I regard the immediate problem as that of the Church, the solution of which will place Christians in a situation where they can tackle the other problems on the basis of a freely developing Christian tradition. The Church was in any case the problem that faced me, and personal thought must arise from one's own personal situation.

I have aimed in writing the book to help others. People have turned to me over the years for guidance. I know how much my decision has pained and upset many who looked to me for help in the confused situation in which all Christians now live. I hope they will not think that I have betrayed them. Whether they agree with my final conclusion or not, my desire is that what I have written will give them some understanding of what I have done and a sufficiently positive vision to strengthen their hope in the future of the Christian Church. At least we shall have in common a love of Christ and of the Church, his Body.

So now I leave my book—and no book I shall ever write will be more my own—for criticism and discussion. I ask for no quarter intellectually. I want to learn from others. But I should be sorry if it met with a merely defensive reaction from Roman Catholics. I have no wish to forestall criticism, but there is a danger when much is at stake of imitating Bossuet, who, according to Friedrich Heer, "was a perfect man of the baroque, preserving what he knew was false because he was afraid of what might replace it."[1]

[1] *The Intellectual History of Europe*, (Weidenfeld and Nicolson, London, 1966), p. 390.

INDEX

273